Ontario
1610-1985

A political and economic history

Randall White

Ontario Heritage Foundation
Local History Series #1

Dundurn Press
Toronto and London
1985

The writing of this manuscript and the publication of this book were made possible by support from several sources. The author is grateful to the Ontario Heritage Foundation, an agency of the Ontario Ministry of Citizenship and Culture for technical support and for a research grant. The author and publisher wish to acknowledge as well the generous assistance and ongoing support of the Canada Council and the Ontario Arts Council.

J. Kirk Howard, Publisher

Editor: Roger Riendeau
Design and Production: Ron and Ron Design Photography
Typesetting: The Coach House Press
Printing and Binding: T.H. Best Printing Company, Canada

Dundurn Press Limited

1558 Queen Street East   71 Great Russell Street
Toronto, Canada   London, England
M4L 1E8   WC1B 3BN

Canadian Cataloguing in Publication Data

White, Randall.
  Ontario, a political and economic history,
1610-1985

Bibliography: p.
Includes index.
ISBN 0-919670-99-7 (bound). - ISBN 0-919670-98-9 (pbk.)

1. Ontario - Politics and government. 2. Ontario -
Economic conditions. I. Title.

FC 3061.W45 1985   971.3   C85-099330-X
F1058.W45 1985

British Library Cataloguing in Publication Data

White, Randall.
  Ontario : a political and economic history,
1610-1985.
1. Ontario----History
I. Title
971.3   F1058

ISBN 0-919670-99-7
ISBN 0-919670-98-9 Pbk

Dedication

To Gordon Hepditch, former Assessment Commissioner of the now historic Ontario County, in lieu of another book project that was lost in a shuffle a long time ago, and to the memories of Mae Churchill, Marguerite Craig, Donald James MacDonald, Nellie Webbe, and Lieutenant Sidney White – all historic "Ontario people", three of whom were born in other places.

Foreword

It is a great pleasure to introduce Randall White's *Ontario 1610-1985*, the first volume in the *Ontario Heritage Foundation Local History Series*. Although a number of books have been published over the last thirty years investigating the history of Canada from its earliest exploration to the present, this is the only modern treatment to look specifically at Ontario over the same period, placing it in its regional context. The absence of such a context has often worked to the detriment of local history writing in Ontario, casting authors unfamiliar with the provincial or regional terrain adrift in an often unhelpful national framework. This work will therefore be of interest to the local historian and the general reader alike. Mr White not only demonstrates a clear grasp of the main currents of Ontario's past but does so in a popular, eminently readable manner.

The *Ontario Heritage Foundation Local History Series* is a programme of financial and technical assistance towards the publication of original works on the province of a local or regional nature. The Board of Directors hopes over the next few years to be able to assist both individuals and organizations alike with publishing their own books under the Series' umbrella. By distributing copies of these works to select public institutions, the Board further hopes to give greater visibility to local history and thereby to encourage a broader interest in the province's past. We have with *Ontario 1610-1985* begun well. Dundurn Press, the publisher, deserves our thanks for its foresight in recognizing the value of the present volume and for agreeing to its inclusion as the first publication in the *Ontario Heritage Foundation Local History Series*.

John White, Chairman
Ontario Heritage Foundation

Table of Contents

6

7

Preface

This book represents the first effort at a general history of Canada's most populous province since Jesse Middleton and Fred Landon's four-volume *The Province of Ontario: A History* was published in 1927. That almost sixty years should have elapsed between the two endeavours could be attributed to a certain elusive quality in Ontario's past and present. In the late 1960s the Ontario-born historian, Arthur Lower, observed: "Ontario's variety and the different times at which its parts were settled make it hard to describe briefly." And in the mid-1970s the writer Max Braithwaite, born and raised in Saskatchewan, declared: "When you speak of the Ontario character to me, you must define your terms. Which Ontario citizen do you mean?"

In the face of such testimony, I have persevered in an attempt to tell the province's rich and varied story, spanning some 375 years, in a single volume. The exercise has placed limitations on my treatment of the subject. Though the book does not ignore major aspects of Ontario's social development, it stresses the region's changing political and economic culture. This focus perhaps partly reflects my training in political economy at the University of Toronto, among the last vestiges of an academic setting shaped by Harold Innis in the 1930s and 1940s. It owes something as well to a decade I spent in the Ontario public service, initially with the Department of Municipal Affairs and eventually as a Senior Economist with the Ministry of Treasury and Economics.

Similarly, it seems to me impossible to write about Ontario's political and economic development without touching periodically on the history of other parts of Canada, the United States, the United Kingdom (and what used to be called the British empire), and France. This perhaps partly reflects my own particular fascination with the extent to which Ontario has been shaped by larger national and international forces. Like Lower and Braithwaite, however, I am equally fascinated by the great diversity of people and places inside the region itself. I can only hope that I do some rough justice to all the varied elements of Ontario's past.

R.W.
Toronto
September 1985

Acknowledgements

Numerous individuals and organizations have kindly responded to queries and requests for material in connection with the preparation of this book, and I would like to thank them all in a general way. I am indebted as well to several personal friends and colleagues, who should remain anonymous, but who provided valued support and encouragement in my struggles with a rather large task. More specifically, Jeanne MacDonald has provided many different kinds of assistance and support from the beginnings of a long project and has read and commented on the manuscript from the standpoint of a general reader with an interest in the subject.

The Ontario Heritage Foundation has provided generous financial assistance for the preparation and publication of the book, and I am personally indebted to Lorne Ste. Croix and Lois Chipper of the Foundation staff for various forms of helpful advice and encouragement. I am similarly indebted to Kirk Howard, President of Dundurn Press, as well as his staff. Finally, Roger Riendeau of Innis College, University of Toronto, has been a vigilant, assiduous, and stimulating editor, reading and commenting on the manuscript from the standpoint of a professional historian.

Part One

Wilderness Romance, 1610-1791

"There is not, perhaps, a country on the globe, where there is so much excellent water communication."
John Strachan

"... some countries have too much history, we have too much geography."
William Lyon Mackenzie King

"One thing has deeply impressed me as I swept through the history of North America.... The seeds or roots of almost everything we have today may be discerned in the English, French, and Spanish colonies as early as 1660."
Samuel Eliot Morison

"Un français devenait sauvage avant qu'un sauvage ne devienne français."
Marie de l'Incarnation

Niagara Falls, an eighteenth-century engraving: before industrial pollution, hydroelectric projects, and modern urban development had dimmed its original splendour.

1

The Territory

As a name for the region west of the Ottawa River and north of the Great Lakes, "Ontario" only dates from the Canadian Confederation of 1867. Before then, the place was known as Canada West, and before 1841 Upper Canada. Before 1791 it was called "the upper parts of the Province of Quebec", and before 1763 it was simply "le pays d'en haut" – the upper country of New France.

When British imperial officials pondered what the region should be called in 1867, they observed that Quebec City was the capital of the new Province of Quebec to the east of the Ottawa River. On the same principle, they proposed that the area to the west, with its capital at the City of Toronto, should be known as the Province of Toronto. Even in 1867, however, it was clear to people who lived in the region that this would be wrong. The Manitoba-born historian, W.L. Morton, has suggested that the place was finally called "Ontario, the name of the lake on which Toronto stood, to avoid, it may be supposed, a duplication that had no such historical justification as that of the city and province of Quebec."

Ontario is said to be an Indian word that means "rocks standing by water" and probably refers to the Lake Ontario shoreline to the north and west of Niagara Falls, where the Niagara Escarpment looms in the distance. Since 1783 it had been clear that the southeasterly boundary of what became Ontario in 1867 was an imaginary line running through the middle of the upper St. Lawrence River

14

and the Great Lakes (excluding Lake Michigan). But the exact northwesterly boundary of the province would remain uncertain until 1889, and Ontario would not arrive at its present boundaries until 1912.

Yet even today Ontario means a place rather than a particular group of people or an idea about society. Like other regional jurisdictions in North America, its history can only be the story of the territory marked off by its modern boundaries. Though people have been living in this territory for more than 10,000 years the place has an important geological history preceeding human settlement. In the 1930s Harold Innis began a classic short account of Ontario's economic development with the declaration: "Geological history is a prerequisite to the study of later history." Innis went on to sketch the impact of the last ice age on "the formation of large bodies of water in the region," and concluded noting that it is only "recorded history" in Ontario which "begins with the appearance of Europeans" in the early 1600s.

The Native Waterways

Innis' concern to show the origins of large bodies of water in the region flowed from his sense that water is perhaps the single most important geographic element in Ontario history. Ontario is bounded on the south by the freshwater inland seas of the Great Lakes and on the north by the salt water of Hudson Bay. In a less comprehensive sense, it is bounded on the east by the Ottawa River and on the west by the Lake of the Woods. In between are almost literally countless small lakes and rivers (though the phenomenon is less pronounced in the southwestern Great Lakes Peninsula). And, all told, water accounts for just under twelve per cent of Ontario's total geographic area.

The historically important point is not so much that there was a large amount of water in and around Ontario when Europeans first arrived in the early 1600s. It is that water transportation routes linked Ontario with the coasts of western Europe at one end and the heartland of the North American continent at the other. Moreover, the particular geography of the waterways which effected these links gave a particular pattern to the European-oriented

15

civilization that would gradually expand throughout the modern Ontario territory[1].

In an earlier era, this was obvious to people who lived in the region. It is less so today, when water is no longer the dominant mode of transportation and when travel by air has liberated us from at least some earlier implications of earthbound geography. In modern Ontario, however (as in some adjacent parts of both Canada and the United States), virtually all major highway and rail transportation corridors follow the historic waterways of a more romantic age.

The connection between modern ground transportation corridors and historic waterways is common enough in Europe itself. Yet in Ontario, knowledge of these waterways and technology of travelling on them was not introduced by Europeans but inherited by them from the region's Indian peoples. Europeans did not so much discover Ontario's waterways as learn about them from the Indians.

Similarly, the ocean-going European vessels that linked the region with the coasts of western Europe stopped at Hudson Bay in the north. In the south they stopped outside Ontario itself – principally at the St. Lawrence River seaport of Montreal and the more southerly Atlantic seaport of New York City. Throughout the first 175 years of European involvement in the region, the dominant mode of travel within and through Ontario was the traditional Indian technology of the canoe and the portage. This seems part of what Innis was alluding to when he declared in 1930: "We have not yet realized that the Indian and his culture were fundamental to the growth of Canadian institutions."

The first of the "native" waterways used by Europeans in the early 1600s would continue to be of prime importance in Canadian history. It starts at the island of Montreal in the St. Lawrence River and then moves northwest up the Ottawa River to the Mattawa River, to Lake Nipissing, and then along the French River to Georgian Bay. From here it is possible either to move south to the lower Great Lakes (Ontario and Erie) or to continue northwest on the upper Great Lakes (Huron and Superior). By canoe and portage, the northwest route can be followed past

16

Lake Superior, along to the Rainy River and the Lake of the Woods, then to Lake Winnipeg and the start of the prairie of western Canada, and even ultimately to the far Canadian north.

In the 1930s the Ontario-born historian of "the Empire of the St. Lawrence", Donald Creighton, dubbed this Ottawa-French River canoe waterway, the route of the historic Canadian "economy of the north". In broad outline, it marks the path though Ontario followed by the first transcontinental Canadian Pacific Railway of the later nineteenth century and the modern Trans-Canada Highway completed after the Second World War. The Ontario country of the upper lakes thus linked to western Europe via the St. Lawrence River seaport of Montreal can also be linked to Europe via the salt water coast of Hudson and James bays in the far north, into which several large inland water systems drain, including the Severn, Albany, and Moose rivers. This northern outlet was much more important in an earlier era of the region's history than it has subsequently become. But even today, its earlier significance survives in the Ontario Northland Railway that runs from North Bay on Lake Nipissing to Moosonee on James Bay.

It is also possible to reach the lower Great Lakes via the Ottawa-French River route, and this seems to be how the first Europeans reached Lake Ontario. But the more direct route from Montreal to the lower lakes follows the upper St. Lawrence River, which meets Lake Ontario by Kingston. The significance of "upper" here – and presumably in such phrases as "upper country" and "Upper Canada" – is straightforward: the journey is literally uphill. The surface of Lake Ontario is some 75 meters (250 feet) higher than the surface of the St. Lawrence River at Montreal. Lake Erie is higher than Lake Ontario by a somewhat greater distance again.

Two key difficulties in the upper St. Lawrence waterway to the lower lakes were fierce rapids on the upper parts of the river itself and then the awesome cataract at Niagara Falls, about half way up the Niagara River, which links Lake Ontario and Lake Erie. These were not insurmountable for the technology of the canoe and the portage[2]. But they inspired a long subsequent history of canal building, culminating with the modern St. Lawrence Seaway project

17

in the late 1950s. In broad outline, today the route marks the path of southern Ontario's major passenger rail corridor and the multilane, restricted-access Highway 401 – the main street of southern Ontario in the age of the automobile. The most straightforward route from the lower lakes of the south to the upper lakes of the north is via the Detroit River, Lake St. Clair, and the St. Clair River, which together link Lake Erie and Lake Huron. Several shortcuts, however, are also possible. Perhaps the most important historically was the "Toronto Passage" from Georgian Bay to Lake Ontario via the (southern) Severn River, Lake Simcoe, and the Holland and Humber or Rouge rivers. The exact extent to which the Toronto Passage was used during Ontario's earliest history has been a subject of debate. But it was the unambiguous inspiration for one of the region's first European roads in the late eighteenth century, Yonge Street (from Toronto to Lake Simcoe) and for the Great Northern Railway (from Toronto to Collingwood on Georgian Bay) in the mid-nineteenth century. In the late twentieth century, it marks the corridor followed by the multilane Highway 400.

Kingston can be linked to the north as well via the Kawartha Lakes waterway to Georgian Bay (subsequently the Trent-Severn canal). Via what subsequently became the Rideau canal, Kingston can also be linked to the Ottawa River at Ottawa.

Finally, the lower lakes can be linked to points south. From the south shore of Lake Erie, it is possible to reach the Mississippi River by canoe and portage and then to follow the Mississippi all the way down to the Gulf of Mexico. From the south shore of Lake Ontario, it is possible to travel east across the Mohawk River Valley to the Hudson River (discovered by the same European who discovered Hudson Bay) and then to follow the Hudson River south to the seaport of New York City. This route was subsequently improved by the Erie Canal, and today it marks the major rail and highway transportation corridor of New York State – linked with Ontario by rail and by the multilane Queen Elizabeth Way, which runs from Fort Erie to Toronto.

Ontario entered the Canadian Confederation of 1867 as Canada's most populous province, and this has

18

remained the focus of its regional identity. From as early as the seventeenth century, however, it has been a place where political, economic, social, and cultural currents from the east, west, north, and south of North America have mixed and mingled. The economic history of Ontario, Innis suggested in the mid-1930s, has been much influenced by a "struggle between New York and Montreal" for control over trade and development in the region north of the Great Lakes. The ultimate root of the struggle was the region's natural geography of water transportation.

The Virgin Forest and the Canadian Shield

Beyond the ubiquitous lakes and rivers, the first Europeans who arrived in Ontario in the 1600s confronted an immense virgin forest that gave much of the region an appearance quite different from the one it has now. This forest remained fundamentally intact for almost the first two centuries of European involvement in the Ontario territory. But by the early nineteenth century, it had begun to disappear in parts of the south. It has gradually receded northward until it now survives only in the more remote north, and even there the virgin forest is not like what it once was in more southern places.

A forest tends to grow back after it has been cut down, and there are still many trees even in the south (as well as some systematically reforested tracts of land). In the most southwesterly part of Ontario, north of Lake Erie and west of Lake Ontario, the native forest is a predominantly deciduous or hardwood growth, sometimes termed "Carolinian". From here north to a line about midway through Lake Superior is the home of the "Great Lakes-St. Lawrence" forest – a mixed hardwood and softwood (or deciduous and coniferous) growth, dominated by maple, birches, beeches, and oaks, with pine, hemlock, cedar, and other evergreens. From here north to a line somewhat south of James Bay (beyond which all forest vegetation tends to wither under the rigors of a sub-Arctic climate) is the "boreal forest", a largely softwood or coniferous growth dominated by white and black spruce.

Even the virgin forest was subject to periodic waves of destruction through fires ignited by lightning, a hazard

19

Tom Thomson, martyr of the Group of Seven, on a painting expedition in the bush, about 1910. Thomson made his living as a commercial artist at Grip Limited in Toronto. But even from Ontario's largest city one can escape into the wilderness.

that remains in many parts of northern Ontario today. The initial motivation for deliberate destruction by human hands was to clear land for agricultural settlement. In southern Ontario this had been started in a very modest way by Indians before the appearance of Europeans, though it did not begin in earnest until the late eighteenth century. By the early nineteenth century, the work of cutting down trees to feed an export lumber industry had begun as well.

The destruction of virgin forests seems an almost inevitable accompaniment of modern development. It happened in Europe before it happened in North America, and it is happening in such parts of the "Third World" as Nigeria and the Philippines today. Even with systematic reforestation, the regrown forest cannot match the size and splendour of its primeval state. In Ontario today, only the writings of earlier generations convey something of what has been lost. In 1851 W.H. Smith observed that in the western part of what is now Metropolitan Toronto, the "trees were large and widely spaced and rose to a height of fifty feet or more without a limb. The interior of the woods was dim and cool, with hardly any underbrush, but with a deep covering of duff over the forest floor".

It would be wrong to picture all the virgin forest of Ontario as a tranquil idyll. Something of the original Carolinian hardwood forest of the southwest has survived in small patches at Rondeau Provincial Park on Lake Erie. And journalist Robert Thomas Allen has observed:

> Despite its inviting and romantic appearance, this is not an easy forest to move around in. It is thickly overgrown with tangled vines and roots and the mosquitoes are murderous. Even the Indians did not move through them by choice; they followed worn trails whenever possible.

Beyond swarms of mosquitoes, much of the original Ontario forest was home for the more murderous scourge of the black fly, which can still dampen the joys of the summer in some more northern parts of the region today. A French Rècollet Brother who journeyed up the Ottawa River, when it was still a place known to only a few Europeans (in the early 1620s), wrote that the black fly was "the worst martyrdom I suffered in this country".

For well over 200 years the Ontario forest did tend to hide a fundamental geological fact from even the aggressive apostles of European civilization who transformed the landscape of southern Ontario in the nineteenth century. Almost seventy per cent of the modern Ontario territory is covered by the Precambrian or Archaean (very old) rock of the Canadian Shield. The Shield dominates northern Ontario. A triangular-shaped wedge of it reaches straight down into the eastern part of southern Ontario and crosses the St. Lawrence River to become the "Adirondack Dome" of upstate New York.

The Shield is also a profound legacy of geological history that Ontario shares with the largest part of Quebec, a northeastern slice of western Canada (including about half of Manitoba), and a sizable chunk of the modern Canadian Northwest Territories. As elsewhere, it brings to the region an irresistable sense of wilderness and even, in its more northerly reaches, what has been called "primitive terror". Trees (especially softwoods) can grow on the Shield, though in the far north much of it is covered by swampy muskeg. Since the late nineteenth century, it has proved a treasure chest of mineral wealth. In Ontario's earliest history, it was important as a natural habitat for such easily trapped fur-bearing animals as martens, weasels, muskrats, and beavers.

The Archaean rock of the Canadian Shield, however, is completely unsuited to agriculture. Even before the arrival of Europeans, it tended to resist permanent human settlement. This limitation has only gradually become clear to the people who have pioneered the mass settlement of Ontario during the past two centuries. Systematic geological exploration of the region did not begin until the mid-nineteenth century. And even in 1930 Innis could say: "We are only beginning to realize the central position of the Canadian Shield."

Even though it has resisted mass settlement, the furs, forests, and the minerals of the Shield have made it a major source of economic wealth and prosperity in Ontario. The Shield has also brought a sense of the wilderness to the regional imagination, even in an era when most people (even in the north) live in cities and suburbs. The more southerly extensions of the Shield eventually became "cottage country". And they inspired Ontario's first authentic school of regional landscape painters, the "Group of Seven", who began to create innovative interpretations of the scenery on the Shield during the years just before and after the First World War. The Group of Seven was dominated by men who made their living as commercial artists, working in cities. Critics have occasionally objected that some of their paintings depict the Canadian Shield as it might appear in a Walt Disney movie. But others confront the primitive terror (and often dramatic beauty) of the rocky wilderness in a more direct way[3].

Primitive terror is an odd emotion in a modern society. There is perhaps still a sense in which modern Ontario has not quite come to grips with the geographic legacy of the Shield.

Settlement Areas off the Shield

The total area of the modern Ontario territory is somewhat more than one million square kilometers (or 412,000 square miles). This makes it the second largest province in Canada (after Quebec, with British Columbia a close third). It also makes it considerably larger than either California or Texas in the United States or France and the United Kingdom combined, about the same size as Egypt, and more than half the size of Mexico.

It has been suggested, however, that the significance of Ontario's geographic size for human settlement can be better understood if the more than two thirds of the territory taken up by the Canadian Shield is viewed as a form of desert. The analogy is not exact. But the history of mass settlement in the region has been overwhelmingly focused on relatively small parts of the territory that lie off the Shield.

Starting in the far north, the first large area off the Shield is the Hudson Bay Lowlands. But a sub-Arctic climate helps make this area a uniquely fragile environment, unsuited to intensive settlement for nongeological reasons. Today only a few people, mostly Indian and a few Inuit, live in the Hudson Bay Lowlands. They pursue an existence that is at least in some ways closer to life in Ontario when Europeans first arrived in the early 1600s than to that of the modern region.

To the south of the Hudson Bay Lowlands, the northern Ontario Shield is relieved in various places by large deposits of clay. In an earlier era it was thought that these "Clay Belts" held out the prospect of major agricultural settlement in northern Ontario. In fact, they have helped give the north more and better agricultural land than is sometimes recognized. But if the Clay Belts relieve the northern Shield, it seems that they cannot quite overcome its fundamental antipathy to intensive settlement.

Despite great enthusiasm for and vigorous efforts at northern agricultural development in the very late nineteenth and early twentieth centuries, the enterprise has never lived up to the high hopes once entertained for it. Today, only somewhat less than ten per cent of all Ontario people live north of the French River (though this amounts to a population only somewhat less than that of the province of Nova Scotia), and most are concentrated in urban areas that ultimately depend on forestry and mining.

The area of earliest mass European agricultural settlement in Ontario is to the east of the Shield's southern extension in a zone bounded by the Ottawa River, the upper St. Lawrence River, and the edge of the Shield itself. This "Ottawa-St. Lawrence Valley" is in effect an extension of the adjacent geography in the province of Quebec. It is the Ontario part of the historic "central Canada" of John A. Macdonald and Georges Etienne Cartier in the 1860s – the society of the St. Lawrence River valley that stretches from Quebec City to Kingston and is dominated economically by Montreal. Historically, it has been a focus both for "British-American" United Empire Loyalist migrations in the late eighteenth century and for French Canadian migrations in the nineteenth century.

The Ottawa-St. Lawrence Valley is not remarkable for first-class agricultural land. But much of it is suited to various forms of farming. Today, eastern Ontario (or, more strictly, southeastern Ontario) has a somewhat larger population than northern Ontario. But to those who study economic growth, both the east and the north are Ontario's modern "lagging regions" (and, others would argue, most

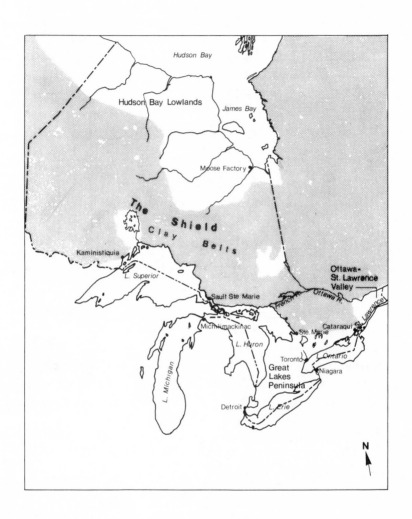

Map: The modern Ontario territory in the seventeenth and eighteenth centuries.

culturally vigorous places). The one unambiguous centre of prosperity in the southeast today is the Canadian national capital region that surrounds Ottawa.

The part of Ontario that has been most hospitable to mass settlement is the "Great Lakes Peninsula" to the west of the Shield's southern extension – or, roughly, west of the Kawartha Lakes waterway that stretches from Kingston to the southeast corner of Georgian Bay. Today, well over three-quarters of all people in Ontario live in this area. And on the available evidence, it seems that the largest part of the region's population also lived in the Great Lakes Peninsula when Europeans first arrived in the early 1600s.

The peninsula itself is divided into two very roughly equal parts by a "giant's rib" of rock known as the Niagara Escarpment, stretching from Niagara Falls in the southeast to the Bruce County area in the northwest. The area to the east of the Escarpment and west of the southern extension of the Canadian Shield is perhaps not what it sometimes takes itself to be – the modern central Canada; but it is at least "central Ontario". It contains three of modern Ontario's four largest metropolitan areas (Toronto, Hamilton, and St. Catharines-Niagara) and is by far and away the most populous part of the province today.

Central Ontario also contains large amounts of high quality farm land. One of Toronto's historic advantages in the early rivalry among Ontario urban centres was that (unlike Kingston in the east, for instance) it was surrounded by a prosperous agricultural hinterland. The area between the Niagara Escarpment and Lake Ontario, immediately northwest of Niagara Falls, is peculiarly suited to tender fruit cultivation and has become a centre for Ontario's modern domestic wine industry.

The area to the west of the Escarpment (southwestern Ontario) contains Ontario's best agricultural land. It was the heartland of the nineteenth-century Ontario wheat economy, which subsequently moved to western Canada. Today, it is the most prosperous centre of modern Ontario mixed farming, with corn (the old staple of Ontario's agricultural Indians) as the principal field crop.

Just as southeastern Ontario is an extension of the adjacent geography of Quebec, southwestern Ontario is an extension of the adjacent geography of the midwest United States. It has been a centre for a Canadian-American influence that has played an important role in Ontario history since the beginnings of mass settlement in the late eighteenth century. As in the US midwest, the German culture of central Europe has also been historically important, especially in the Waterloo County area at the hinge of central and southwestern Ontario. In the first half of the nineteenth century, the southwest was also a haven for Black American refugees from slavery.

Winter, Spring, Summer and Fall

As in Canada at large, winter is perhaps the one season most closely associated with Ontario by people outside the region. In the middle of the eighteenth century, when France and England were at war in North America, the French writer Voltaire dismissed Canada as "a few acres of snow" not worth fighting for. In the late nineteenth century Ottawa was described by Goldwin Smith, one of Ontario's most famous English immigrants, as "the last lumber village before the North Pole."

With only a few exceptions in the deepest southwest, frost lingers in the ground throughout the region for more than half the year. The Great Lakes tend to freeze over in the winter. One of the historic difficulties of the St. Lawrence waterway, with its port at Montreal, is that it must shut down for the winter (though in the Ontario pioneer era of the nineteenth century, winter also opened up possibilities for land travel that did not exist in other seasons). Winter ice is an even greater problem on the sub-Arctic coastline of Hudson Bay. In Ontario, as elsewhere in Canada, the native sport is ice hockey.

At the same time, Ontario contains the most southerly parts of Canada (which may be one geographic reason why it is also Canada's most populous province). There is a major contrast between the relatively benign "Humid Continental Interior" climate of the more southerly parts of the region and the cold "Taiga" climate north of Lake Huron and Lake Superior, with its sub-Arctic overtones on the shores of Hudson Bay. Similarly, the average frost-free period in Thunder Bay on the northwest shore of Lake

Superior is just over three months, and in Kapuskasing it is even less. The frost-free period in Toronto lasts for five and a half months, and in the Windsor area of the southwest it approaches half a year.

The English geographers W.R.Mead and E.H. Brown have reported that in Ontario, as in adjacent parts of both Canada and the United States, "spring in the West European sense of the term does not appear in the climate." In Ontario, spring is when the snow and ice melt, the leaves reappear on the hardwood trees, the grass starts to grow again, and the birds which have gone south for the winter return. Not long after this, it suddenly seems to be summer.

The contrast between winter and summer in the region is dramatic. Sudbury in the more southerly part of the Shield, has a higher maximum normal temperature in July than San Francisco in northern California. Ottawa tends to get hotter than Sudbury; Toronto gets somewhat hotter than Ottawa; and Windsor gets hotter than Toronto. But all three tend to get almost as hot as New York City in the middle of summer. In 1976 the highest recorded temperature in the northern Ontario city of Sault Ste. Marie, at the gateway from Lake Huron to Lake Superior, matched that of the Solomon Islands in the south Pacific Ocean.

Almost all the more settled parts of modern Ontario share the "New England Autumn" common throughout the northeastern part of North America. The needle-like vegetation on the evergreen trees of the boreal forest in the far north remains in place all year. But in the Great Lakes-St. Lawrence and Carolinian forests to the south, the first frosts of fall turn the leaves on the hardwood trees (if it is a good year) into a riot of colour. Then, the leaves fall from the trees, and winter sets in with the first snowfall. The process begins progressively earlier as one moves north. Ontario, like other parts of Canada, celebrates Thanksgiving, the modern commemoration of the mythical first European winter in the North American wilderness, about six weeks earlier than in the United States.

Climate seems to be something that human beings cannot deliberately change. Not everyone in the late twentieth century, however, would agree with Wilfred Laurier's dictum: "You cannot legislate against geography." In the 1960s a former Ontario civil servant, with his eye on "the continental thirst for fresh water", suggested a scheme "to dam Hudson Bay, pump out the salt water and use the basin as a freshwater reservoir for the streams and rivers in the Hudson Bay drainage area". Assuming it is remotely practicable, in some ways the suggestion still has attractions. But the "ecological crisis", journalist Barbara Moon argued in the early 1970s, "has made it clear how mischievous such schemes can be, and how subtle and far-reaching their effects."

Those who take the ecological crisis most seriously have more recently suggested that human industrial progress during the past 200 years has been heating up the atmosphere of the earth. According to a *Globe and Mail* report, a resulting "greenhouse effect" could produce "a climatic upheaval as great as any since the last ice age", with "dramatic changes ... taking place in the next century". From the particular standpoint of Ontario, studies from the early 1980s have suggested that there "will be less water in the Great Lakes...but the Hudson Bay Lowlands could become a foodbasket."

It is difficult for someone who is not a specialist to know just what to make of such claims (and perhaps even more difficult to judge just how seriously the specialists are to be taken). But if such things do happen, the Ontario society that responds to the new challenges and opportunities will be one shaped and influenced by the same geography that confronted the first Europeans in the early 1600s.

2

Ontario's Forgotten History

Ontario's recorded history begins with a long period of French and Indian wilderness romance, a misty prelude to the more recent history of English-speaking mass settlement that starts in the late eighteenth century. The period lasts for more than 150 years, and is part of what British colonial officials of 200 years ago viewed as the "antient" history of Canada. Former Premier Leslie Frost has aptly called the the French and Indian period "Ontario's forgotten history...."

The period is sometimes dated from 1613-1615, which marks the first journeys into the modern Ontario territory by Samuel de Champlain, the founder of New France. A stronger case can perhaps be made for the year 1610. This marks the first appearance in Ontario by Champlain's younger lieutenant, Etienne Brûlé. It marks as well the discovery of Hudson Bay by the Englishman Henry Hudson (though it would be another sixty years before English fur traders became active in northern Ontario). 1610 has also been proposed as the date of a significant event for the Indians who formed the overwhelming majority of the Ontario population throughout the French and Indian period. According to the historical anthropologist, Bruce Trigger, about 1610 an Indian nation known as the Tahontaenrat joined the Attignawantan, the Attingueenongnahac, and the Ahrendarrhonon to complete the ancient Huron Confederacy, whose adventures during the next forty years dominate

"Sainte-Marie-aux-Hurons": the modern reconstruction. The mission is located on the Wye River, just south of Georgian Bay. Archaeological excavation at the site began in the 1950s, supported by the Royal Ontario Museum, the Society of Jesus in Upper Canada, and the University of Western Ontario. It attracted as many as 50,000 visitors a year during its later phases. Work on systematic and extensive reconstruction, sponsored by the Government of Ontario, began in 1964.

the earliest written records of human life in the region. Whatever the exact year, recorded history in the Ontario territory begins not long after the founding of the capital of New France at Quebec City in 1608 or the establishment in 1607 of Jamestown, Virginia – the first of what would later become the original Thirteen Colonies of the British empire in North America.

The Algonkian and Iroquoian Peoples

The exact number of Indians living in the modern Ontario territory when Europeans first appeared in 1610 can perhaps never be known with certainty. A combination of archaeological evidence and the available written records for the subsequent two decades, however, suggests at least about 50,000 and almost certainly no more than 100,000 people. It is now believed that the Indians originally emigrated from Asia to North America and first appeared in southern Ontario about 9,000 BC. By the early seventeenth century there were two main groups of these people, each in more or less separate parts of the territory. The geographic distinction is a blend of north and south and areas on and off the Canadian Shield. According to J.V.Wright, a leading archaeological authority on Ontario prehistory, the "available evidence suggests that the prehistory of these two regions or culture areas has been distinct and different from the earliest beginnings to the historic period".

On the Shield to the north were smaller numbers of Algonkian "hunters and gatherers" or "wandering peoples". They included the Algonquin, the Ottawa, the Nipissing, the Mississauga, the Ojibway (or Chippewa), and (to the far north) the Cree[1]. The Algonkian peoples lived in temporary settlements moving from place to place in response to the exigencies of an economy based on hunting, fishing, and gathering (chiefly wild fruits and nuts). But they were also the makers of the finest of all bark canoes, constructed from lightweight birch-bark not available in the deeper south and highly valued by other peoples in trade.

Before the start of mass settlement in the 1780s, Algonkian peoples moved into southern Ontario. Many early English-speaking settlers in the south believed that they had been the area's original peoples. Yet in 1610 the area off the Shield to the south, in the Great Lakes Peninsula, was the home of Iroquoian agricultural peoples, who significantly outnumbered the Algonkians to the north.

The largest group of "Ontario Iroquois" in the early 1600s was the Huron Confederacy (which called itself the "Wendat"), located at the north end of the Toronto Passage between Lake Simcoe and Georgian Bay. When French-speaking Europeans first arrived in Ontario, the Huron Confederacy included perhaps 20,000 or more people, living in about twenty villages, some half dozen of which were large fortified settlements. The land surrounding the Huron villages had been cleared, and agriculture accounted for as much as three-quarters of the Huron food supply, with the remainder provided by hunting, gathering, fishing, and trade. Corn (or maize) was the most important crop. But the Huron also grew beans and squash (and some tobacco), and cultivated sunflower seeds for their oil.

To the west of the Huron, near what is now the Blue Mountain area of the Niagara Escarpment, was another group of agricultural Ontario Iroquois, known as the Petun or Tobacco Nation. The Petun (like Huron, a French name – they called themselves "Tionantati") were less numerous than the Huron, living in about nine villages, only one or two of which were of any size. They spoke the same language as the Huron; and by around 1640 the Huron and the Petun had negotiated a formal treaty of friendship.

Small numbers of Algonkian peoples inhabited the Georgian Bay area to the west of the Petun. To the south, on the north shore of Lake Erie, was a third group of Ontario Iroquois, known to the Huron as the "Attiwandaron" (meaning "people who speak a slightly different language") and to the French as Les Neutres or the Neutral Nation. They were also corn-growing agricultural people, though hunting and gathering may have been more important for them than for the Huron. It seems that they were somewhat less numerous than the Huron. But they are said to have occupied as many as forty villages scattered along the north shore of Lake Erie.

The Neutrals were so called by the French because they refused to take sides in a longstanding tradition of warfare between the Huron and the "Five Nations Iroquois", who lived south of Lake Ontario in what is now western New York State. The most easterly of the Five Nations, the Mohawks, also seem to have had influence in the country south of the upper St. Lawrence to the west of Montreal. There are reports of Iroquoian peoples in the St. Lawrence valley part of Ontario, east of the southern Shield, before the early 1600s. By the time Brûlé and Champlain arrived, however, Algonkian peoples were dominant in the area.

It has been speculated that Iroquois who once lived along the St. Lawrence later became part of both the Five Nations Iroquois and the Huron Confederacy. It has been speculated as well that part of the Huron Confederacy was once located at the south end of the Toronto Passage, on the site of modern Metropolitan Toronto (and archaeologists have discovered the remains of prehistoric Iroquoian settlements in the area). But by the early 1600s both the north shore of Lake Ontario and the interior of the southwest were uninhabited hunting grounds.

Huronia: The Country of the Wendat

The Huron Confederacy was the strongest political organization in the Ontario territory when Brûlé and Champlain arrived in the early 1600s. Economically, the language of the Huron was the *lingua franca* of a quite large trading network that extended beyond the modern boundaries of Ontario.

The Huron had close trading relationships with the Algonkians to their north, including the Nipissing (on Lake Nipissing), who travelled as far north as James Bay every summer. They were in touch with Algonkian peoples as far east as Tadoussac, east of Quebec City on the St. Lawrence River. They traded with the Winnebago as far west as Lake Michigan, and they seem to have had quite close relationships with the Susquehannah to the south in the vicinity of what would later become Philadelphia. They had also begun to deal with French fur traders on the lower St. Lawrence as early as 1600. As the first

Frenchmen were arriving in Ontario, the Confederacy of the Wendat was consolidating its role as principal middleman of the newly developing fur trade between France and the upper country of the Great Lakes. It was in this context that Brûlé, Champlain, and other ambassadors from the new French settlements in the lower St. Lawrence valley made the journey to the country of the Wendat.

The French travelled in canoes with Indian guides, and they followed the Ottawa-French River route to Georgian Bay. From here they travelled south on the Bay (part of the Lac des Hurons) to Huronia in what is now northern Simcoe County, roughly between Orillia and Midland. Having been accustomed to the simpler Algonkian societies of the St. Lawrence valley, the French were struck by the complexity and sophistication of the Iroquoian society of the Huron. According to Trigger, they came to regard "the intelligence of the Huron" as "superior to that of peasants in their own country". The encounter between the European civilization of seventeenth-century France and the North American wilderness culture of the Confederacy of the Wendat from about 1610 to 1650 marks the first major episode in the recorded history of Ontario.

The French were particularly struck by a complex network of Huron political institutions. These reached from the grass roots of the family (or extended family) to the highest places of the Confederacy, providing a vigorous and benign blend of freedom and order, without recourse to police powers or capital punishment. The optimistic French political thought of the eighteenth century, with its conception of man as "born free" in a "state of nature" (especially identified with Jean-Jacques Rousseau), owes at least something to the French encounter with the Huron Indians of North America in the earlier seventeenth century.

At the same time, Huron society had features which grate against the sensibilities of Ontario society today. Men undertook the arduous labour of clearing fields for agriculture under stone-age technology when Huron villages were moved to cope with soil exhaustion every ten to twenty years. Otherwise, all the work of the agricultural economy was the responsibility of women. Men hunted, fished, and made weapons, tools, and houses; they also traded with their neighbours, and made war on their enemies. Warfare tended to be chronic among the agricultural Iroquoians of northeastern North America, though it was not especially violent or aggressive. Before the arrival of European weapons, Huron warriors wore wooden armour into battle. But a prime objective was to seize captives, who were then taken to the captors' village and put to death by ceremonial torture, which it was the captured warrior's duty to accept stoically and even with a degree of wit[2].

For the Huron, the chief attraction of contact with the French was the fur trade. It brought them European manufactured goods, especially iron and copper domestic utensils, that greatly enhanced the convenience of their day to day life. But, jealously guarding their role as middlemen of the fur trade in the upper country, they were suspicious of French fur traders who ventured into their own region. They gave a warmer welcome to members of French religious orders, who began to arrive in the 1620s with the objective of converting the Indians to Catholicism.

Both the Récollet and Sulpician orders would gradually become active in what is now southern Ontario. But the most successful mission to the country of the Huron was undertaken by the Jesuits, known to the Indians as "Black Robes". The Huron generally were not avid converts. A few became Christians, however, and in 1639 the Jesuits constructed a mission settlement known as "Ste. Marie among the Hurons", near what is now Midland. It contained more than two dozen buildings, including a log church and a hospital. It was sometimes occupied by as many as fifty to sixty Frenchmen, at a time when the French settlements on the lower St. Lawrence River had a total population of not many more than 200 Europeans.

Not long before the construction of Ste. Marie, epidemics had swept through Huronia, similar to those which often accompanied early European contacts elsewhere in the New World. And by about 1640, the traditional warfare betwen the Huron and the Five Nations Iroquois had become entangled with new economic rivalries, linked with the European-oriented fur trade. The Huron to the north had become middlemen for the French fur trade based on the lower St. Lawrence River at Quebec City and Montreal (established in 1642). The Five Nations Iroquois to the south had become middlemen for a Dutch fur trade based on the Hudson River, at New Amsterdam (which would become the English city of New York in 1664) and Fort Orange (the modern capital of New York State at Albany).

Control over the rich fur resources of the upper country north of the Great Lakes became a new focus for the old Huron-Iroquois warfare. At stake was the flow of vital European manufactured goods, on which the Indians had become quickly dependent for their survival. The Iroquois were particularly aggressive because the fur resources of their area were diminishing. They extended their lines of trade northward, clashing with those of the Hurons and the French. Accessibility to European guns now rendered warfare more deadly than before.

By 1648 the Five Nations were pressing hard on the perimeters of Huronia itself. The Jesuit mission villages of St. Joseph, St. Ignace, and St. Louis were obliterated, and Fathers Jean Brébeuf and Gabriel Lalement became heroic martyrs. In the spring of 1649 the Huron, with many warriors dead and their population already much depleted by the epidemics of the later 1630s, decided to abandon their villages. The Jesuits abandoned Ste. Marie, setting it on fire as they left[3]. Some Huron returned with most of the French to the lower St. Lawrence, where their descendants still live today. Others fled to the north and west.

By the early 1650s the Five Nations Iroquois had managed to expel the Petun and the Neutral from the Great Lakes Peninsula as well. It would be another generation or more before the French and their northern Indian allies regained effective control over what is now southern Ontario. According to Innis, the "struggle waged between the Iroquois and the Hurons was a prelude to the struggle between New York and Montreal, which dominated the economic history of Ontario."

The Early Canadian Fur Trade
and the Ontario Regional Economy

A fashion for expensive beaver hats among the upper classes of western Europe helped stimulate the seventeenth-century European fur trade in northern North America. Above all else the fur trade first opened up much of Canada (and much of the northern United States) to the influence of Europe. The trade was a dominant economic force in the Ontario territory from the end of the Huron-Iroquois War in 1650 down to the 1780s, and it remained important until about a decade after the War of 1812 (after which it lived on in western Canada).

The long, slow development of the early Canadian fur trade also helped shape the more complex Ontario regional economy, that would gradually develop after the start of mass settlement in the late eighteenth century. Through the fur trade, Europeans learned about Ontario's geography and its transportation corridors along the native waterways, typically travelled by "canot de maître" until virtually the start of mass settlement. A half dozen strategic outposts of the fur trade would ultimately become the modern Ontario urban centres of Kingston, Toronto, Niagara, Windsor, Sault Ste. Marie, and Thunder Bay. From 1650 to 1750, the Ontario territory itself was a kind of hub, around which the gradual expansion of the early Canadian fur trade took shape.

The initial impact of the final Huron-Iroquois War was to push the Ottawa-French River trade to the north and west of the abandoned mission at Ste. Marie, following the flight of the Huron. During the 1660s and 1670s new French outposts (and Jesuit missions) were established at Sault Ste. Marie between Lake Huron and Lake Superior as well as in several places in what are now the states of Michigan and Wisconsin. The French also became the first Europeans to establish a presence in modern Illinois. At first, the Ottawa-French River route remained the one link between this new trade on the upper Great Lakes (and the more westerly Lake Michigan) and the French settlements on the lower St. Lawrence River. The interior centre of the trade, however, gravitated toward an outpost just outside the modern Ontario territory at Michilimackinac, between

Lake Huron and Lake Michigan in what is now the state of Michigan.

After the final Huron-Iroquois War, some Huron united with the Petun to become the Wyandot (a corruption of Wendat), who eventually scattered as far south as Oklahoma. Some still known as the Hurons remained a part of the fur trade. But by the later seventeenth century, they are described in the French sources as "reduced to a very small number", though still "with a turn for intrigue and a capacity for large undertakings". The Hurons' earlier role as native middlemen in the fur trade based on the lower St. Lawrence was inherited by the Algonkian nation of the Ottawa, who (much later events would show) also developed their own large capacity and skill at intrigue.

Some Frenchmen from the lower St. Lawrence became active in the work of paddling canots de maître as well. They began the wilderness romance of the voyageur or "coureur de bois", who, as historian Francis Parkman noted, "liked the woods because they emancipated him from restraint ... the lounging ease of the camp-fire, and the licence of Indian villages." When not at his lounging ease, the coureur de bois travelled from seventy to eighty miles a day by canoe and portage, bearing trade goods from Europe on the yearly trip from Montreal into the interior and bales of furs on the return journey. Some tended to remain in the interior, and (like other Europeans at later stages of the fur trade) they took Indian wives. The result was the unique culture of the "Métis", a blend of European and North American Indian culture. Though the Métis would not aspire to political expression until the appearance of Louis Riel in western Canada during the nineteenth century, they had their origins in the upper country of Ontario and the northeastern American midwest during the seventeenth and eighteenth centuries.

The upper or managerial levels of the early Canadian fur trade were subject to highly regulated forms of French "bureaucratic commerce" in the absolutist age of the Sun King, Louis xiv, who ruled France and its colonial possessions from 1661 to 1715. In the 1660s the bureaucratic commercial regime of New France proved particularly irksome to two French traders active along the Ottawa-French

River route – Pierre-Esprit Radisson and Médard Chouart des Groseilliers. They conceived a plan to tap the rich fur resources in the upper country of the Great Lakes via the watershed that drained into Hudson Bay. Radisson's philosophy was "where that there is lucre, there are people enough to be had."

Radisson and Groseilliers travelled to London, England to seek English financial backing for their project. Their efforts led to the establishment of the Hudson's Bay Company in 1670. The Company constructed posts at the mouths of several rivers on Hudson and James bays and quickly reaped attractive profits from the North American trade in furs.

The immediate French response to this new English competition from the far north was to move onto Hudson Bay themselves. For a time, in the 1680s, Radisson switched back to the side of the bureaucratic commercial regime of New France. During the later seventeenth and early eighteenth centuries, there were periodic skirmishes between small groups of French and English in the sub-Arctic wilderness, and possession of the posts on Hudson and James bays from time to time switched hands. The conflict did not begin to fade until Louis XIV formally acknowledged the English claim to the territories drained by Hudson Bay as part of the Treaty of Utrecht in 1713.

A more long-term French response was to expand the Montreal-based fur trade of the upper Great Lakes to the northwest into what is now western Canada, while the merchants of the Hudson's Bay Company waited for the Indians to bring furs to their posts on Hudson and James bays. Not long after the Treaty of Utrecht, the French had become very familiar with the waterway from Lake Superior to Lake Winnipeg. By the 1730s Pierre Gaultier de Varennes et de La Vérendrye was using a fur-trading outpost at "Kaministiquia", now Thunder Bay, on the northwest shore of Lake Superior as a base in his search for "the Western Sea". He would never reach the Pacific Ocean. But in 1743 La Vérendrye and four of his sons arrived at the Rocky Mountains.

The early Canadian fur trade on the Ottawa-French River route also faced English competition from the south. After the end of the Huron-Iroquois War in the early

Old Fort Niagara, on the east bank of the Niagara River, in what is now western New York State. Built by the French in Canada more than 250 years ago; captured for the British by William Johnson of the Mohawks in 1759; and surrendered by the British to the forces of the new American republic in 1796.

1650s, the Five Nations Iroquois established villages on the north shore of Lake Ontario. "Teiaigon" and "Ganatsekwyagon" were at either end of modern Metropolitan Toronto at the mouths of the Humber and the Rouge Rivers. "Ganaraske" was near Port Hope and "Ganneious" near Napanee on the Bay of Quinte.

Via the Toronto Passage and the Kawartha waterway, the Iroquois siphoned trade away from the Montreal-based Ottawa-French River route and sent furs to the European traders on the Hudson River. When the English New York succeeded the Dutch New Amsterdam in 1664, the Five Nations Iroquois became staunch allies of the new English fur traders. By the time of the Treaty of Utrecht, the Five Nations themselves had become the Six Nations, as the Tuscarora from what is now North Carolina joined the Seneca, Cayuga, Onondaga, Oneida, and Mohawks in what is now western New York[4].

The French began to assert their own presence in southern Ontario when the Marquis de Tracy and the Carignan-Salières Regiment defeated Iroquois war parties blocking the upper St. Lawrence waterway in the early 1660s. Later in the decade French Sulpician missionaries were sent to the Iroquois villages on the north shore of Lake Ontario. In 1673 a French fort was established at "Cataraqui", now Kingston, where the St. Lawrence River meets Lake Ontario. Antoine de La Mothe Cadillac established a major French outpost at Detroit on the Detroit River between Lake Erie and Lake St. Clair in 1701, and this replaced Michilimackinac as capital of the upper country.

By this time, the Iroquois villages had begun to disappear from the north shore of Lake Ontario, and Algonkian allies of the French (especially the Mississauga and Ojibway or Chippewa) had begun to move into southern Ontario. During the 1720s, as Innis points out, "Ontario was being hammered by French policy into a fortified unit, guaranteeing control for the lower St. Lawrence." A three-storey stone fort was erected on the east bank of the Niagara River at the edge of Lake Ontario. A small trading post was established on Lake Ontario at the southern end of the Toronto Passage as "a dependency of Niagara". The English fur traders of New York built a competing fort at the mouth of the Oswego River on the south shore of Lake Ontario. But the French had established primacy in southern Ontario itself. In the early 1750s the trading outpost at Toronto was succeeded by a log fort with a small French garrison.

The French presence in southern Ontario provided leverage for expansion southward into the Mississipppi valley as well. The enterprise had been started by René Robert Cavalier Sieur de La Salle in the 1670s and 1680s. Using the new outpost at Cataraqui (called Fort Frontenac) as a base of operations, La Salle led a series of dramatic canoe voyages[5] through the wilderness, which ultimately took him down the Mississippi River to the Gulf of Mexico. He named the Mississippi Valley "Louisiana", claiming it for Louis xiv. Less than forty years later, in 1718, New Orleans was established at the mouth of the Mississippi River.

Detroit, the capital of the French Canadian upper country of the Great Lakes, was also an important link of communication between Canada and Louisiana. Though located just outside the boundaries of modern Ontario, Detroit is a part of its early history. As late as 1793, maps of the new British province of Upper Canada included Detroit within the boundaries of the province as part of the county of Kent[6]. Detroit would remain predominantly French Canadian into the early nineteenth century; and down to the present, the modern American city has exerted an important economic and cultural influence in southwestern Ontario.

The Culture of French and Indian Ontario and its Fate

Even at the height of the French empire in North America in the early 1750s, the European (or even European and Métis) population of Ontario was not very large. Indians (mostly Algonkians) still formed the overwhelming majority. Moreover, it seems clear that the population of the region as a whole was significantly smaller than it had been during the final era of the Ontario Iroquois in the earlier seventeenth century.

By the 1740s the French American empire, stretching in a giant arc from Quebec City and Montreal on the lower St. Lawrence to New Orleans at the mouth of the Mississippi, was starting to feel pressure from the much more populous British American Thirteen Colonies, stretching along the Atlantic seaboard south of the St. Lawrence valley. To strengthen the linchpin of the wilderness commercial regime at Detroit, by the later 1740s French officials had begun to encourage French Canadian farmers from the lower St. Lawrence to settle at the capital of the upper country. Some of those who responded took up land on the south shore of the Detroit River, opposite the fort and trading outpost, on the site of present-day Windsor. They pioneered the first permanent European agricultural settlements in the modern Ontario territory.

The culture of French and Indian Ontario at large, however, was different from the New World replica of feudal France that had taken root on the lower St. Lawrence. Indians as well as coureur de bois were indispensable participants in the labour force of early Ontario's fur trade economy. During the later seventeenth century a few wealthy individuals in the French settlements on the lower St. Lawrence had begun to import black African slaves to act as domestic servants. Not long after Cadillac founded Detroit in 1701, a few black Africans were also living in the new capital of the upper country[7]. In essence, French and Indian Ontario was a "polyethnic" world.

3

e for Mastery
eat Lakes

ury the Ontario wilderness
nded struggle for control not
of the North American heart-
t the opponents in this strug-
he English. The historically
defeat of the forces of the
y those of the British empire.
Canada and the United States
would be one country today.

The fundamental opponents were two different North American worlds of the earlier eighteenth century. On the one side was an immense French and Indian commercial wilderness, stretching from Quebec City to New Orleans and west to the Rocky Mountains – anchored by a cluster of some 60,000 French Catholics along the lower St. Lawrence River. On the other side was the expanding Anglo-American settlement frontier, anchored by more than a million English Protestants between the Atlantic Ocean and the Allegheny Mountains, from Massachusetts south to Georgia[1].

The struggle began with what American historian William P. Taylor has characterized as "the almost insane grandiosity of French colonial ambition" pitted against the equally wild demonic energy of the Anglo-American frontier. It ended in a more complicated way. Indian warriors played important roles on both sides in the first wave of the

45

conflict, known as the Seven Years War (1756-1763) or the British conquest of New France. In the second wave, the American War of Independence (1776-1783), they were concentrated on one side. In between the two waves, the British and French empires switched sides.

In both waves of the struggle, the modern Ontario territory was on the periphery of the actual fighting that took place, rather than at its centre. Similarly, to the south of the Great Lakes, the final results of the struggle were decisive. To the north, the results were more ambiguous (though they would ultimately prove equally decisive in a somewhat different way). The struggle for mastery in the Great Lakes saw two different worlds collide. Ontario history after the late eighteenth century is a creation of the collision.

The Last French and Indian War
and Pontiac's Conspiracy

What is usually known in the history of the United States as the French and Indian War – and in Canada by its more European name of the Seven Years War – was in fact only the last in a series of periodic military conflicts between France and England in North America, starting in the seventeenth century. The earlier conflicts, however, were skirmishes in the wilderness or in the backwoods of more easterly settlement frontiers with only partial results. One example was a conflict on the Atlantic coast that added Nova Scotia to the British empire. Another was the fighting on Hudson and James bays, that gave the British Empire (and its agent the Hudson's Bay Company) formal title to what is now the northern part of northern Ontario as a result of the Treaty of Utrecht in 1713. The North American war betwen France and England that began in the mid 1750s and ended with the Peace of Paris on 10 February 1763 was much more conclusive. In the eyes of the nations of Europe, it brought all of what is now Canada east of the Rocky Mountains (and thus the remainder of what is now Ontario) into the British empire. And with only a few exceptions, it ended the historic French empire in America.

46

Private in the French Canadian militia, engraving, 1758.

From a very broad point of view, the war was only part of a much larger struggle that eventually involved all the major European powers of the day in several regions of the globe; Samuel Eliot Morison maintains it "should really have been called the First World War." The English won major victories against the French on the subcontinent of India, just two years before their decisive victories in North America. At the Peace of Paris in 1763 the French colony of Louisiana was ceded to the King of Spain, who also got back Manila in the Philippines from the United Kingdom[2].

The defeats suffered during the Seven Years War by the "Ancien Regime" in France (now under Louis xv) were part of the path to the French Revolution a quarter century later. But under Louis xvi (1774-1792), old France had a last revenge on the King of England, by playing the decisive military role in the final triumph of the patriot republicans in the American War of Independence which broke out just twelve years after the Peace of Paris was signed.

In North America, as elsewhere, Europeans and people of European descent did not fight alone in the Seven Years War, but with native allies. On the eve of the war, in June 1754, representatives from British New York, Pennsylvania, Maryland, and the New England colonies met with the Six Nations Iroquois at Albany, to work out a joint plan of defense by Indian and British colonial forces against the advances of the French. Just over a year later, almost 1,500 British scarlet-coated regulars and blue-coated Virginians were defeated at the Battle of Monongahela River, near present day Pittsburgh, by a force of 637 braves (perhaps led by Pontiac, a chief of the Ottawa) and about 150 French Canadian militia led by 72 French officers and regulars.

The war in North America emanated from stirrings in the Anglo-American settlement frontier just to the west of the Thirteen Colonies. In the late 1740s a group of land-speculating notables from Virginia (including the father of Thomas Jefferson) had formed the Ohio Company, with a plan to settle the Ohio valley wilderness to the south of the Great Lakes. The officials of New France took this as a threat to French communications between Montreal and New Orleans that could not be ignored. In Europe the war was an imperial struggle between two great powers – England and France. In North America, it was a struggle for control of the continental heartland between the Anglo-American settlement frontier and the French and Indian wilderness romance.

In 1749 an expedition from the lower St. Lawrence had occupied the Ohio valley for the King of France. Matters came to a head in 1753 when the Marquis Duquesne, Governor of Canada, ordered the construction of a chain of log forts on the Allegheny and upper Ohio rivers in what is now western Pennsylvania. The Governor of Virginia (then the most populous of the Thirteen Colonies) sent a 22-year-old George Washington to the forks of the Ohio River with a formal protest. The French ignored the protest and fighting broke out in 1754. War was formally declared the following year.

The defeat of the British redcoats and Virginia blue-coats at the Battle of the Monongahela River in 1755 was, according to Morison:

> the Pearl Harbor of the Seven Years' War. It ... threw back the effective English frontier hundreds of miles, and exposed new settlements to a series of devastating Indian attacks. Thousands of men, women, and children who had settled the Shenandoah valley in the last forty years lost all they had, and were lucky to escape with their lives.

In 1756 French forces captured the English fort at Oswego on the south shore of Lake Ontario and took Fort William Henry to the north of Albany, New York a year later. The French and their Indian allies continued to hold the upper hand in the North American fighting until 1758, when British Secretary of State William Pitt, bolstered by success in India, strengthened the British war effort.

In the late summer of 1758 a New England force captured the French post at Cataraqui, and Oswego was recaptured. In the autumn the main French positions in the Ohio valley fell to British forces. William Johnson of the Mohawks from New York captured the three-storey stone fort at Niagara in July 1759. News of the fall of Niagara prompted the small French garrison at Toronto (following

49

an earlier plan) to abandon their position, setting fire to the fort as they fled to Montreal.

The British General James Wolfe's defeat of the Marquis de Montcalm on the Plains of Abraham at Quebec City in September 1759, during a brief battle in which both men died, proved the decisive event of the Seven Years War in North America. French forces at Detroit, however, did not surrender until the late fall of 1760, and some of the more westerly fur-trade outposts remained in French hands until the following year. Moreover, as the Peace of Paris was signed in 1763, the new British forces in the upper country of Canada faced a new challenge from the former Indian allies of the King of France.

When British forces and British American fur traders began to take over the outposts of the Canadian fur trade, the unprecedented extent of the French defeat became clear to the tribes of the interior. Fears for the ultimate future of the wilderness commerce from which both French and Indians had profitted and broader fears about the future of life in the forest gained strength. By 1762 Pontiac, a chief of the Ottawa nation, had begun to voice these fears.

He won enormous support from the Algonkian peoples in what is now Ontario and the more westerly Great Lakes, from Indian nations as far south as the lower Mississippi, and even from the Seneca, most westerly of the Six Nations Iroquois. As the ink was drying on the Peace of Paris, he orchestrated a dramatic protest that showed just how much the Ottawa had inherited of the old Huron "turn for intrigue" and "capacity for large undertakings". Starting at Detroit in the spring of 1763, for more than a year the conspiracy of Pontiac terrorized the newly-acquired British posts of the north and west. A truce of sorts was arranged at Niagara late in 1764. Pontiac himself formally made peace at Detroit in the summer of 1765 and finally concluded a treaty with William Johnson at Oswego on 23 July 1766. But in the eyes of the officials of the British empire, his resistance had made an important point.

The impact of Pontiac's bold protest in the western wilderness was felt almost immediately in the British Royal Proclamation of 1763, which provided a new British government for the defeated colony of New France. The

50

Proclamation defined the boundaries of the British Province of Quebec very narrowly, from Gaspé on the Atlantic coast to a line just west of the Ottawa River. The Great Lakes region (including most of Ontario) became part of a far-flung "Indian Territory", west of a line (throughout British North America from Quebec to Florida) beyond which new European settlement was to be discouraged.

In the eyes of those living on the Anglo-American frontier, the British imperial administration had taken the place of the French in the New World but somehow forgotten to change French policy. The Royal Proclamation of 1763 became a first step in an unexpectedly short journey toward the birth of an independent, English-speaking United States of America. The dozen years from the outbreak of the Conspiracy of Pontiac to the start of the American War of Independence form a crowded period in which the Ontario territory plays only an incidental part. The same might be said for the War of Independence that broke out in 1775 and ended with the Peace of Versailles in 1783. Nonetheless, the course of events outside the region would profoundly affect Ontario's future.

The Second Wave of Change

One of these events was the passing of the Quebec Act by British Parliament in 1774. Among other things, this measure gave official recognition to the culture and institutions of the French Catholic civilization entrenched and multiplying rapidly east of the Ottawa River.

The Quebec Act also entrenched a variation on the Indian Territory of the Proclamation of 1763. It extended the boundary of the Province of Quebec to include all of what is now southern Ontario, the more southerly part of northern Ontario, and all of present day Ohio, Indiana, Michigan, Illinois, and Wisconsin. Under the protection of the British Crown, the French and the Indians would continue to hold the Ohio valley area south of the Great Lakes that Duquesne's forts of 1753 had been erected to defend from the British Americans.

Lord North, the British Prime Minister, argued that this new boundary merely acknowledged "the ancient limits of Canada". Moreover, even if it did extend somewhat

51

beyond these limits, "the country to which it is extended is the habitation of bears and beavers". But in British North America, the Quebec Act became among the last in a series of "Intolerable Acts" by imperial authorities, that led to the first Continental Congress of British American colonies at Philadelphia on 5 September 1774, then to the American Declaration of Independence on 4 July 1776, and finally to the formal birth of a new American republic at the Peace of Versailles on 3 September 1783.

The progress of the American War of Independence also had profound implications for the struggle between New York and Montreal, that had helped shape the Ontario regional economy throughout the French and Indian period and would continue to shape the new future that lay ahead. The boundary provisions of the Quebec Act were not directly addressed to the French and the Indians but to the interests of an English-speaking mercantile community in Montreal and Quebec City, with agents at such upper country outposts as Cataraqui, Niagara, Detroit, and Michilimackinac. These merchants had taken over the financing and management of the old French economy of the north in the wake of the British conquest, and their influence helped ensure that Canada would remain in British hands at the end of the War of Independence.

By 1784 the fur merchants of Montreal trading in the upper country had acquired a loosely-knit corporate identity as the North West Company. In the Ontario territory, this was simply the ancient French and Indian fur trade, managed by British instead of French clerks and merchants. A few French Canadians – like the Bâby family with particular interests at Detroit and in the Toronto area – remained influential.

The boundary between British Canada and the new American republic that finally appeared in the Peace of Versailles of 1783 created some difficulties for the new North West Company. British and American negotiators had set the southern boundary of what is now Ontario along a line running through the middle of the Great Lakes. In the language of John Bartlett Brebner, historian of "the North Atlantic Triangle", this had the effect of "cutting in two Montreal's fur empire in the Great Lakes Basin". Several of the historic outposts of the Canadian fur trade in the upper country, such as Niagara and Detroit, fell on the American side of the line.

Immediate problems were avoided by a British decision to delay the surrender of the western posts in the Great Lakes to the forces of the republic. The pretext was that the new United States was not meeting its treaty commitments to compensate Loyalist supporters of the Crown, who had suffered losses in the War of Independence. The British did not surrender the posts until 1796. For more than a dozen years after the formal conclusion of the war, the might of the British army continued to shelter the Great Lakes fur traders of Montreal from their historic competition in New York.

Even in 1784, however, there were partners in the Montreal-based North West Company who understood that the British could not hold the western posts forever. They helped organize two particular responses to the new boundary line. They turned the Company's forward vision away from the Great Lakes and toward the country of the far northwest that La Vérendrye had begun to open up some half a century before. In the Ontario territory, the enormous westward reach of Montreal that the new forward vision implied drew attention to the characteristic Canadian problem of transportation costs. The old Ottawa-French River canoe route, with its "upwards of Forty" portages, was expensive and not easily integrated with the large-boat traffic that was starting to appear on the Great Lakes. In searching for another alternative to the lower-lakes route that straddled the new boundary line, the North West Company took a new interest in the Toronto Passage. By 1787 the British Crown had purchased land following the canoe portage from Lake Ontario to Georgian Bay from the Mississauga and Chippewa or Ojibway Indians. In 1788 Captain Gother Mann of the Royal Engineers walked off into the forest by the mouth of the Humber River (not too far from the charred remains of the earlier French fort) and made the first official survey and plan for a town at Toronto.

Northwest Company canoe on the Mattawa River, engraving from a painting by Frances Hopkins. An early expression of what the modern American jounalist, Edith Terry, has dubbed the "Canadian ... image of pristine wilderness and macho outdoorsmanship."

The Loyalists of Upper Canada:
Red, White, and Black

According to an earlier tradition in Ontario history, the arrival of Loyalist refugees in the wake of the War of Independence marks the founding moment of the region's modern political society – the birth of the particular political culture of "British Canada". Research since the Second World War has characterized the coming of the Loyalists in more exact and inevitably more complex ways. The complexities begin with the meaning of loyalism in the War of Independence itself.

The early 1770s movement for political change in the Thirteen Colonies had envisioned reforms in imperial administration. But when it began, the cause of the United States did not envision independence from the United Kingdom. Morison notes that the first American flag raised by George Washington near Boston on New Years Day, 1775, "carried thirteen stripes to mark the union of the colonies, but still displayed the Union Jack in the canton as a symbol of union with Great Britain."

At Westminster, Charles Fox and the liberal Whig Opposition were ready to accept the demands of the Continental Congress at Philadelphia for a reorganization of the British empire that would accommodate colonial autonomy. On the other hand, Lord North and the conservative Tory government were not. But it was only as Tory intransigence hardened that the Englishman Tom Paine and the American Thomas Jefferson helped legitimize the colonial drive to independence by linking it with the popular democratic philosophy of the "Rights of Man". With the Declaration of Independence of 4 July 1776, British Whigs in America became Patriots, and Tories became "Loyalists" (to whom the Patriots were "Rebels"). In the ensuing civil war within the Thirteen Colonies, not more than ten per cent of the population was actively Loyalist, about forty percent actively Patriot, and about fifty per cent indifferent or neutral.

The war created bitter memories among some Loyalist and Patriot partisans. But it is estimated that less than 100,000 Loyalists left the new United States when the fighting ended. Some went to the United Kingdom. Some went to the West Indies. Perhaps as many as 30,000 settled among the "neutral Yankees" in the British province of Nova Scotia (including present-day New Brunswick). A few settled in Quebec. According to British imperial records, by 1786 less than 6,000 "United Empire Loyalists" had arrived in what is now Ontario.

A deeper complexity in the old tradition is that the Loyalist migrations in Ontario brought an English-speaking mirror image of the polyethnic French and Indian world that had already been evolving in the region for at least a century. The first large group of Loyalist refugees to arrive were a few thousand Six Nations Iroquois led by Thayendanegea, or Joseph Brant. They were not included in the official imperial count. But they were granted lands in the Bay of Quinte area to the east and the Grand River valley to the west as rewards for faithful service to the British Crown in the War of Independence.

Well before the war ended in the early 1780s, small groups of refugees of European descent had begun to arrive at Niagara and Detroit, where British forces were stationed. Along with various British peoples, they included Huguenots or French Protestants and migrants from the German-American settlements of Pennsylvania, They had remained loyal to the British Crown, like the Six Nations, for reasons that transcended ethnicity. They settled on the British side of the new boundary line. Like Joseph Brant, a few brought Black slaves.

The largest Loyalist settlements took place in southeastern Ontario. During the late spring and early summer of 1784, some 1,500 men, 625 women, and 1,500 children were settled along the upper St. Lawrence River and in the Bay of Quinte area. They included many refugees from New York and soldiers from disbanded imperial regiments. They were largely English-speaking people. But their old world backgrounds were diverse. A group of settlers along the upper St. Lawrence were, as historian Gerald Craig points out, "divided, at their own request, according to race and religion ... Catholic Highlanders, Scottish Presbyterians, German Calvinists, German Lutherans, and Anglicans." A report in 1786 indicated that the Loyalists in Ontario "with a few exceptions do not consist of Persons of great Property or consequence. They are chiefly landholders, Farmers and others from the Inland parts of the Continent."

If the largest Loyalist settlements of 1784 did not exactly mark the founding moment of the modern Ontario political community, they did signal the start of large-scale mass settlement in the Ontario territory. And particularly for many older Ontario-born people the Loyalist migration has been seen as a formative event in the province's history.

The historic United Empire Loyalists of eastern Ontario were settled in two ranges of numbered townships, intended to fit into the seignorial system of Quebec. The first five of the "Royal Townships" along the upper St. Lawrence immediately west of the Ottawa River went to the first battalion of Royal Yorkers led by John Johnson, son of William Johnson of the Mohawks. The remaining Royal Townships went to Major Jessup's corps. The "Cataraqui Townships" in the Bay of Quinte area went to Sir John Johnson's second battalion, to other members of Major Jessup's corps, to members of Major Roger's corps, to a party from New York City led by Captain Grass, and to another party from New York City led by Major Van Alstine.

It seems that the largest number of Loyalists in Ontario were farmers from the back parts of New York and Pennsylvania. Others, however, came from such places as Maryland, Georgia, New Jersey, and Rhode Island. Though perhaps most had been people of only modest means and position in the former Thirteen Colonies, some had been part of the governing group in Virginia.

Finally, not long after the post-war wave of Loyalist refugees had subsided, southern Ontario, like the Great Lakes region at large, began to receive its first influx of inhabitants from the American frontier. These new migrants, the Ontario archivist J.J.Talman has noted, "included many non-Loyalists who quickly joined the Loyalist movement and became almost indistinguishable from it." An important attraction was a British imperial decision of 1787 to grant 200 acres of land to the sons and daughters of Loyalist settlers when they came of age or at the time of their marriage. This marks the origins of a Loyalist Register linked with land grants, that would remain an object of great private interest and public controversy until the early 1800s.

Above all else, the overwhelming majority of the new arrivals of the 1780s were not migrants from across the Atlantic Ocean, but people who had moved from one part of North America to another. They established the same pioneer agricultural homesteads in the new west of the Great Lakes that they had left behind in the east. The one final formative element that the Loyalist migrations brought to the history of Ontario was not the British connection. (The North West Company and the British army had already started that some twenty years before, or the Hudson's Bay Company much earlier still). It was the English-speaking society of the Anglo-American frontier. The long wilderness romance of the Canadian fur trade in French and Indian Ontario was ending. A new age had begun.

Part Two

Southern Frontier, 1791-1867

"It is to be remembered that there is in Canada no counteract-ing influence of an ancient Aristocracy, of a great landed interest or even of a wealthy agricultural class; there is little in short but the presumed good sense, and good feeling of an uneducated multitude (which may be too much tempted) to stand between almost universal suffrage and those institu-tions, which proudly and happily distinguish Britons...."
John Beverly Robinson

"...The fact is beyond dispute that the higher classes, to whom the Times *alludes in terms of approval, are the authors of the greatest mischief in Canada. They have formed a bureau-cracy, and by boundless corruption carried on in alliance with London bankers, have retained the control of affairs.... Our farmers and mechanics whom the* Times *would con-sider too low in the social scale to be entrusted with the fran-chise, are our best politicians....*

We, too, are Americans. On us, as well as on them, lies the duty of preserving the honour of the continent. On us, as on them, rests the noble trust of shielding free institutions."
George Brown

Log-house.

Engraving of a log house, from Catharine Parr Traill's The Backwoods of Canada, *first published in 1836. Even at Con-federation in 1867, log dwellings accounted for almost half the total housing stock in Ontario.*

4

Pioneer Settlement

With few exceptions, the settlers of the 1780s entered an immense virgin forest, which would not start to disappear even in the most southerly parts of the region for another two generations. Along with free land, British authorities gave the Loyalist refugees some help with provisions and tools. Historical geographer, Kenneth Kelly, has described the early settler or pioneer "farmscape" in southern Ontario:

> The cleared area was small, most of the lot remained under forest. The one or two small fields were stumpy, untidy and unlevelled. They were under a wide range of crops reflecting a diversified subsistence economy, which were choked and overtopped by recolonizing forest plants. The only fences were trees felled in line along the edge of the cleared land and roughly trimmed. Because harvests were small there were no real barns. Livestock were raised but no accommodations were provided for them. For most of the year they foraged in the forest, and during the winter they picked around the land being cleared. Most houses were simply rough shanties.

Mass agricultural settlement started in the most southerly parts of the region and would only gradually spread northward. Indians still formed the majority of the population in the modern Ontario territory as a whole until the final years of the eighteenth century. But by the late 1780s the new English-speaking settlers overwhelmingly outnumbered the few French-speaking Canadians concentrated in the Detroit area, though also sparsely represented at other outposts of the early fur trade[1]. Beyond Indians, Métis, and a few hundred Blacks, by about 1790 there were perhaps as many as 12,000 white people, some 10,000 of whom were recent migrants from the old Thirteen Colonies, living in what is now Ontario.

The Birth of a New Province

The English-speaking settlers had one immediate grievance to which British authorities were sympathetic. They still lived in the upper parts of the Province of Quebec and were subject to the French civil law and seignorial land tenures as established in the Quebec Act. In contrast to the French, the new Loyalist settlers saw land not as a feudal obligation but as a "freehold" commodity that could be bought and sold. Like the Loyalists who had moved to Nova Scotia or New Brunswick, they wished to live under the English institutions, and especially the "free and common socage" land tenures with which they were familiar.

In response, the King's government at Westminster divided the Province of Quebec into "the two Canadas" in the late spring of 1791. "Lower Canada" to the east of the Ottawa River retained the French (and largely Catholic) institutions of the Quebec Act, with some modifications in deference to the English-speaking commercial minority in Quebec City and Montreal as well as to the few American Loyalists who had settled in the lower St. Lawrence valley. English (and largely Protestant) institutions were prescribed for "Upper Canada" to the west of the Ottawa River.

As a legal entity, the new British Province of Upper Canada would only exist for half a century. It is the constitutional forerunner of the modern Province of Ontario, however, and it marks the early beginnings of the public institutions that prevail in the region today. Echoes of French and Indian Ontario would live on and even grow modestly in the future. But something of what the region had become by the end of the eighteenth century is reflected in the official seal of the Province of Upper

63

Canada. It included a crown and Union Jack, though no reference to loyalty. Talman points out that it also included "two cornucopia 'charged with fruits and corn'", recalling the Pilgrim fathers of New England, and a "a calumet, or pipe of peace" in"tribute to the Indian allies of the Crown."

The southern boundary of the new Province had been defined by the Peace of Versailles in 1783. From here, the British Order-in-Council that technically divided the two Canadas simply drew a line along the Ottawa River to Lake Timiskaming and then extended the line due north. Upper Canada was defined as " all the territory to the west-ward and the northward of the said line to the utmost extent of the country commonly called or known by the name of Canada." The exact legal meaning of this language would not be clarified until 1889, long after the Province of Upper Canada had ceased to exist. But it was known that the boundary of the province to the north and west was hedged in some degree by the claim of the Hudson's Bay Company to all the land drained by Hudson Bay (the exact extent of which was also unclear). As a prac-tical matter, the Hudson's Bay Company would exercise what effective jurisdiction there was over what is now northern Ontario until the late nineteenth century. Until the early 1820s, the rival North West Company based in Montreal would play a similar role in the more southerly parts of the north and west.

Throughout its half century as a legal entity, the effective practical jurisdiction of the Government of Upper Canada was focused on what is now southern Ontario. The Constitutional Act of 1791, the British parlia-mentary legislation which defined the public institutions of the new province, provided for representative assemblies in both Upper and Lower Canada. The Legislative Assem-bly was to be elected by those adult males who owned land in freehold with an "annual value" of at least forty shil-lings[2]. Yet the key figure in the Government of Upper Canada was to be a Lieutenant-Governor, appointed by the British Crown and reporting to a Governor General for the two Canadas at Quebec City. The Lieutenant-Governor appointed as his advisors a Legislative Council (whose members would hold their position for life) and an Executive Council (the nature and duties of which were never defined). The Lieutenant-Governor could effectively reject the advice of the Assembly and his Councils if he saw fit.

The Act also authorized the King to issue hereditary titles of honour in Upper Canada, which might include "an Hereditary Right of being summoned to the Legislative Council" on the model of the British House of Lords. The Act contained as well broad hints that the Anglican Church of England was to be the "established church" of Upper Canada, as it had been in such former southern colonies as Maryland, Virginia, the Carolinas, and Georgia before the War of Independence. One-seventh of the lands granted new settlers was to be set aside for "the Support and Maintenance of a Protestant Clergy", and some of this land could be used to erect parsonages "according to the Establishment of the Church of England". Finally, British officials at Westminster had decided that another one-seventh of the lands granted in Upper Canada was to be set aside as "Crown Reserves". These were to provide the Lieutenant-Governor with a revenue source independent of the elected representative assembly's power over money bills, which had so marred the government of the lost colonies.

The Constitutional Act of 1791 itself was in large measure a reaction to the American War of Independence. In the eyes of the British imperial officials who drafted the Act, the revolt of the American colonies owed a great deal to the development of colonial institutions that overemphasized the democratic elements in the "balanced" British Constitution of the day, and underemphasized the aristocratic and monarchic elements. In Upper Canada, as in other parts of the "Second British Empire", an effort would be made to strengthen the aristocratic and monarchic elements in the colonial government in the hope of preventing future wars of independence in what remained of British North America.

The first Lieutenant-Governor of Upper Canada appointed by the British Crown was John Graves Simcoe, who had commanded a regiment known as the Queen's Rangers in the War of Independence. He arrived in the province during the early summer of 1792, with his energetic and quite remarkable wife, Elizabeth. He stopped first at Kingston, the former Cataraqui, which with some fifty houses was then Upper Canada's largest town. He then went on to the small Lake Ontario settlement on the west bank of the Niagara River, across from the old French stone fort on the east bank (which would continue to be held by British forces until 1796). Simcoe called the place Newark. It served as temporary capital of the new province until 1793 when the capital was moved across Lake Ontario to Toronto, which Simcoe renamed York[3].

Lieutenant-Governor Simcoe has been something of a controversial figure in Ontario history. To an earlier generation of historians, like Arthur Lower, he was a man whose "reactionary convictions ... love for monarchy, aristocracy, and the Church of England" made him a "Tory to the tips of his fingers", who left a profound mark on the future of Upper Canada. Though he was only in the province for four years, his appointment as Lieutenant-Governor was the first in his career as a colonial administrator, and above all else he was determined to make a strong impression. None of the British Lieutenant-Governors of Upper Canada who succeeded him had his energy or his commitment to the office and the region. His contribution to early Upper Canada was to breathe life into the rather conservative provisions of the Constitutional Act of 1791 with unusual vigor and enthusiasm.

Simcoe's legacy had two main parts. One did involve a particular vision of society and politics, though even this was two-sided. On the one side, as the Constitutional Act implied he ought to, Simcoe tried to promote, if not exactly a territorial aristocracy in the backwoods north of the Great Lakes, then at least a group of men who received much larger land grants from the Crown than other men. Similarly, there never actually would be hereditary titles in Upper Canada. But Simcoe did his best to imbue his appointees to the Executive and Legislative councils with a sense of their mission as a governing class, helping to set the stage for political conflicts almost a generation after his departure from the province.

Simcoe also probably did make the strains of British Tory idealism implicit in some parts of the Constitutional Act more important in the official political culture of early Upper Canada than a less enthusiastic first Lieutenant-

Governor might have. He did what little he could, for instance, to promote an established Church of England, as a spiritual bulwark for the authority of his new governing class. And he added to the concept the notion of a future Anglican university to which the "Gentlemen of Upper Canada" could send their sons for an education that would stress "British principles" (as opposed to those of the new American republic which Simcoe held in great disdain). Unlike the American republic, Upper Canada enjoyed a constitution that was the "very image and transcript" of the British Constitution, which explicitly recognized "the subordination necessary to civilized society".

On the other side of Simcoe's social and political vision, even the reverence he promoted for Upper Canada's British Constitution would ultimately have progressive implications. Similarly, his High Tory idealism was rooted in a pragmatic realism, appropriate to a man of his time and place. (Nothing, he once declared, "is more essential than to profess Correct Opinions, unless to possess a Correct Acquaintance"). And it was Simcoe's realism that prompted him to promote immigration to Upper Canada from the despised American republic, when it became clear that, for the moment at least, mass British immigration from overseas was impossible.

Moreover, like many European conservatives of his day, Simcoe abhorred slavery. Though more than a few of the governing class of Gentlemen that he was trying to promote in the backwoods employed Black slaves as domestic servants, Simcoe convinced them that slavery was uncivilized subordination and thus wrong in principle. In 1793 the legislature of Upper Canada passed "An act to prevent the further introduction of slaves, and to limit the term of contracts for servitude within this province", similar to legislation passed at about the same time by several northern states in the republic to the south.

The other main part of Simcoe's legacy involved the physical and economic development of Upper Canada. He saw his first responsibility as ensuring the defence of the new British province against the prospect of future conflicts between the United Kingdom and the United States. So he made extensive plans for a series of strategic roads and fortified centres in the Great Lakes Peninsula of southern Ontario. Like many of Simcoe's plans, these were never fully realized. But Simcoe had managed to have his old Queen's Rangers regiment accompany him to Upper Canada. Along with a few local contractors, the soldiers of the Queen's Rangers made a start on the dim outlines of a provincial road network.

By the time of Simcoe's departure in 1796, work had started (and in some cases been completed) on very rough pioneer roads from Montreal to Kingston, from Kingston to the new provincial capital at the Town of York, from York north to Lake Simcoe, and from York southwest to the forks of the Thames River. Simcoe envisioned a future city of London at the forks of the Thames River; and as another of his unrealized plans, he maintained that this was where the ultimate "Capital of Upper Canada ... ought to be Situated ... for every purpose of Civilization, command of the Indians, and general Defence."

Simcoe's plans also called for – in the interests of both defence and the province's future prosperity – a "numerous and Agricultural people" (by which he meant more English-speaking settlers of European descent). And realist that he was, on this account he offered free land to pioneers on the great westward wave of the Anglo-American frontier that followed the War of Independence – or at least to those among them "who shall prefer the British Constitution in Upper Canada".

The Anglo-American Frontier in Upper Canada

The Napoleonic Wars that the French Revolution brought to most of western Europe between 1793 and 1815 made mass emigration to Upper Canada from Great Britain itself impractical. Only a smattering of retired soldiers (or "half-pay officers") and other second sons of the minor gentry arrived from the United Kingdom before the 1820s. A somewhat wild suggestion that the population of the British Province of Newfoundland be transplanted to Upper Canada was not acted on.

As a practical matter, Simcoe and the lieutenant-governors who succeeded him embraced the only real supply of a numerous and agricultural people at hand. They looked to the great wave of the American frontier that was

68

settling western New York and the Ohio Territory and that had already begun to drift north of the lakes by the late 1780s. In Upper Canada "a benevolent government" would grant at least 200 acres of land, subject only to modest registration fees, settlement duties, and an oath of loyalty to the King[4]. By 1815 the policy had helped to swell the English-speaking population of the province to nearly 100,000, at least eight times more than there had been at the time of the Constitutional Act.

The Anglo-American frontier in Upper Canada had its peculiarities. As part of the effort to build an aspiring Anglican gentry in Upper Canada, Simcoe had begun the practice of granting as much as 5,000 acres of land to "leading families" among the Loyalists of the 1780s and the few new arrivals from the gentry of the old English countryside (as well as former officers in the King's army). And two-sevenths of all lands granted were being set aside as Crown and Clergy reserves. Moreover, the deadline for enrolment on the Loyalist register of the 1780s was eventually extended to 1798. A man who arrived in Upper Canada as much as fifteen years after the War of Independence had ended, but who could convincingly claim to have once stood up for the King in a place far away, acquired rights to 200 acres of free land for each of his children. The Loyalist Register became a vehicle for the enthusiastic real estate speculation that marked the Anglo-American frontier virtually everywhere it went. In 1805 the Provincial Solicitor-General, D'Arcy Boulton, complained that "three quarters of his Majesty's bounty" had been "lavishly thrown away".

Though sometimes fancifully termed "late Loyalists", it seems clear that the overwhelming majority of the new frontier settlers of the 1790s and early 1800s were not particularly attracted by the province's British Constitution. They "came to find a suitable field for their talents and energies", notes Craig. And they were "ready to find that field anywhere on the continent. Now it was Upper Canada, but in twenty years time some of their kind would be ready to move into the Mexican province of Texas". It has been estimated that by about 1810 the frontier pioneers of the 1790s and early 1800s outnumbered the Loyalists of the 1780s and the few British immigrants to the province by as much as four to one.

Geographically, the settlement pattern of the new arrivals had a pronounced western tilt. The Loyalists of the 1780s remained dominant along the upper St. Lawrence and in the Bay of Quinte area to the east. The more opportunistic frontier of the 1790s and early 1800s spread through the area off the Canadian Shield to the west. Francis Gore, Lieutenant-Governor of Upper Canada from 1806 to 1811, saw the region from Kingston eastward as loyal to the King. But the region from York west to Long Point on Lake Erie was dominated by "Persons who have emigrated from the States of America and of consequence retain those ideas of equality and insubordination ... so prevalent in that country."

The approximate northern boundaries of the early settlement frontier at large are suggested by the extent of Indian land purchases. Simcoe had explained to the Six Nations Iroquois that the triumph of British arms in the region related only to France. Imperial policy assumed that the Indians still "owned" the land. Even the grants to the Iroquois had first been purchased from the Mississauga. By 1811 an additional ten purchases from the Mississauga and the Chippewa or Ojibway had taken place. Together they formed a continuous band along the upper St. Lawrence, Lake Ontario, and Lake Erie shorelines. The only significant northward penetration followed Yonge Street along the path of the old Toronto Passage.

The new arrivals brought changes to the place that Simcoe had found when he arrived in 1792. By the early 1800s Methodists formed the single largest Protestant denomination in Upper Canada whose aspiring Anglican gentry believed in an established Church of England. Baptists, Quakers, and Mennonites had been added to the existing mix of Presbyterians, Catholics, Calvinists, Lutherans, and Anglicans. The French Canadians in the Detroit area were still dominant in the far west. But the German strains in the Loyalist migrations of the 1780s were strengthened when Pennsylvania "Dutch" migrants started the first inland settlements in the province near what would later become Berlin (now Kitchener).

In 1807 Hugh Gray, a visiting British writer, found the pioneer settlers of Upper Canada "active, industrious, hardy, and enterprising to a degree that is scarcely to be credited till ocular demonstration convinces you of the fact". Some places were starting to leave the very worst of the struggle in the forest behind. More commodious log cabins, barns, and a few frame houses were beginning to appear. But many rough edges of the frontier survived. Barnabas Bidwell, who arrived in the province from New England in 1810, found that as in other "new countries people generally make too free use of ardent spirits". And there were periodic outbreaks of the "vulgar practice of pugilism ... the avenging of private wrongs, by personal violence, under the immediate impulse of excited passions."

The right to vote in elections for the Legislative Assembly was subject to the same property qualifications that in the United Kingdom effectively disenfranchised the vast majority of the population. But in Upper Canada a settlement policy that gave away 200 acre farms to pioneers on the Anglo-American frontier also gave away votes. From the first election in 1792 on, men "in lower degrees of life" were elected to the Upper Canadian Assembly. The Assembly's role as a centre for popular pressure on the Government of Upper Canada did not become a major political issue until after the War of 1812. But the province's first "anti-government paper", the *Upper Canadian Guardian or Freeman's Journal*, was established in 1807 at Simcoe's Newark, which was now calling itself Niagara (or "New Niagara"). An ill-organized faction openly critical of the Government and its more ardent Loyalist Tory supporters had appeared by the end of the early pioneer period.

In 1809 an 18-year-old John Beverly Robinson, son of a distinguished Virginian family and later to become an admired leader of the Upper Canadian Tories, observed that the last general election before the War of 1812 had produced an Assembly "nearly equally divided between Blackguards and Gentlemen". Like the customs and manners and the people themselves, the political habits of a new "Valley of Democracy" in the northern and midwestern parts of the American republic had crossed the border.

71

The War of 1812

By the early 1800s so many people from the United States had crossed the border that interested parties inside and outside Upper Canada began to have doubts (and fears) about the province's political future in the British Empire. By the middle of the first decade of the 1800s, the two Canadas, and especially Upper Canada, were caught in the middle of political tensions between the English-speaking mother country and her former colonies in America. There was a war scare toward the end of Thomas Jefferson's second term as President in 1807 followed by five years of shaky efforts to preserve peace. Then on 19 June 1812, President James Madison of the United States declared war on the United Kingdom. It was understood by everyone that Upper Canada would be a crucial battleground.

In 1812 the still youthful American republic was protesting the old mother country's view that she retained the right to "impress" sailors on American ships as a means of manning the Royal Navy, which was protecting the shipping of the world during the Napoleonic Wars. In this sense, the War of 1812 was a successor to the American War of Independence. In the Great Lakes region, however, there was a more important sense in which the War became a successor to the Conspiracy of Pontiac in the early 1760s.

Concern by British officials for the defence of the Canadas during the earlier 1800s had prompted a revival of the interest in the Indian allies of the Crown. This went beyond the old loyal Iroquois and the Algonkians in the region to embrace the Shawnee, who had launched a final protest against the Anglo-American frontier in the Ohio valley south of the Great Lakes. At the same time, the North West Company came to believe that a war which pitted the British and the Indians in Canada against the American frontier in the United States could recover Montreal's lost fur empire in the Great Lakes basin from the clutches of New York-based fur traders led by John Jacob Astor.

In the United States there was an undercurrent of vigorous pro-British sentiment that opposed Madison's declaration of war. But this was concentrated in the New England states and New York, where economic and senti-

The War of 1812 on the Great Lakes. Whatever else, military conflict between the United Kingdom and the United States marked a watershed in the life of the Province of Upper Canada. Several years later, the British traveller, John Howison, noted that people in the region dated every event as "before or after the war".

mental ties with the United Kingdom still flourished. Support for the war was strong from Pennsylvania south to Georgia and rampant in the new western states of Tennessee, Kentucky, and Ohio. A war to expel the British from Canada became an emotional crusade for the "agrarian cupidity" of the new frontier in the republic. It would liberate the brethren who had settled north of the Lakes from the old tyranny of the Empire. And as Jefferson himself had declared, it would save "our women and children forever from the tomahawk and scalping knife, by removing those who excite them".

On the eve of the war, there were some declared supporters of annexation by the American republic among "the Blackguards" in the elected Legislative Assembly of Upper Canada. "Canadian" was still a term largely reserved for the French-speaking people who lived in the Detroit area and in Lower Canada. The Indians, freed Black slaves, agents of the Montreal merchants (like the Cartwrights in Kingston or the Bâby family in Windsor), and many among the Loyalist Tories of the 1780s were straunch supporters of the Crown. But among the more numerous frontier pioneers of the 1790s and early 1800s, perhaps a clear majority anticipated that Upper Canada would become part of the United States in the struggle that lay ahead. When the British General, Isaac Brock, arrived to take command of the region's defence, he found that the "population is essentially bad.... A full belief possesses them all that this Province must inevitably succumb".

After some two and a half years of intermittent fighting, the popular belief had been defied. The province remained in the hands of the British Crown, largely as a result of the fierce bravery of the Indian allies, the inexperience of American soldiers, and the professional military might of imperial forces.

Three victories by British forces in the first six months of the war, at Michilimackinac, Detroit, and Queenston Heights in the Niagara area, quickly dampened expressions of popular support for the cause of the republic. The forces of the United States enjoyed ambiguous successes in 1813. They defeated the Shawnee chief, Tecumseh, at the Battle of the Thames River[5], and briefly captured the British capital at York. The pioneer Parliament Buildings were

74

burned at York, and much of Niagara (Simcoe's Newark) was burned to the ground. In the "Western District" of Upper Canada, private homes, barns, and other buildings were burned and plundered, and some suspected Loyalist partisans were shot. The incidents were later censured by a Congressional investigation at Washington. But they bred anti-American feeling north of the Great Lakes among many who had begun the war happy enough to imagine a republican victory.

British forces regained control in 1814. Eight men were hanged for treason at Burlington Heights on 20 July, only five days before a major British victory at Lundy's Lane near Niagara Falls. The British regained control not just of all Upper Canada but of the adjacent Michigan Territory in the United States as well. (And they burned parts of Buffalo and Washington in retaliation for the burnings at York and Niagara).

Peace negotiations had begun early in 1814 at Ghent in Belgium. British negotiators refused to even discuss the impressment of American sailors. At first, they also demanded both an Indian satellite state north of the Ohio River[6] and changes in the Great Lakes boundary of 1783 that would restore Montreal's lost fur empire in the upper lakes. American successes in the east-coast naval war late in the year prompted the British to drop the last two demands. Except for a few small islands, the Treaty of Ghent signed on Christmas Eve 1814 simply restored all boundaries in effect before the start of the war.

For the United States and the United Kingdom, the War of 1812 had proved futile and unnecessary, though it had the long-term effect of confirming the American republic's complete independence from its former mother country. In Upper Canada, the war was a decisive turning point. The Indians and the fur merchants of Montreal had lost in the end. But the Government of Upper Canada and the Loyalist Tories of the 1780s had won.

On both sides of the border, militia regiments had proved testy and unreliable, concerned chiefly to protect their hard-earned homesteads. The refusal of the New York militia to advance beyond the boundaries of their state had been a key to the British victory at Queenston Heights in 1812. Among the frontier pioneers of the 1790s and early 1800s in Upper Canada, the triumph of British arms had a limited significance. The Blackguards would remain in the Assembly, and they would not concede that "the Gentlemen" had won everything. But the option of annexation by the American republic had been dealt a blow from which it could never quite recover.

The Regional Economy: New Wine in Old Bottles

In Upper Canada the War of 1812 marked the beginnings of an end for both the Indian "lords of the lakes and forests" and the ancient Canadian fur trade. Montreal lost its historic control over the trade when the Northwest Company became part of the Hudson's Bay Company in 1821. The reorganized Hudson's Bay Company took over the old North West Company posts and remained active in the more northerly parts of the modern Ontario territory. But the centre of the fur trade moved to the Hudson Bay port of York Factory in what is now Manitoba.

The beginnings of pioneer settlement in the south during the late eighteenth and early nineteenth centuries, however, had been accompanied by a last energetic golden age of the Canadian fur trade in the Ontario territory as a whole. And this strengthened transportation routes and commercial practices that would help form the framework for a post-war economy dominated by the "new staples" of square timber and wheat.

By the early 1790s, large European boats had challenged the ancient primacy of the native canoe on Ontario waterways. The extent to which the North West Company used the Toronto Passage as an alternative to the Ottawa-French River route has been debated. Yonge Street, the new road from York to Lake Simcoe, began as no more than a stumpy path through the forest. But at least some fur trade cargoes travelled the Toronto Passage on sleighs in winter from York to Georgian Bay. From records of the day, it has been estimated that the cost of carrying a ton of trade goods from Montreal to Sault Ste. Marie was some £18 less on bateaux by Kingston, York, and Lake Simcoe than on canot de maître by Ottawa. The North West Company also linked large-boat traffic on Lake Ontario and Lake Erie by an improvement on the old canoe portage

Fort William: the modern reconstruction of the last great centre for the high romance of the Canadian fur trade in Ontario. Its golden age had ended by the early 1820s, but it would not shut its doors for the last time until 1883. By 1902 the original structure had been levelled to the ground. The modern reconstruction, undertaken in the 1970s, includes all forty of the original buildings.

around Niagara Falls. The new farmers in the Niagara area were hired to haul freight by horse and wagon over a rugged frontier road.

The Company built canoe locks and a road to improve access around the rapids at Sault Ste. Marie between Lake Huron and Lake Superior. In 1803 it moved its Lake Superior headquarters from Grand Portage on the American side of the 1783 boundary line to the old French outpost at Kaministiquia, which subsequently became Fort William. In the early 1800s Fort William was the site of the North West Company's annual mid-summer "Great Rendezvous", where the merchants of Montreal met with the "hommes du nord" – Scottish, French, Métis, and Indian – who worked the lakes and forests of the northwest[7].

The British had surrendered Niagara, Detroit, and the other western posts to the American forces in the summer of 1796 (including Oswego on the south shore of Lake Ontario). So the main branch of the Canadian fur trade turned to the new British northwest, as marked by the move from Grand Portage to Fort William some half dozen years later. As the North West Company revived La Vérendrye's old adventure in western Canada, it faced new competition from an expansive Hudson's Bay Company in the far north. For a time, it faced new competition as well from a dissenting Montreal-based organization known as the xy Company.

Meanwhile, the new settlers in Upper Canada were preoccupied with the arduous toil of establishing pioneer farms in a raw wilderness. But when they did need to look beyond the stumps in their freshly-cleared fields, they confronted a regional economy dominated by the North West Company and agents of the Montreal merchants in Upper Canada. Richard Cartwright of Kingston was an early leading figure in a "Tory shopkeeper aristocracy" that had aroused some popular resentment by the early 1800s.

In the early 1790s, John Graves Simcoe himself had worried about the commercial armlock that the British Canadian merchants on the lower St. Lawrence seemed to have on the settlers in the upper country. But he left in 1796, the year when the British finally surrendered the western posts to American forces. By the early 1800s the ancient struggle between New York and Montreal had returned to the region north of the Great Lakes. Some pioneers in Upper Canada found alternative markets among agents of New York merchants trading on Lake Ontario and Lake Erie. In some cases, goods imported from the United States were liable to duty payments. But Barnabas Bidwell acknowledged: "In such an extended line of water communication there are places of landing, where, it is supposed, dutied goods are sometimes smuggled into the province."

By the early 1800s, the merchants of Montreal had also begun to take an interest in the export of Ontario forests that the new settlers were busy cutting down. In 1806 Philemon Wright, a native of Massachusetts, led the first rafts of cut timber down the Ottawa River to the lower St. Lawrence, ushering in a new era of resource development north of the Great Lakes.

5

Growth and Conflict

At the end of the War of 1812, Upper Canada's population of less than 100,000 inhabitants were thinly spread out along the north shore of the upper St. Lawrence River, Lake Ontario, and Lake Erie. By 1840, the population was four times larger and pushing northward. Before the war, mass settlement in the region had been dominated by migrants who arrived by land from other parts of North America. After the war, it was dominated by migrants who arrived by ship from across the Atlantic Ocean.

To the world of commerce beyond its borders, the region north of the Great Lakes was still most notable for the resource economy of the fur trade before the War of 1812. After the war it gradually became known for a resource economy dominated by two new staple products: square timber and wheat. Before the war, Upper Canada had no urban centre of any real size. By 1840, it had two centres, Kingston and Toronto, with well over 10,000 people each. This growth also helped stimulate the emerging new regional society's first major political conflicts

The New Migrations

The population of Upper Canada doubled to nearly 200,000 people in the late 1820s and then doubled again to just under 400,000 by the late 1830s. Part of the growth was accounted for by natural increase among those already in the province. But much flowed from a first wave of mass

Kingston, 1828. The "loyal old town of Kingston" was Upper Canada's largest urban centre, from the province's beginnings in the 1790s virtually to its official demise in the early 1840s. Though only a smaller Ontario city today, it retains a cultural importance disproportionate to its size.

immigration from the United Kingdom that began in the 1820s and would continue (with some periodic interruptions) into the 1850s.

After the War of 1812 the Government of Upper Canada took steps to halt immigration from the "Red Republican" United States. It also promoted a controversy over the citizenship status of the frontier pioneers who had arrived during the previous two decades, that was not resolved until the later 1820s. The elected Legislative Assembly challenged the anti-American thrust of postwar government policy. Some people from the United States continued to move north of the Great Lakes, especially small urban businessmen who started such enterprises as tanneries, iron works, and hotels and taverns.

But the longstanding desire of the Government and its supporters among the aspiring Anglican gentry for a more dependably "British" population was finally fulfilled. The province became a haven for the old world rural population displaced by the rapid progress of the industrial revolution in Great Britain following the end of the Napoleonic Wars.

The new migrations from the United Kingdom were a continental, North American phenomenon. And in Upper Canada, as in neighbouring New York State, the Irish outnumbered the English and Scots. In New York, however, the Irish tended to be Catholics from the south, who despised the Union Jack. In Upper Canada they tended to be Protestant Ulstermen from the north (or "Scotch-Irish"), who brought the Loyal Orange Order with them. Irish Protestants were concentrated in the east among the American Loyalists of the 1780s. Brockville on the upper St. Lawrence River became "the cradle of Canadian Orangeism" and home centre for Ogle Robert Gowan, Grand Master of the Orange Lodge in Upper Canada. The movement was also important elsewhere. The history of the Toronto Orangeman can be dated from the Town of York's first Orange Parade in 1822.

Not all the Irish immigrants to Upper Canada were Protestant and not all the Protestants were Orangemen. Many Scottish immigrants were refugees from the "Highland Clearances" that accompanied the modernization of agriculture in the north of Britain. In the mid-1820s the

Scottish novelist John Galt started the work of settling his less fortunate compatriots in the western Great Lakes Peninsula under the supervision of the controversial Canada Company (which would remain intact as an organization until the 1950s). Some English immigrants were refugees from the repression of political radicalism in the United Kingdom, symbolized by the "Peterloo Massacre" of 1819.

By the 1820s the earlier system of free land grants was virtually at an end. The new British immigrants typically bought their land, either from the government or from private real estate speculators, including many among the governing class. Those who came without the required capital often worked as labourers on the farms of others or in rising new urban centres while saving for farms of their own. Those who bought land began another cycle of the arduous toil of carving agricultural homesteads out of the virgin forest on the new inland frontier, a step back from the earlier southern front along the upper St. Lawrence, Lake Ontario, and Lake Erie. "I never could have the prospects for my family in Britain that I have here", wrote John Inglis of Guelph to his brother across the ocean in 1831: "only one thing is to be remarked, no one need come here ... unless he intend to ... work hard."

On the southern front, the early commercial wheat farmscape was replacing the earlier agrarian frontier in tribute to the progress made by the pioneers of the 1790s and early 1800s. Many fields were still stump-laden. But there were barns, rail fences, and more substantial frame or log houses had become the norm. It has been estimated that in 1831 about three-quarters of the housing in the province was made of some form of log construction (including small shanties in new pioneer settlements), with the remainder wood-frame, brick, or stone.

The early wheat economy and new pioneer settlement stimulated the growth of urban centres. In 1825 only Kingston, York and Niagara had more than 1,000 people. Kingston, a key trans-shipment point on the waterway to Montreal, was about twice the size of York. By 1830 Niagara had fallen behind. The wheat economy in the fertile western Great Lakes Peninsula briefly made Hamilton (at the western end of Lake Ontario) and London (Simcoe's planned city at the forks of the Thames River in

83

the southwest) rivals to the provincial capital at York. York, however, had some 9,000 people when it changed its name back to Toronto in 1834, about three times the size of Hamilton. By the late 1830s Toronto had some 12,000 people, about the same size as Kingston; and a new "square timber" trade in the Ottawa valley had made Bytown a far eastern rival to Hamilton and London.

Roads were expanding and becoming somewhat more suited to travel (though they would remain a source of much complaint throughout the nineteenth century). By the late 1820s Colonel Thomas Talbot had organized the construction of a 300 mile-long road linking the Detroit River and Lake Ontario as part of a grand settlement enterprise in the southwestern peninsula. The first plank road on the continent was laid in 1835-36, leading east from Toronto. In the later 1830s the lakeshore road from Kingston to Napanee and part of Yonge Street near Toronto were macadamized (a process of constructing levelled roads from layers of crushed rock). There were stagecoach services between larger urban centres. One or more taverns every six or seven miles became characteristic in southern Ontario by the 1830s.

The Upper Canadian population in place by the end of the 1830s struck travellers of the day as "exceedingly heterogeneous and exotic". By the early 1820s Black Americans arriving on the Underground Railway from points south were adding to the mixture in the central and southwestern parts of the province. To clarify the earlier gradual abolition of slavery, the youthful Upper Canadian Attorney General John Beverly Robinson declared in 1819: "the negroes [are] entitled to personal freedom through residence [in Upper Canada] and any attempt to infringe their rights [will] be resisted in the courts."

By 1836 Indian land had been purchased everywhere south of a somewhat indented line from the base of the Bruce Peninsula in the west to the Pembroke area in the east. Indians were becoming somewhat less visible in the more settled southern parts of the province. The government began to develop a new "paternal reserve policy" in the late 1820s. According to historian R.J.Surtees, it "viewed the Indian as a lost savage to be saved and civilized" and was a major departure from earlier policy "which saw the Indian as useful functionaries or allies in the event of war." Even so, the English "gentlewoman in Upper Canada", Anna Jameson, living in the western suburbs of Toronto, reported that in the winter of 1837 "we had black bass and whitefish, caught in holes in the ice, and brought down by the Indians."[1]

By the 1830s immigration from the United Kingdom had helped end the dominance of American Methodists in the province. In 1839 about a quarter of the population was officially classed as Anglican and somewhat less than a quarter as various forms of Presbyterian. Methodists ranked next (seventeen per cent), followed by Roman Catholics (twelve per cent), Baptists (three per cent), and several smaller denominations (a few thousand each of Mennonites, Quakers, and Lutherans – and six Jews, all in Toronto). The more than 40,000 Roman Catholics included Highland Scots, southern Irish, and some 12,000 French Canadians (now about three per cent of the total population, down from perhaps as much as fifteen per cent in 1790).

In the early 1830s the Methodist preacher Egerton Ryerson (later so influential in the development of the Ontario education system) led a substantial faction of the Upper Canadian Methodists away from the American Church and into a new union with the British Wesleyan Methodists. Ryerson's most recent biographer, Clara Thomas, has noted that even though he was an opponent of the high Compact Toryism personified by the Anglican Archdeacon (and later Bishop) John Strachan, for him, as for Strachan, "England was home ... her institutions and customs were the parent ones ... the picture of order, dignity, decorum, stability, and power."

The New Staples

Two "new staples" in the Great Lakes region, square timber and wheat, more than made up for the loss of the fur trade. The British Canadian merchants of the lower St. Lawrence virtually monopolized the trade in square timber that arose in the Ottawa valley. Demand for spars by the British Royal Navy had stimulated the trade during the Napoleonic Wars. By the early 1820s the "resource proletariat" of "les raftsmen" in the Ottawa valley had adapted the rugged outdoor life of the earlier coureur de bois to the new circumstances of the nineteenth century. By the mid-1820s markets in the United Kingdom beyond the Royal Navy had developed, and the Government of Upper Canada began to license timber rights on Crown land to help raise public revenue.

The early commercial wheat farmscape in Upper Canada was concentrated off the southern extension of the Canadian Shield to the west. From the start, some wheat found its way to New York, especially via the old fur trade outpost at Oswego. But the British Empire's protected system of colonial trade gave wheat exported via Montreal a privileged position in the markets of the United Kingdom, even when it came from the American midwest.

To help finance the new staples, the Bank of Montreal began operations in 1817 (though its government charter was not confirmed until 1822). Interests at both Kingston and York tried to start a Bank of Upper Canada, with the account of the provincial government as a base of operations. Even though Kingston was larger, York's status as provincial capital proved decisive, and the Bank of Upper Canada chartered in 1821 was located there. Like the early American banking system, both the Bank of Montreal and the Bank of Upper Canada were parts of an international financial system headquartered in London, England.

The struggle between New York and Montreal in the region of the lakes reached a new stage when New York interests completed the Erie Canal in 1825. It was an improvement on the old Hudson-Mohawk canoe route that provided a direct waterway from Buffalo at the eastern end of Lake Erie to the port of New York City on the Atlantic Ocean. The Bank and Government of Upper Canada, Montreal merchants, and American interests at Oswego were all involved in the construction of the first Welland Canal, an improvement on the earlier rugged frontier road that by-passed Niagara Falls to link Lake Erie and Lake Ontario. It opened in 1829 as Montreal's answer to New York's rival Erie Canal. Canals were also begun to improve access around the rapids of the upper St. Lawrence River. Largely as a military alternative to the upper St. Lawrence route, the British imperial government completed the Rideau Canal from Kingston to the new lumbering centre of Bytown on the Ottawa River in 1834. Steamboats driven by paddle wheels were common on the lower Great Lakes by the 1820s and on Lake Simcoe and the Kawartha Lakes by the 1830s. At Upper Canadian ports on the Great Lakes, it was difficult to distinguish the American from the British vessels.

Some among the merchants of Montreal saw the expansion of urban centres west of the Ottawa River as a problem rooted in Montreal's political separation from its Upper Canadian hinterland. They had not supported the division of the old Province of Quebec in 1791, and in the early 1820s they urged that the two Canadas be reunited into one province, ostensibly to alleviate the problem of divided jurisdiction over the collection of customs duties. When this failed they urged that Montreal and its western environs be annexed to Upper Canada. This suggestion failed as well. But by the mid-1830s Montreal was still several times larger than either Toronto or Kingston. It commanded a three-way traffic among the British Isles, the United States, and Upper Canada.

Under the guidance of the British Canadian merchants of the lower St. Lawrence (and to a lesser extent the merchants of New York City), the lumbermen in the Ottawa valley and the wheat farmers north of the Great Lakes had joined a new international economy. But in both the United States and the United Kingdom, a period of vigorous growth in the earlier 1830s stumbled on the "Panic of 1837", a financial crisis that began in New York but quickly spread to London, England. And Upper Canada joined the cycle of "boom and bust" to which the new world economy was prone.

The Tory Oligarchy

The new population growth and economic development of the period after the War of 1812 helped set the stage for political conflicts in Upper Canada that mark the origins of modern Ontario political culture. The point of departure for these conflicts was the rise of a ruling oligarchy in the province. Regional ruling oligarchies had been common enough in the old Thirteen Colonies and even in the new states of the American republic. What became known as the "Family Compact" in Upper Canada was an exact contemporary of the "Chateau Clique" in Lower Canada.

In Upper Canada, however, the Constitutional Act of 1791 (and John Graves Simcoe's early efforts to give it practical expression) brought a particular character to the regional oligarchy. The Act did provide for an elected Legislative Assembly in the new province. But concerned to avoid the difficulties that such "democratic" elements in the eighteenth-century British Constitution had created in the former Thirteen Colonies, the Act gave countervailing powers to the lifetime appointed members of the Legislative Council and to a vaguely defined Executive Council as well as a veto power to the Lieutenant-Governor appointed by the British Crown. Moreover, for a time at least, proceeds from the one-seventh of provincial land in the Crown Reserves helped give the appointed executive government a degree of freedom from the Assembly's power over money bills.

Starting with Simcoe's regime in the early 1790s, this constitutional structure promoted the growth of what was derisively termed the Family Compact by its opponents of the 1820s and 1830s. At the core of the Compact in the provincial capital at York was a small group of men who monopolized appointments to the Executive and Legislative councils and the provincial judiciary. Excepting the long regime of Peregrine Maitland (1818-1828), the Lieutenant-Governors sent from the United Kingdom only stayed in the province for short periods of time, and their lack of familiarity with the surroundings tended to make them dependent on the established local oligarchy.

Beyond the "men at York", the Compact reached out to include local"elites of office" (especially judicial office) in other settled parts of the province. Its members included descendants of "the Gentlemen" among the Loyalists of the 1780s and a few well-to-do immigrants from the United Kingdom. In the eyes of imperial and local officials, the mass of pioneer settlers were not qualified for public office because of their lack of education, wealth, and leisure. The oligarchy's social influence had begun to wane as the pace of Anglo-American frontier immigration increased during the decade before the War of 1812. But the war itself was a crucible for the more confident and assertive postwar Compact that sparked the region's first major political conflicts in the 1820s and 1830s.

Among the leading figures of the postwar Compact were John Strachan (the Anglican Archdeacon of York, and later Bishop of Toronto), John Beverly Robinson (also from York), Christopher Hagerman (from Kingston), and Allan MacNab, the "Laird of Dundurn Castle" (from the Hamilton area). The Compact's French Canadian connection was Jacques Bâby from the old French settlement in the Detroit-Windsor area. The unique position of these men leaned heavily on the region's ties with the British Empire, especially on the constitutional power of the Lieutenant-Governor appointed by the British Crown. First and foremost, the Compact stressed the importance of "the British connection" in the Upper Canadian future.

The Compact, however, had a particular "High Tory" view of the British connection. It saw an established Anglican Church with rights to all proceeds of the Clergy Reserves as a bulwark of British institutions in the province – prescribed in fact by the Constitutional Act of 1791. By the late 1820s John Strachan had managed to bring Simcoe's companion concept of an Anglican university to fruition in plans for King's College (the forerunner of the modern University of Toronto, intended to shield the sons of the gentlemen of Upper Canada from the heresies of American republicanism).

Even the Compact's concept of economic progress had some conservative overtones. Though the oligarchy itself aspired more to the status of a social and cultural than an economic elite, it had links with the Tory "shopkeeper aristocracy" that had set down roots in the period before the War of 1812. Strachan especially endorsed the early commercial aspirations of the provincial capital at York (Toronto after 1834), headquarters for the Bank of Upper Canada. But the Compact tried to restrain both New York-oriented commerce with the United States and continuing immigration from the American frontier. It looked first to the protected St. Lawrence commerce presided over by the British merchants of Montreal. It actively supported the development of the Welland Canal and endorsed the British settlement activities of the Canada Company.

The Compact promoted as well a rigorously Tory view of "balanced government" for Upper Canada. The democratic elements in the Constitutional Act of 1791 were to be not just restrained by, but distinctly subordinate to, its aristocratic and monarchic elements. Government, in the Compact's view, did not, as Gerald Craig puts it, "derive its authority from the consent of the governed, but from the King, from history, and from religion". Practically, this meant that the appointed Executive and Legislative councils and the Lieutenant-Governor could virtually ignore the elected Legislative Assembly. Under conditions of almost universal suffrage, to allow otherwise would be to accept that the life of the province should be dominated by the will of the majority, as it was in the republic to the south.

To John Beverly Robinson, a decisive flaw in the life of the republic to the south was its strident materialism:

> trade and revenue are not all that constitute the happiness of a people ... by endangering other objects in the hope of benefitting these, we may find that we have purchased even wealth at too high a price.

The Rise of Reform

Some oppositon to the ruling oligarchy had arisen even before the War of 1812. But for the most part, the population of Upper Canada was still preoccupied with the arduous toil of carving pioneer homesteads out of the wilderness. As the population and the role of the government grew after the war and the resources of the Crown Reserves dwindled, the elected Assembly's constitutional power over money bills gradually made it an increasingly potent instrument in the hands of those inclined to oppose the rule of the oligarchy.

The first organized opposition was stimulated by the Scottish radical Robert Gourlay who arrived in the province in 1817 to collect material for his *Statistical Account of*

Upper Canada. Questionnaires he circulated and public meetings he held to gather information became vehicles for the first widespread popular protest against the oligarchy's power and policy. In 1819 the Government of Upper Canada banished Gourlay from the province. The following year, however, another Scottish radical ("another reptile of the Gourlay species"), William Lyon Mackenzie, settled in the Niagara area. He later moved to the provincial capital at York, where he became editor of a paper known as the *Colonial Advocate*, a controversial member of the Legislative Assembly, the first Mayor of the new City of Toronto in 1834, and Upper Canada's leading critic of the Family Compact.

By the mid-1820s a heterogeneous and ill-organized "Reform" faction, initially united by little more than its opposition to the Compact, had taken root in the elected Legislative Assembly. It won particular support from the Anglo-American frontier migrants of the 1790s and early 1800s, whose legal status in the province was for a time contested by the ruling oligarchy after the War of 1812. Marshall Spring Bidwell, the Reform Speaker of the Assembly in 1828, was the son of a former official in Thomas Jefferson's administration at Washington. The cause of Reform also won support from many among the new British immigrants of the 1820s and 1830s, especially Scottish compatriots of Mackenzie as well as English and Irish refugees from the post-1815 suppression of political radicalism in the United Kingdom. Geographically, Reform support was concentrated in the central and western parts of the province, where American Methodists and Scottish Presbyterians had settled in large numbers.

Even as they developed in the 1820s, the Reformers remained a heterogeneous political faction. Mackenzie was at the radical extreme of the movement, particularly drawn to political agitation among "the farmers and mechanics of Upper Canada". More moderate Reformers, with commercial connections and more focused interests in the operations of government, would ultimately play more decisive roles in practical politics. Among the leading moderate Reformers were the Baldwins (father William and son Robert) and Francis Hincks, all originally from Irish liberal families.

William Warren Baldwin (above) and his son Robert (below): early advocates for the politics of the vital centre. William Warren had been the Town of York's leading professional man – doctor and lawyer – before the War of 1812. Robert would preside over the triumph of moderate Reform, west of the Ottawa River in the later 1840s. In the eyes of their Tory opponents, the Baldwins were among the few real "gentlemen" who supported the Reform cause.

The Reformers' grievances against the Compact were diverse. Government patronage in the form of official jobs and public works contracts could be an important source of economic opportunity in a developing frontier society. For some, the oligarchy's determination to support only its favourites in such matters bred strong resentment.

Economic development policy more generally was another source of conflict. Reform drew support from Upper Canadian commercial interests who looked first to New York and the growing American cities of Buffalo and Detroit rather than the monopolist British merchants of Montreal. It drew support as well from backwoods farmers, who wanted to see public money spent on road construction rather than mercantile water transportation projects like the Welland Canal. This side of Reform in Upper Canada had similarities with the growing protest of French-speaking radicals against the Chateau Clique in Lower Canada. With the blessings of the Baldwins and others, Mackenzie began to develop contacts with Louis Joseph Papineau's Patriote opposition at Quebec City toward the end of the 1820s.

Land policy was still another source of diverse if sometimes misplaced conflict. Gourlay's survey for his *Statistical Account* had shown that some farmers in the province saw the Crown and Clergy Reserves, held back from development in a speculative effort to increase their market value, as a major disincentive to material progress in Upper Canada. Yet by the later 1820s both the Crown and Clergy Reserves were being sold with some dispatch. The Compact's desire to see the proceeds of the Clergy Reserves go exclusively to an established Anglican Church then became a source of rancorous dispute. Though the relative importance of Anglicans in the province actually increased with the rise of British immigration after the War of 1812, even in the later 1830s they accounted for no more than a quarter of the total population. To some Reformers, the Presbyterians, Methodists, and perhaps even Catholics were also entitled to a share in the proceeds from the Clergy Reserves.

To others, the Reserves should be sold quickly, and their proceeds used to teach the children of the farmers and mechanics of Upper Canada to read and write. By the

1830s Upper Canada had only a very modest system of public education much influenced by the High Tory principles of John Strachan. At best, less than ten per cent of the rising generation was acquiring even the most rudimentary acquaintance with reading, writing, and arithmetic.

As the Reformers began to consolidate their position in the Assembly in the 1820s (and as the ruling oligarchy increasingly confronted the Assembly's constitutional power over money bills), the Compact began to take a greater interest in cultivating its own base of Tory mass support. It had always been able to rely on many among the Loyalists of the 1780s and the aspiring Anglican gentry that Simcoe had tried to promote. With the new British immigration of the 1820s, it could look to a broader social coalition. Irish Protestants from Ulster were particularly important. "By the 1830s", historian P.B. Waite notes, "Orangemen had become the storm troopers of the Tories."

Geographically, Tory mass support was concentrated in the east, though it had wider dimensions. It is a peculiarity of Ontario Black history that most of the several thousand refugees from slavery who had arrived by the end of the 1830s were aggressive supporters of the "government party". Militia regiments like the York Dragoons that formed in 1822 revived the earlier heritage of Simcoe's Queen's Rangers and the Loyalist corps of 1784. They would have a long history as popular social as well as military organizations linked with the cause of King and Empire. Tory papers like the *Kingston Gazette* increasingly became embroiled in the violently factional press warfare that came to mark the politics of the 1820s and 1830s.

This reaching out for mass support in the face of the demands of practical politics, however, did not alter the ruling oligarchy's fundamental philosophy of government. At bottom, the Reformers' ultimate unifying grievance was that the Compact ignored popular opinion in the political process. For the moderates, it was not enough for government to rest on the King, on history, and on religion. North of the Great Lakes it must also rest on the consent of the governed. For the most radical, government could in fact rest solely on the consent of the governed as it did in the republic to the south.

The Beginnings of Political Change

The clashes on specific issues between Tories and Reformers in Upper Canada typically involved confused disputes among various ill-defined and shifting coalitions in the Assembly. What developed in the 1820s and 1830s was factional politics rather than party politics in the modern sense.

For the most part, the ruling oligarchy itself had defined the programme of Compact Toryism. Initially, however, the Reformers' unifying issue of the quest for a popular role in government was itself a source of dispute among Reform supporters, whose heterogeneity reflected that of the Upper Canadian population at large. In its broadest context, the quest in Upper Canada was comparable in some limited ways with the popular movement that led to the Great Reform Act of 1832 in the United Kingdom and with the contemporaneous rise of "Jacksonian democracy" in the United States. Yet what finally became the struggle for "responsible government" north of the Great Lakes had quite distinctive features.

Elected members who endorsed the cause of Reform won majorities in the Upper Canadian Legislative Assembly in the elections of 1824, 1828, and 1834. To those moderate Reformers who eventually came to identify with the leadership of William and Robert Baldwin, if the province's British Constitution were to truly reflect the practices of the mother country, these majorities in the Assembly should have given the Reformers control over the reins of government. Following the traditions of cabinet government developed in the United Kingdom in the earlier eighteenth century, the Lieutenant-Governor and his advisors should have been "responsible" to the majority in the elected Assembly. Instead, the Lieutenant-Governor continued to take his advice from the Tory ruling oligarchy, entrenched in the appointed Executive and Legislative councils.

The British Whigs who passed the Great Reform Act of 1832 were not altogether unsympathetic to the Baldwins' views. But their decisive objection was that responsible government in a colony would put the Lieutenant-Governor appointed by the British Crown in the impossible position of having to obey "two masters" –

PROCLAMATION.

BY His Excellency SIR FRANCIS BOND HEAD, Baronet, Lieutenant Governor of Upper Canada, &c. &c.

To the Queen's Faithful Subjects in Upper Canada.

In a time of profound peace, while every one was quietly following his occupations, feeling secure under the protection of our Laws, a band of Rebels, instigated by a few malignant and disloyal men, has had the wickedness and audacity to assemble with Arms, and to attack and Murder the Queen's Subjects on the Highway—to Burn and Destroy their Property—to Rob the Public Mails—and to threaten to Plunder the Banks—and to Fire the City of Toronto.

Brave and Loyal People of Upper Canada, we have been long suffering from the acts and endeavours of concealed Traitors, but this is the first time that Rebellion has dared to shew itself openly in the land, in the absence of invasion by any Foreign Enemy.

Let every man do his duty now, and it will be the last time that we or our children shall see our lives or properties endangered, or the Authority of our Gracious Queen insulted by such treacherous and ungrateful men. MILITIA-MEN OF UPPER CANADA, no Country has ever shewn a finer example of Loyalty and Spirit than YOU have given upon this sudden call of Duty. Young and old of all ranks, are flocking to the Standard of their Country. What has taken place will enable our Queen to know Her Friends from Her Enemies—a public enemy is never so dangerous as a concealed Traitor—and now my friends let us complete well what is begun—let us not return to our rest till Treason and Traitors are revealed to the light of day, and rendered harmless throughout the land.

Be vigilant, patient and active—leave punishment to the Laws—our first object is, to arrest and secure all those who have been guilty of Rebellion, Murder and Robbery.—And to aid us in this, a Reward is hereby offered of

One Thousand Pounds,

to any one who will apprehend, and deliver up to Justice, WILLIAM LYON MACKENZE; and FIVE HUNDRED POUNDS to any one who will apprehend, and deliver up to Justice, DAVID GIBSON—or SAMUEL LOUNT—or JESSE LLOYD—or SILAS FLETCHER—and the same reward and a free pardon will be given to any of their accomplices who will render this public service, except he or they shall have committed, in his own person, the crime of Murder or Arson.

And all, but the Leaders above-named, who have been seduced to join in this unnatural Rebellion, are hereby called to return to their duty to their Sovereign—to obey the Laws—and to live henceforward as good and faithful Subjects—and they will find the Government of their Queen as indulgent as it is just.

GOD SAVE THE QUEEN.

Thursday, 3 o'clock, P. M.
7th Dec.

☞ The Party of Rebels, under their Chief Leaders, is wholly dispersed, and flying before the Loyal Militia. The only thing that remains to be done, is to find them, and arrest them.

R. STANTON, Printer to the QUEEN'S Most Excellent Majesty.

Notice of reward for the capture of William Lyon Mackenzie.

96

the majority in the local elected Assembly on the one hand and the home government at Westminster on the other. Among other things, this would make it impossible for the home government to regulate the protected commerce of the Empire.

Moreover, the reform movement of the 1820s and 1830s in the United Kingdom had virtually nothing to do with responsible government, already long established there. It focused instead on increasing the size of the electorate entitled to vote for members of Parliament. Yet even the Act of 1832 created an electorate accounting for a much smaller percentage of the population than in Upper Canada, where the North Americn frontier society was dominated by a property-owning "middle class" of family farmers. With almost universal suffrage, responsible government in the British colony of Upper Canada implied something much closer to a kind of "democracy" that was well beyond the pale of practical British politics in the first half of the nineteenth century. This was a point especially stressed by the Upper Canadian Compact Tories: genuine responsible government could only mean the destruction of "British institutions" in the province and a surrender to the despised "American model".

Not all the Reformers appreciated the subtleties and potential of British traditions of constitutional development as well as the Baldwins. Some advocated an elected Legislative Council as a solution to Upper Canada's political problems. Radicals like Mackenzie also became increasingly impatient with the unwillingness of British imperial officials at Westminster to act on the moderate Reform programme and increasingly persuaded that the quest for a popular role in government in Upper Canada probably must mean some form of American-style republicanism.

Mackenzie's own views were intensified by the Upper Canada elections of 1830 and 1836 when the Tory ruling oligarchy itself managed to secure majorities in the Legislative Assembly, especially by appealing to the loyalty of the new wave of recent British immigrants to the province. In 1836 the Lieutenant-Governor Francis Bond Head had actively campaigned for the Tories (now calling themselves the "Constitutional party") on a platform that stressed the disloyalty of the Reform movement and a programme of local public works. Mackenzie himself was defeated in the election.

In the same year, there was a dramatic illustration of how political violence could effectively achieve popular rule on the American republican model in the Mexican province of Texas. During the previous two decades, Texas had been settled by the Anglo-American frontier, just as the British province of Upper Canada had been settled before the War of 1812. The new settlers had grown increasingly restive under Mexican rule. And as the culminating act in an armed insurrection, in April 1836 Sam Houston defeated a Mexican army at the Battle of San Jacinto and founded the Lone Star Republic.

Louis Joseph Papineau's French-speaking Patriote opposition at Quebec City, with which Mackenzie was in touch, began to make plans for a comparable armed insurrection in Lower Canada. Bad harvests in 1835 and 1836 and the financial panic of 1837 also helped create restless anger among some farmers and mechanics west of the Ottawa River. By the summer of 1837 Mackenzie and associates in the central and western parts of the province were making plans for a rebellion in Upper Canada. Papineau's insurrection in Lower Canada broke out in November 1837, buoyed by the extra energy of longstanding French resentment towards alien English rule. Early in December, Mackenzie and several hundred vaguely-armed supporters made a confused attack on the provincial capital at Toronto. Dr. Charles Duncombe and a smaller group made equally confused efforts to challenge authority in the London district.

Government forces quickly defeated the rebels. At most, the uprising in Upper Canada lasted for a few days. Mackenzie and other leaders escaped to the United States, as did Papineau and other leaders from Lower Canada where the fighting had been more prolonged and bitter. The Canadian rebels were warmly received by newly-formed American Patriot organizations, eager to emulate in the north the republican example of Texas. Late in 1837 and in 1838, the Canadian rebellions threatened to turn into a re-enactment of the War of 1812. But to the south of the Great Lakes, Jacksonian democracy had ended with the election of Martin Van Buren as President in the fall of 1836. The governments of the United Kingdom and the United States cooperated in suppressing political violence along the Canadian border.

In Upper Canada, the Government and its Tory supporters seemed to have prevailed. The Habeas Corpus Act was suspended. Two participants in the attack on Toronto, Samuel Lount and Peter Matthews, were hanged for treason. From the standpoint of government authorities, this was a rather moderate response to acts of armed rebellion. But for a time, it created an atmosphere of real political repression. Some radical Reform partisans felt it prudent to follow Mackenzie and other leaders into the United States. Even the quite moderate Reformer Francis Hincks (who would later be John A. Macdonald's Minister of Finance) briefly became involved in plans for a settlement of Upper Canada Reformers in the new Iowa territory of the American midwest.

The ruling oligarchy's final triumph, however, was short-lived. As rebellions go, the Rebellion of 1837 in Upper Canada was a tame affair. But along with Papineau's stronger and more bitter protest in Lower Canada, it did at last convince British imperial authorities that something must be done about the problems of government in the Canadian colonies. In 1838 the Whig Government at Westminster sent Lord Durham, "Radical Jack" to his friends in London, to investigate "the adjustment of certain important questions depending in the Provinces of Upper and Lower Canada, respecting the form and future Government of the said Provinces". Durham's report was widely published in Upper Canadian newspapers in the spring of 1839. It astonished the Compact Tories and dramatically transformed the climate of political life in the province. In its sections dealing with Upper Canada, it amounted to at least a qualified endorsement of the programme advocated by such moderate Reformers as the Baldwins and Hincks.

Durham recommended colonial responsible government for local and regional affairs, with the imperial government retaining its prerogatives in such fields as defence and foreign trade. Lord Melbourne's Whig government of the day would not go quite that far. But it promised a new regime of "harmony" between the executive and the elected legislature.

Durham also recommended that the two Canadas be reunited as a first step toward the eventual anglicization of the French-speaking population in Lower Canada. In his view, this was the only realistic approach to resolving the French-English antagonism that had made the Canadian rebellions so much stonger and more bitter to the east of the Ottawa River. This recommendation was accepted by Lord Melbourne's government without reservation. On 23 July 1840 the British Parliament at Westminster passed the Act of Union, setting the stage for a new regime of harmony in "The United Province of Canada".

6

"This Progressive, Well-Farmed Country ... "

The United Province of Canada officially began what would prove to be its brief quarter-century history with a crash of canon in Toronto and Montreal at noon on 10 February 1841. Upper Canada disappeared as a political organization, though the name was in popular use for another half century. At the same time, there remained an important administrative distinction between the old Lower Canada, renamed Canada East, and the old Upper Canada, now called Canada West.

Though Canada East had some 190,000 more people than Canada West in 1841, each section was given equal representation in the new United Parliament to encourage anglicization of predominantly French-speaking Canada East. French, which had been an official language of government record in Lower Canada, was abolished in the United Province. The ultimate success of Lord Durham's recommendations on responsible government, however, spelled the ultimate failure of his recommendations on anglicizing French Canada. In 1839 the moderate Upper Canadian Reformer Francis Hincks had written to the moderate Lower Canadian Reformer Louis Hippolyte Lafontaine arguing that the elected Assembly in a United Parliament would have "an immense Reform majority". In 1848 (also a year of revolution and political change in Europe) Lafontaine and Robert Baldwin presided over the final realization of colonial self-government – a triumph for a new French and English Reform alliance. By the following year, the official use of French as a language of government record had been restored. The "union was intended to annihilate the French Canadians", Lafontaine declared in 1851. "But the result has been very different."

This achievement also made certain that Canada East and Canada West would remain very different kinds of societies as well. By the mid-1850s the French and English Reform alliance had come apart. "Reform" remained the most frequent voice of the majority in Canada West. But United Canada became a complex exercise in political and cultural dualism, ruled by unstable coalition governments. In the late 1850s and early 1860s, a resurgent French Catholic conservatism, allied with a new and more moderate Upper Canada Toryism, had the most success in forming governments. But it could not keep them together.

The search for a solution to political deadlock in the Canadas became an important force behind the creation of a larger British North American Confederation in 1867. With Confederation, the two Canadas were liberated from the bonds of legislative union. Canada East returned to the old name of Quebec, and Canada West became the Province of Ontario.

The New World of Canada West

The population of Canada West increased dramatically during the quarter century preceding Confederation. The half million people of the early 1840s had risen to a million people by the early 1850s and a million and a half people by the mid-1860s. In 1840 the French-speaking population of Canada East alone had been somewhat larger than the total population of Canada West. Shortly after 1850 the population of Canada West was larger than that of all Canada East.

By 1860 almost twenty per cent of the population of Canada West lived in cities, towns, and villages. The mechanics of Upper Canada and several thousand small industrial establishments were concentrated in these urban places. The mechanics were typically independent tradesmen who owned their own tools. The new industrial

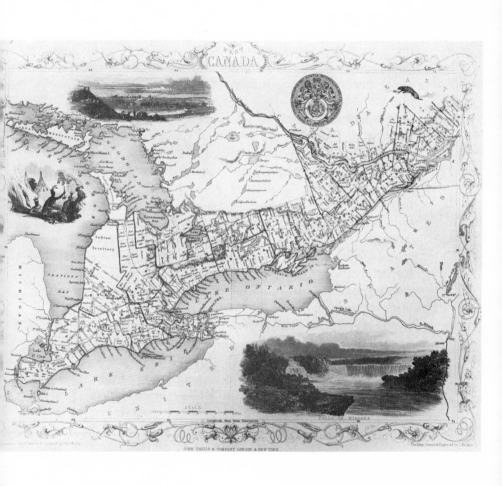

Map: Canada West, about 1850. Drawn by J. Rapkin, published by John Tallis & Company, London and New York. The old official seal of Upper Canada still appears in the illustrated crest, and Kingston is still pictured as the region's leading urban centre.

establishments seldom employed more than a few people each, and well over half the early industrial labour force worked in sawmills and gristmills. A propertyless labouring class had become important in lumbering as well as railway and canal construction. A small salaried class had appeared, working in various early "service" occupations in the larger urban centres. Local manufacturing in farm machinery, shoes and clothing, and foundries and machine shops was starting to show progress by the later 1860s. The Trades Assembly that formed at Hamilton in 1863 marked the beginnings of a regional labour movement.

By the 1860s the agricultural settlement frontier was starting to flounder on the rocky Canadian Shield. New government policies to promote the Muskoka and Haliburton districts were developed in the 1850s. But in 1863 a Committee of the Legislative Assembly reported: "settlement has been unreasonably pushed in some locations quite unfit to become the permanent residence of an agricultural population." The first (or southern) settlement frontier was close to its geographic limits by the time of Confederation. But even in 1861 some eighty per cent of the population in Canada West lived in rural areas. Widespread small property ownership and the commercial enterprise of the family farm formed the dominant mode of earning a living. Southern Ontario would remain fundamentally agricultural until the later nineteenth century. Early farm machinery and the new mobility of a new railway age lightened some of the burden and isolation of the agrarian frontier in the earlier pioneer period. Log dwellings still accounted for some sixty-two per cent of the total housing stock in 1841 but only forty-seven per cent in 1861. By 1860 the romantic splendour of the virgin forest (with its mosquitoes and black flies) had been pushed back to at least the most northerly parts of the south.

In the 1840s and 1850s immigration from the United Kingdom (and to a lesser extent the United States) continued to help develop the unsettled parts of Canada West still suited to an agricultural population. According to the census of 1851, just under sixty per cent of the people in Canada West had been born in the region. Another eighteen per cent had been born in Ireland, nine per cent in

England and Wales, eight per cent in Scotland, and five per cent in the United States. The Irish potato famine of the later 1840s increased the numbers of Irish Catholics, though Protestant Ulstermen were still dominant. Some of the German emigration to the United States after the failure of the 1848 revolutions in Europe spilled over into earlier areas of German settlement in the western Great Lakes Peninsula. In the American republic, a new Fugitive Slave Act took effect in 1850, and by the end of the decade an estimated 30,000 Black refugees were living north of the Great Lakes. Indians were still a strong presence as little as 100 kilometres (or about 60 miles) north of Toronto. But their numbers had dwindled, and even in some northern areas the retreat to the reservation had begun. By the 1860s, however, new French Canadian migrations from Canada East had started in the eastern part of Canada West and along the Ottawa River route of the historic economy of the north.

An unprecedented economic boom had developed by the early 1850s. The English-Canadian society that would typify Ontario in the late nineteenth and early twentieth centuries had begun to take shape. From a distance, it was a British Empire variation on North American themes, with an increasingly pronounced Anglo-Protestant mainstream. Up close, English-speaking Canada West was still a place where a vigorous cultural mosaic and large numbers of recent immigrants brought great variety (and conflict) to the wider community life stimulated by a new railway age.

Though economic hard times sometimes induced American annexationist sentiment, Canada West was more securely British than Upper Canada had been on the eve of the War of 1812. But like the neighbouring American midwest, it had "a population to whom philistinism came as naturally as breathing". In the 1860s the *British Daily Whig* of Kingston complained: "the generality of Canadian readers admire bosh and nonsense ... like the Yankees with whose domestic habits they assimilate."

By 1860 the cultural mosaic had acquired distinctive geographic clusterings that would persist well into the twentieth century. Yet even the regionalism of Canada West had important diversities. The east was awash with Tory Loyalism and the Orange Order. But it was also a centre of Scottish and French Catholic influence. The western Great Lakes Peninsula was a stronghold of American agrarianism, "the Scotch" and early nineteenth-century British radicalism, Black refugees from slavery, and the German civilization of central Europe. But the loyal Tory Colonel Talbot and the land speculators of the Canada Company endured.

Charles Dickens had briefly visited Canada West on his first North American tour in the early 1840s. He found the "wild and rabid Toryism of Toronto ... *appalling*". Even in the 1850s and 1860s, "Tory Toronto" was a stronghold of militia regiments and the Orange Parade on the 12th of July. But it was equally a centre for the independent mechanic, Irish Catholics, and Reform politics. In 1851 Toronto hosted the first "Great North American Convention of Coloured People". From 1851 to 1860 its Roman Catholic Bishop, Armand François Marie Comte de Charbonnel, was from France.

The old Upper Canadian capital was also the home of *The Globe*, the most widely read daily newspaper in all Canada West by 1860. It had been founded in 1844 by George Brown, a Scottish Presbyterian from Edinburgh who spent half a dozen years in New York City before settling in Toronto. Brown combined enthusiasm for the Victorian colonial culture of the British Empire with deep admiration for Abraham Lincoln and "the rural population, the reading population who rule in the United States". More than any other single public figure of the pre-Confederation era, he spoke with the new "voice of Upper Canada".

The Age of Steam and the Rise of Toronto

The United Province at first seemed to realize the ambitions of the English-speaking merchants of Montreal who had urged that the two Canadas be reunited in the 1820s. The new political capital began in Kingston (Montreal's old satellite in the upper country) and then moved to Montreal itself in 1844. In 1846, however, Great Britiain abolished its historic Corn Laws and preferential duties on timber imported from its North American colonies. The protected commerce of the British Empire was abandoned for a new policy of free trade. Upper Canadian wheat and timber exported via Montreal lost its privileged position in the imperial markets. Another period of economic stess in the United Kingdom and the United States marked the later 1840s, and many British Canadian merchants of the lower St. Lawrence urged annexation by the American republic.

By 1850 the larger world economy had improved dramatically. In 1854 the imperial government negotiated a Reciprocity Treaty with the United States, providing for free trade in resource products between the American republic and the British North American colonies. This helped revive the fortunes of the merchants of Montreal. But it also strengthened Toronto's growing links with the commerce of New York. The old capital of Upper Canada set off on its own long quest for a metropolitan status which would rival that of Montreal. Toronto would ultimately carve out a zone of commercial influence by playing off the longstanding competition between New York and Montreal.

By the later 1850s a system of decimal coinage based on a new Canadian dollar had replaced the pound sterling as the official currency of the United Province. New trade with the United States helped bring a resounding economic boom to the Ontario territory, that would not be equalled for another century. Even though demand for square timber in the United Kingdom remained strong despite the end of imperial preference, by the later 1840s a new demand for sawn timber had arisen in the rapidly growing cities of the northeastern United States. This helped spread lumbering to the more central and even western parts of Canada West. Sawmilling had become the largest employer in the region's industrial economy by the 1860s.

By mid-century the Ontario wheat economy was in its prime, particularly in the western Great Lakes Peninsula. In more developed areas, stumps had disappeared, fields were level, drainage was common, and farm machinery had begun to appear. Many smaller Ontario centres became thriving wheat markets, and Toronto and Hamilton became major grain export centres. In 1855 the "Toronto Exchange" was organized as a stock exchange and especially as an exchange for the trade in wheat.

Small farm machinery factories started by Daniel and Hart Massey at Newcastle in 1847 and Allanson and John Harris at Beamsville in 1857 marked a turning point in the early history of industrial manufacturing. Oil was discovered in southwestern Ontario in the later 1850s, though it was not yet the important world resource that it would later become. By 1858 Oil Springs in Enniskillen Township (not far from Sarnia) had become the site of North America's first successful oil well.

The Canadian canal system begun in the 1820s to support Montreal's empire of the St. Lawrence was completed in 1848 with the opening of new canals on the upper St. Lawrence River. But railways were the new transportation technology. Four major lines completed in the 1850s brought the age of steam to Canada West and began to transform economic and social life in the region. By 1855 the Great Western Railway had linked Windsor (and Detroit) and Hamilton, while a branch line also linked Toronto, Hamilton, and Niagara. In the same year the Northern Railway was completed, linking Collingwood on Georgian Bay with Toronto, thus reviving in a new form the old Toronto Passage. It brought grain from the upper lakes of the American midwest and a tremendous lumber trade to Toronto. The British-backed Grand Trunk Railway had linked Montreal and Toronto by 1856 as well as Toronto and Sarnia by 1859. Early in 1858 Buffalo interests completed the Buffalo and Lake Huron Railway, linking Goderich on Lake Huron with Fort Erie on the Niagara River.

Although still half the size of Montreal, Toronto was far and away the largest city in Canada West by the 1850s. The first decennial census of 1851 reported its population at 30,775, more than twice the size of its nearest rival, Hamilton, which had 14,112 people. Kingston, the largest urban centre in Upper Canada until the 1840s, ranked third in 1851 with 11,697 people. There were 7,760 people in the lumbering centre of Bytown (which was renamed Ottawa in 1855), and London followed with a population of 7,035.

Just as Toronto's Northern Railway was completed in 1855, American interests completed a canal at Sault Ste. Marie. This was a major improvement over the old North

Desjardins Canal Disaster, 1857. The railway age in southern Ontario was less than a decade old when the new technology demonstrated its capacity for bringing new kinds of grief along with new blessings. A railway bridge over the Desjardins Canal in the Hamilton area collapsed while a Great Western passenger train crossed over it, and some sixty people perished.

West Company canoe locks around the rapids between Lake Huron and Lake Superior. It transformed travel on Lake Superior and gradually brought a new era of commerce to Fort William and the Thunder Bay area. By 1850 some among the merchants of Toronto had begun to see the commercial conquest of "the northwest" as part of their city's destiny. Toronto's Great Northern Railway would perform notable service for three decades as part of a combined water-rail route to northern Ontario and western Canada. On the day after Christmas in 1856, George Brown declared in the pages of *The Globe*:

> Let the merchants of Toronto consider, that if their city is ever to be made really great – if it is ever to rise above the rank of a fifth rate American town – it must be by the development of the great British territory lying to the north and west.

As George Brown understood, if either Toronto or Montreal were to play a role in the future of the northwest, the territory had to remain in British hands. Indian lands north of Lake Superior and Lake Huron had been purchased in the treaties of 1850, negotiated by John Beverly Robinson's brother, William. Doubts arose about the ability of the Hudson's Bay Company's commercial regime to resist American expansionism in the area to the west of Lake Superior. In 1856 British troops were sent to the Red River district that would become the Province of Manitoba in 1870. The following year the Government of the United Province of Canada sent Simon Dawson and Henry Hind to explore the region between Lake Superior and Lake Winnipeg. In 1860 John Prince was appointed the first judge of the new provisional judicial district of Algoma, headquartered at Sault Ste. Marie.

Suddenly the great boom of the mid-nineteenth century began to falter. Throughout North America, the surge of prosperity in the earlier 1850s stumbled on a new period of financial stress known as the "Panic of 1857". In Canada West the early railway network had overexpanded. The start of the American Civil War in April 1861 brought new uncertainty north of the Great Lakes. Land and railway values were falling. In an effort to strengthen the largest Canadian financial institution, early in 1864 government funds in the Bank of Upper Canada were transferred to the Bank of Montreal.

In 1866 the Bank of Upper Canada failed. The Canadian Bank of Commerce, founded at about the same time by William McMaster and others, became Toronto's leading rival to the Bank of Montreal. It was closely connected with the import and export trade via New York and was complemented by the smaller Bank of Toronto which had been chartered in 1855. As the Civil War progressed to the south of the Great Lakes, British relations with Abraham Lincoln's Union government of the north deteriorated, and in 1866 the American republic refused to renew its Reciprocity Treaty with the British North American colonies. Economic stress became another force pressing toward a larger northern North American confederation in 1867.

The Achievement of Responsible Government

The first eight years in the political history of the United Province of Canada were dominated by the old Upper Canadian moderate Reformers' quest for responsible government. The quest gained considerable momentum when the moderate Reformers from predominantly English-speaking Canada West combined with moderate Reformers from French-speaking Canada East in the new Legislative Assembly of the United Province.

Lord Sydenham, the first British governor of the United Province, was a man of considerably more sophisticated political talents and broader experience than the earlier Lieutenant-Governors of Upper Canada. He had instructions from imperial authorities to prepare the ground for colonial responsible government in practice without actually conceding it in principle. Under the old Tory ruling oligarchy, the particular role of the Executive Council had been ambiguous. Sydenham turned the Executive Council into an ancestor of the modern Cabinet. He chose its members so as to represent at least a balance of political forces in the elected Legislative Assembly, and each member of the Executive Council was assigned responsibility for a particular administrative department

111

of government. In effect, he served as his own prime minister and, according to J.M.S. Careless, skillfully ran a "half-way, all party system of harmony". The Legislative Council, meanwhile, began a long evolution into obscurity.

The administrative machine of the United Province ultimately became rigorously divided along lines of geography and language. Most departments, and thus places on the Executive Council, would have separate Canada West and Canada East divisions. The responsible cabinets that developed in the province after 1848 would also be known by double-headed French and English names: "Lafontaine-Baldwin", "Hincks-Morin", "Cartier-Macdonald", "Brown-Dorion", and so forth.

Lord Sydenham himself, however, did not live to see a thoroughly responsible French and English system. Something much closer to the complete system was achieved briefly under Sydenham's successor as governor, Charles Bagot. Both French and English Reformers had won majorities in elections held in 1841, and Baldwin and Lafontaine began the work of building the historic French and English Reform alliance[1]. Bagot was less politically adroit than Sydenham; by 1843 he had found it impossible to manage the Assembly without conceding virtual control of the Executive Council to the Reform alliance. According to J.M.S. Careless, "for all practical purposes, Canada was being governed in Bagot's final months of office by a virtual Reform cabinet under Lafontaine and Baldwin."

Bagot was succeeded as governor by Charles Metcalfe, an appointee of Robert Peel's new Conservative Government in the United Kingdom. Metcalfe was instructed to slow down the sudden burst of progress toward colonial responsible government, an instruction which matched his own political views. When he refused to surrender control of government appointments and patronage to the Executive Council dominated by Baldwin and Lafontaine, all except one member of council resigned. Returning to a variation on Sydenham's system, Metcalfe now organized his own ministry, led by William Henry Draper from Canada West and Denis Benjamin Viger from Canada East. Draper was in the forefront of a group of Upper Canadian Tories who were forging a new more moderate conservatism, adapted to the changes that the late 1830s had wrought in the region's political climate. Viger was a disciple of Papineau (still himself in exile from the old Lower Canada). Draper-Viger was an "unholy alliance" between English conservatives and French radical "nationalists", that would have at least a few subsequent echoes in Canadian history.

In elections held in 1844, Governor Metcalfe actively campaigned for the Draper-Viger ministry he had created, resorting to a more moderate version of the "loyalty" platform that Francis Bond Head had advanced in the Upper Canadian election of 1836. Once again, the Reformers were defeated in Canada West (though Lafontaine held majority support in Canada East). Ironically, however, in one sense the Draper-Viger ministry became the first responsible cabinet. It commanded a slim majority in the elected Assembly for United Canada as a whole, and Metcalfe took its advice as a matter of course. Moreover, by 1845 Metcalfe himself had become ill, letting his responsibilities for appointments and patronage devolve upon Draper.

Even Draper's more moderate conservatism did not actually endorse or demand recognition of the principle of responsible government. Yet in 1846 the Whigs returned to power at Westminster, now ready to concede the principle without reservation. With the repeal of the Corn Laws and the move to imperial free trade in the same year, it was no longer necessary to regulate the protected commerce of the empire. The earlier decisive objection to colonial responsible government had disappeared.

In 1847 the Scottish peer Lord Elgin arrived to succeed Metcalfe as governor of the United Province of Canada, with instructions to implement the complete system. Then, major electoral victories in both eastern and western sections of the province at last brought in the first thoroughly responsible Reform government under Baldwin and Lafontaine, which took office on 11 March 1848. Lafontaine's supporters had more seats in the Assembly, and Baldwin properly conceded formal seniority to his French partner. But the partners communicated only in English (Baldwin being unable to speak French). Similarly, as confirmation of the growing tradition of rigorous administrative dualism, in effect Lafontaine was premier of Canada East, and Baldwin was premier of Canada West.

As one of the first acts of their new government, Lafontaine and Baldwin put through the Rebellion Losses Bill to compensate Patriote leaders in Canada East who had lost property in 1837 and 1838. (A parallel bill for Canada West had been passed in the earlier 1840s). Lord Elgin's refusal to use the governor's veto on this bill, on the grounds that it had been duly passed by a majority of the Assembly, is traditionally viewed as the ultimate triumph of responsible government.

Coming on the heels of imperial free trade and the economic stress of the late 1840s, however, the official recognition of responsible government was more than the English-speaking Tories in the United Canadian capital of Montreal could bear. Riots broke out and Montreal's parliament buildings were set on fire while the Assembly was still in session. Lord Elgin could not appear in public without fear of physical violence for several weeks, and Lafontaine's house was vandalized. When the tumult died down, the Assembly decided that henceforth the capital city of United Canada would alternate between Toronto and Quebec City on a four-year cycle. The Assembly opened at Toronto in 1850. For the next fifteen years, the legislature, the executive, and much of a growing civil service periodically packed its records and its furniture and moved back and forth between the two cities.

The Emergence of Modern Provincial Institutions

Lafontaine's and Baldwin's government passed almost 200 separate bills during its first six months in office. Much of the legislation for Canada West was of lasting importance for the Province of Ontario that would appear some twenty years later. Though no one could quite have put it this way at the time, in several respects the institutions of old Upper Canada were transformed into those of modern Ontario during the late 1840s and early 1850s.

Local government in Upper Canada, for instance, had largely been the responsibility of district judicial bodies known as Courts of Quarter Sessions, presided over by justices of the peace appointed by the Lieutenant-

Governor and his advisors. In the 1830s these were supplemented by statutory municipal corporations, with elected councils, in several of the larger urban centres. And in 1841 a District Councils Act, inspired by Lord Sydenham, established district municipalities with elected councils, presided over by wardens appointed by the governor (a kind of local version of the half-way "harmony" system of government operated by Sydenham at the provincial level).

The Municipal Act of 1849 (customarily known as the Baldwin Act) reorganized these early institutions into a complete system of local self-government for Canada West, with strictly elected councils in counties, cities, towns, villages, and townships. The system was viewed as a local parallel to responsible government at the provincial level, though legally the new municipalities were "creatures of the province" – without the constitutional rights to "home rule" enjoyed by local governments in the republic to the south. The Municipal Act of 1849 provided a basic framework for local self-government in Ontario that, with the partial exception of the regional government experiments of the later 1960s and earlier 1970s, has remained fundamentally in place down to the present.

The Common School Act of 1850 likewise consolidated the earliest beginnings of modern Ontario's system of state-supported mass education. The old Upper Canadian education system that John Strachan had come to preside over had its earliest roots in a District Grammar School Act of 1807 and a Common School Act of 1816. But it was only modestly assisted by government, relying heavily on fees from the parents of pupils, with some provision for scholarships. It was essentially a system designed for the children of the most affluent segments of the community. And under Strachan's influence, much of the system had particular links with the Anglican Church.

The more generously assisted and broadly based mass education system consolidated in 1850 can be traced back to as early as the Common School Act of 1841, a hastily-contrived companion to the District Councils Act of the same year. But the new system began in earnest with legislation that appeared during the brief early approximation of responsible government under Charles Bagot – the

Common School Act of 1843, known as the Hincks Act, the first of a series of frank imitations of American school laws.

In 1844 Egerton Ryerson became the public official responsible for the administration of the new system, which he would preside over for the next thirty-two years. Ryerson himself drafted both a new Act of 1846 and the Act of 1850, giving full expression to Ontario's particular variation on the original model. The system was accountable to elected local school boards and funded by general provincial and municipal taxes (and a modest supplementary tax levy on the parents of the pupils).

Finally, as a higher symbol of the new spirit that Baldwin's triumph of Reform brought to the region west of the Ottawa River, the University Act of 1849 replaced John Strachan's Anglican King's College with a state-supported, non-sectarian University of Toronto. As a sign of the new twists of fate that lay ahead, however, by 1860 the secular University of Toronto of 1849 had become a secular University College, with potential for affiliation with Bishop Strachan's new Trinity College, Bishop Charbonnel's new St. Michael's College, and the Wesleyan Methodist Victoria College in Cobourg – all supplemented by a Presbyterian Queen's University at Kingston.

The New Political Forces

By the early 1850s, Robert Baldwin had been struggling for the principle of responsible government for some quarter of a century. His interests were more those of a political thinker than a political actor. With the principle at last won, he was ready to retire from the wars of politics to the joys of private life. Baldwin and Louis Hippolyte Lafontaine had also become great personal friends during the struggles of the 1840s, and Lafontaine was similarly inclined. In 1851 the two pioneering leaders of the French and English moderate Reform alliance resigned.

The alliance had spoken for electoral majorities in both eastern and western sections of the United Province. For a time, it remained intact, under the new leadership of Francis Hincks and Augustin-Norbert Morin. And for many in Canada West, Hincks' premiership was not without virtue. In 1852 he arranged a Railway Guarantee

116

and Municipal Loan Fund, which historian William Ormsby describes as "a means of encouraging railway building and fostering economic expansion under Canadian governmental leadership". Though Lord Elgin led the formal negotiations, Hincks was also an important force behind the Reciprocity Treaty of 1854 with the United States.

At the same time, Hincks found himself unable to move ahead on the contentious issue of the old Upper Canadian Clergy Reserves. This gradually weakened his support in Canada West, and in 1854 the Hincks-Morin administration was defeated in the Assembly. The unifying force of the struggle for responsible government had disappeared, and the French and English Reform alliance disappeared with it. The United Province now entered a period of dramatic political instability that would see ten different governments in as many years.

At the bottom of the difficulties was an innate sectionalism that the struggle for responsible government had temporarily papered over and that its triumph unleashed with fresh energy. The setting for sectional conflict was complicated by the economic stress of the late 1850s and by the outbreak of the American Civil War in 1861. For what would become the Province of Ontario, the project of a wider British North American Confederation ultimately emerged as the best possible solution to all the difficulties involved.

The start of the difficulties of the 1850s and 1860s was a resurgence of radicalism brought on by the triumph of responsible government and symbolized by the return from exile of Mackenzie, Papineau, and other radical leaders from the era of the rebellions. In Canada West, Mackenzie would not regain his importance of the 1820s and 1830s, but his return helped stimulate a new wave of enthusiasm for "Old Reform" principles and "the American model".

By 1850 the purest exponents of the new enthusiasm had christened themselves the "Clear Grits". Their heartland was the agrarian stronghold of the western Great Lakes Peninsula, and their newspaper was *The North American*, published by William McDougall in Toronto. Their base of support had similarities with the "free society" coalition of "greasy mechanics, filthy operatives, small-fisted farmers, and moon-struck theorists" that Abraham Lincoln was building at the same time in the northern United States.

The Clear Grits advocated a radical democratic extension of the political change achieved under Baldwin and Lafontaine, based largely on American precedents and including such reforms as representation by population, biennial fixed elections, and complete universal suffrage. In its purest expression, however, Clear Grittism remained perhaps too American for the public life of even a self-governing British colony. In 1852 George Brown of *The Globe* entered the Assembly as an independent Reformer, critical of the Hincks-Morin regime for its lack of attention to strict Reform principles on issues related to separation of church and state. By the later 1850s he had tamed the Clear Grits and won "our farmers and mechanics" over to a North American variation on the new themes of nineteenth-century British liberalism. As in the northern United States, under "Brownite Reform" agrarian radicalism co-existed with commercial interests attached to the rising North American financial centre of New York City. William McMaster of Toronto's Canadian Bank of Commerce became a prominent figure in the new British-American Reform Party that George Brown would bequeath to Ontario.

Brown was a passionate opponent of slavery. His reformism also retained two key ingredients in the original Clear Grit programme that brought his new "voice of Upper Canada" into fundamental conflict with the French Catholic majority in the eastern section of the United Province – representation by population and a rigorous conception of the separation of church and state. With the Civil War brewing in the American republic, George Brown looked for "the overthrow of two equally baleful dominions – the Slavocracy of the South and the French Priestocracy of the North".

Brown would become the political leader with the single largest following in Canada West. But in the Government of United Canada, the immediate beneficiaries of the new radicalism west of the Ottawa River were the old Upper Canadian Tories. In the 1840s the best western

118

allies for a French Canadian eastern majority concerned above all else with French survival had been the moderate Reformers. As the Canada West Reformers grew more radical, however, they also grew more distant from the traditional society of French Catholic Canada. And the French Canadian majority looked to more conservative English partners, who had some sympathy with the case for an established Church.

The ultimate beneficiary was John A. Macdonald from "the loyal old town of Kingston", who would eventually dominate the creation of the Confederation compromise. Macdonald was a protege of William Henry Draper and continued Draper's efforts to forge a new, more moderate conservatism from the ashes of the old Compact Toryism. Macdonald's political base in Canada West looked to three disparate blocs of support: the Orange Order, the Roman Catholics, and the Wesleyan Methodists. Geographically, it had a bias toward the old Tory stronghold of eastern Ontario. "The Peninsula", Macdonald declared in a private letter of 1856 (meaning the western Great Lakes Peninsula, stronghold of George Brown's Grit Reformers), "must not get command of the ship. It is occupied by Yankees and Covenanters, in fact the most yeasty and unsafe of populations".

What Macdonald came to call his "Liberal Conservative" Party retained the earlier Tory ideal of the British connection as a leading theme. But it eschewed the old Compact's concern to foster the growth of a social and cultural elite and took a much franker interest in the problems of commerce and the fledgling Canadian industrial sector. It is an over-simplification to say that Macdonald's new Conservatives looked first to industry and the established commercial interests of Montreal whereas Brown's new Reformers looked first to agriculture and the rising commercial interests of Toronto. But it is not altogether incorrect.

John A. Macdonald was not the commanding figure in the politics of Canada West that he would become in Canadian federal politics after 1867. Brown, not Macdonald, was the leading politician west of the Ottawa River. Macdonald's political importance in the 1850s and 1860s depended fundamentally on an alliance with the French in

George Brown: Premier of Canada West for only forty-eight hours, but the "voice of Upper Canada" nonetheless.

John Sandfield Macdonald: the "Laird of Glengarry", married to a lady from Louisiana – a central Canadian idealist, in whose house French was spoken as often as English.

Canada East in which he was only the junior partner.

In the early 1860s, John Sandfield Macdonald – the "Laird of Glengarry" – made an unsuccessful attempt to bridge the gap between Brown and John A. Macdonald by reviving something of the spirit of the old moderate Reform alliance of Baldwin and Lafontaine. Like John A. Macdonald, John Sandfield Macdonald was from the eastern part of Canada West. He was a Scottish Catholic who had married a French girl from Louisiana. He deeply believed in a French and English Canadian Union, run on a "Double Majority" principle, whereby key acts of government required majorities in both predominantly French Canada East and English Canada West. And he won the support of the *London Free Press* in the western Great Lakes Peninsula. That he could not in fact make the principle work in the early 1860s would not prevent him from becoming the first premier of the new Province of Ontario in 1867.

Each of the new political groupings of the 1850s and 1860s in Canada West had "natural partners" in predominantly French-speaking Canada East. George Brown was against established churches, not "anti-French"; so his allies east of the Ottawa River were Antoine-Aimé Dorion's "Rouges" – vaguely anti-clerical legatees of Papineau who, as Careless points out, "dreamed rosily of a French democratic nation within the republican sisterhood of the American states." Dorion's Rouges were a radical minority in French Catholic Canada. From the mid-1850s onward, the majority followed Georges Etienne Cartier's "Bleus" – the natural allies of John A. Macdonald to the west of the Ottawa River. Finally, the "Mauves" under Louis-Victor Sicotte joined briefly with John Sandfield Macdonald in the unsuccessful Double Majority experiment of the early 1860s.

Sectional and Sectarian Disputes

In Canada West, the key issue in the defeat of Hincks-Morin had been the secularization of the Upper Canadian Clergy Reserves, an old cause for the new radicalism of the 1850s that ultimately grew into George Brown's Grit

Reform party. Hincks' chief difficulty had been the fears of his moderate French Reform allies that secularizing the Clergy Reserves in Upper Canada would threaten the status of the Catholic Church as the bulwark of French Canada.

The coalition of moderate French (and a few English) Reformers and Upper Canadian Tories that succeeded Hincks-Morin (MacNab-Morin) helped allay French fears. And it in fact did manage to secularize the Clergy Reserves in Canada West, by a compromise that gradually phased out existing church funding while allocating the bulk of the proceeds from the reserves to the new municipalities created in 1849.

John A. Macdonald was the guiding light in MacNab-Morin's secularization of the Upper Canadian Clergy Reserves. By 1854 he appeared as co-premier with Cartier in a coalition of new French and English conservatives that would prove the most stable regime which the United Province was capable of producing in the 1850s and 1860s. The 1840 Act of Union, however, had prescribed equal numbers of seats for Canada West and Canada East in the Assembly of United Canada. The trouble with the Cartier-Macdonald majority in the United Province as a whole was that it typically depended on majority French support in Canada East while George Brown's Grit Reformers had become the leading political force in Canada West.

In one sense, the underlying problem was that John A. Macdonald's conservative minority in Canada West was considerably larger than Antoine-Aimé Dorion's radical minority in Canada East. Brown and Dorion actually formed a government in 1858. But it lasted only forty-eight hours, after which Cartier-Macdonald returned to office. Brown's lieutenant, Oliver Mowat, protested that the politics of the United Province had developed into a "system ... of tyranny towards Upper Canada", which was "ruled by a minority of Upper Canadians".

In the eyes of many Upper Canadians, the tyranny was illustrated most vividly by the fate of state-supported mass education in Canada West. When the new system west of the Ottawa River began to develop in the 1840s, it was based on secular or non-sectarian schools open to all religious and other groups, with modest provisions for some

122

public funding of Anglican, Catholic, and Negro separate schools[2].

To the most ardent Grit Reformers, progress meant that the system would develop along increasingly secular lines. The votes of French Catholics in Canada East, however, helped move events in the opposite direction. French Canada believed that the rights of the Catholic minority in Canada West should equal those of the English Protestant minority in Canada East. By 1860 the Irish, Scottish, and French Catholic minority in Canada West had won a much larger state-supported separate school system than the Upper Canadian Protestant majority would have conceded on its own. And it was a new Upper Canadian Separate School Act in 1863 that finally made even the brief Sandfield Macdonald-Louis Sicotte experiment in Double Majority government impossible.

George Brown's initial response to the underlying dilemma was to argue that the equal number of Assembly seats for Canada East and Canada West prescribed by the 1840 Act of Union should be replaced by "representation by population". The population of Canada West had grown larger than that of Canada East by the early 1850s. And what Lord Elgin had called "this progressive, well-farmed country" west of the Ottawa River was continuing to grow more quickly than the older homeland of French Canadian Catholics. Representation by population would give Canada West an ultimate majority in the United Province, liberating it from the tyranny of John A. Macdonald's alliance with the French.

No French faction in Canada East, not even Brown's natural allies the Rouges, could realistically move in this direction. But in 1856 Dorion became the first to propose a form of federal union for the two Canadas, with each section following its own instincts on education and other regional issues while preserving some larger attachment on issues "common to both sections". By the "Great Reform" convention of 1859, Brown and the Grit Reformers in Canada West had at least endorsed a version of the principle as a tactical manoeuvre.

In 1858 the Cartier-Macdonald regime had made tentative queries to British imperial officials about the prospects of a wider federal union of Canada West, Canada

East, and the Maritime Provinces, as an alternative solution to increasing sectional tensions in the United Province. The concept had been proposed by the Montreal business-man Alexander Galt. To many Grit Reformers, like so much else associated with Cartier-Macdonald, it ignored the economic development aspirations of Canada West and the rising commercial centre of Toronto.

As Brown himself had urged, the economic future of Toronto depended to no small extent on the Hudson's Bay Company territories of the British northwest, which Hind and Dawson had been sent to explore in 1857. The Anglo-American frontier in Minneapolis-St. Paul was already coveting the region. Farmers in the western Great Lakes Peninsula, where the end of the frontier was already in sight, saw the British northwest as a new zone of settlement for their children. One stream of Grit sentiment urged that the Hudson's Bay Company territories be quickly annexed to Canada West on the argument that this was in any case implicit in the definition of Upper Canada set out when the province had been created in 1791. But the annexation of the British northwest by the English in Upper Canada was no more acceptable to the French in Lower Canada than representation by population.

By 1864, few believed that the United Province of Canada by itself could ever produce stable governments. After the defeat of the second Cartier-Macdonald govern-ment in 1862, John Sandfield Macdonald and Louis Victor Sicotte had attempted their unsuccessful experiment in formal Double Majority government. When this met defeat in the Assembly in May 1863, Sandfield Macdonald formed a new government that bowed more deeply to the forces of Brownite Reform by allying with Dorion in Canada East and by bringing Brown's lieutenant, Oliver Mowat, into the Executive Council. In effect, the theory was that a French and English Reform alliance with Sandfield Macdonald acting as proxy for George Brown could win fresh French support from Canada East. By March 1864 the theory had been disproved. As a last act of faith a Taché-Macdonald government was formed, with the old warhorse Etienne-Pascal Taché acting as proxy for Cartier in a test of the converse of Sandfield Macdonald-

Dorion. This too had proved a failure about three months later.

It was at this point that George Brown responded with his historic act of statesmanship, proposing a wider British North American Confederation that would include the two Canadas, the Maritime Provinces, and the British northwest territories (as a unit separate from Canada West). The confederation would have a general or federal government for issues common to all sections, but each section would also have its own provincial government to deal with issues of interest strictly in its own region – a version of the principles illustrated by the federal system of the United States. The proposal served as the unifying issue for the "Great Coalition" government of Brown, Cartier, and John A. Macdonald. And the great coalition travelled east to Charlottetown, Prince Edward Island in the summer of 1864 to begin the formal discussions with the Maritime Provinces that ultimately led to Confederation in 1867.

Confederation and the American Civil War

When the Cartier-Macdonald regime had queried British imperial officials about the possiblity of a wider British North American federal union in 1858 (in a letter to Sir Edward Bulwer-Lytton, Secretary for the Colonies, signed by G.E. Cartier, John Ross, and A.T. Galt), the response was lukewarm or at least very prudent. It was noted, for instance, that none of "the other North American Provinces" had raised the matter. Only a few years later, circumstances had changed. And this had much to do with the outbreak of the American Civil War in April 1861.

The war would prove to be the bloodiest military conflict in North American history, before or since. At least several thousand Canadians actually fought in Abraham Lincoln's Union Army of the North and only a few hundred in the army of the defeated Confederacy of the South. In Canada West, the Grit Reform leader, George Brown, was a staunch supporter of Lincoln's cause. *The Globe* frequently reported war news under the headline, "The American Revolution". But the imperial government, the Liberal Conservatives of Macdonald and Cartier,

Fenian Raid Volunteers and their friends at Thorold in the Niagara border region, about 1866. For a time, it seemed that the American Civil War might spread into "the true north, strong and free".

and the conservative regional press had sympathies with the South. The Trent Affair in 1861 and the St. Albans Raid in 1864 raised prospects of military conflict between Britain and the United States[3].

These propects seemed real enough to prompt a group of Canadians fighting in Lincoln's army to inform the President himself that they would be unwilling to fight against the British North American colonies should this prove part of the Union's design. By 1864 it had also become clear that irritation with the British Empire would prompt the Union to abrogate its 1854 Reciprocity Treaty with the British colonies, and the Treaty was duly terminated in 1866. After the war ended in April 1865, "Fenian" Irish Nationalists disbanded from the northern army made brief attacks at various points along the U.S. border with British North America, including an attempted "invasion" near Fort Erie.

Above all else, the Civil War made it clear that dramatic winds of change were blowing on the North American continent. At Westminster in the United Kingdom, in the Maritime Provinces, and in the United Province of Canada, this opened minds to new dangers, new possibilities, and perhaps even new necessities, creating a much more receptive climate for a British North American Confederation than had existed in the late 1850s. In the end, the American Civil War helped make Confederation in British North America a matter of practical politics.

Meanwhile, George Brown resigned from the Great Coalition in 1865, ostensibly over a dispute on efforts to renegotiate the Reciprocity Treaty with the United States. But he continued to support the project of the new Confederation. With Brown's continuing support (and in continuing collaboration with Georges Etienne Cartier), John A. Macdonald became the dominant figure in both the Great Coalition and the wider imperial political process that worked out the details of the Confederation bargain.

Support for the new Confederation was stronger in Canada West than in the other founding provinces; fifty-four of sixty-four Canada West members had cried "yea" (compared with thirty-seven of sixty-five Canada East members) when the issue was put to a vote in the Assembly of the old United Province in March 1865. Yet it seems clear that even north of the Great Lakes the new Confederation did not take shape on a great tide of popular enthusiasm. It was a compromise addressed to the resolution of practical problems. As much as anything else, it liberated what became the Province of Ontario from the bonds of legislative union with the old Lower Canada. The new Ontario was also the most populous of the founding provinces, and it no doubt had some sense of its destiny as an important actor in a new kind of Canadian future. But as elsewhere, few people could anticipate just how this future would unfold.

Nonetheless, after almost three years of discussion, debate, and negotiation, the new Confederation of Nova Scotia, New Brunswick, Quebec (the old Canada East), and Ontario (the old Canada West) was officially proclaimed on 1 July 1867. It was to be known as the Dominion of Canada. The name "Canada", Morton notes, was chosen "without trouble; a Maritimer proposed it". The Confederation would be the first "British Dominion" in what would later become the Commonwealth of Nations. It was a novel constitutional status – much more than a colony in any traditional sense but still less than an independent sovereign state. At the heart of the Empire, *The Times* of London tried hard to strike the right note:

> political faith overreaches itself in a conception so vast and so loose, in frontiers so extensive, and in conditions so infinitely varied.... But that fears are as often disappointed as hopes ... we should scarcely venture to estimate the destiny of this Confederation. However, there it is.... There is strength even in weakness.... The freer and less binding relations sometimes last the longest.

Part Three

Old Ontario, 1867-1905

"Immense progress has been made towards the Christian Ideal since Christ died on the cross; the 19th century is far in advance of the first; and...of every century since the first. The goal unhappily is far from being reached yet."
Oliver Mowat

"... this prosy old province of Ontario.... We have made business and politics a very large portion of our provincial life."
C.C. James

Old Ontario Farmhouse, built about 1880. (The photograph has similarities with a painting of the same name by Carl Schaefer). The winds of a new industrialism and new urbanism had begun to blow. But for the Ontario majority, the generation after Confederation was a last golden age of the agrarian society and the yeoman democracy of the family farm.

7

Reform in Power

From Ontario's standpoint, the Confederation of 1867 was to no small extent a response to perceived repressions of Upper Canadian aspirations in the United Province of Canada during the 1850s and 1860s. One part of the response was a broader field for ambition in the new kind of Canada defined by the wider Confederation. Another part was, in effect, a return to the region of its own provincial government, something it had enjoyed for half a century after 1791 and then lost in 1841.

The political forces in pre-Confederation Ontario represented by John A. Macdonald's Liberal Conservative party would ultimately find their strongest expression in the enterprise of building a new Candian nation, "from sea to sea". After a brief, unsuccessful flirtation with "national power", the forces represented by George Brown's Grit Reformers, albeit under a quite different kind of leadership, would realize their aspirations in the new Province of Ontario.

The Province, like the Dominion of Canada, would retain the British political institutions of its past[1]. Yet unlike the United Kingdom, the Canadian Confederation was a federal state – a political system in which two levels of government, national (or federal) and regional (or provincial), each had claims on "sovereign power", with regard to different government responsibilities. The British North America Act of 1867, the act of the Imperial Parliament that defined the Confederation bargain, also defined the formal distribution of power between federal and provincial governments.

In 1867 the only working example of a federal state on a continental scale virtually anywhere else in the world was the American republic. In this context, one striking feature of Canadian history between 1865 and 1873 is the extent to which John A. Macdonald (in close collaboration with Georges Etienne Cartier) dominated the political process of Confederation. And Macdonald believed that the American Civil War had shown the ultimate folly of allowing too much power to the regional governments in a federal state.

This belief was reflected in the British North America Act, which seemed to imply that all decisive power in the new Confederation lay with the federal government at Ottawa. But the "Canadian constitution", according to J.R. Mallory, a leading authority on the subject, "is a product of negotiation and bargaining, of a feeling that practical operation is more important than the letter of the law, and that the spirit supersedes the letter of the agreement". As a practical matter, Macdonald's view of the Confederation was not the only one, and it was particularly not the view of the initial four provincial partners.

Nova Scotia and New Brunswick were wary of a federal government inevitably dominated by the much larger populations of the old two Canadas. The new Province of Quebec would become the anchor of French Catholic Canada, wary of a federal government dominated by English Protestants. By the 1870s Ontario itself had begun to pioneer what would much later be called "province building" – an important ingredient in the history of Canadian development.

The Patent Combination

The formation of the first Ontario provincial government reflected John A. Macdonald's domination of the Confederation process. Governor-General Viscount Monck had asked Macdonald to become Prime Minister of the new Canadian federal government proclaimed on 1 July 1867, since he had been the elected chairman of the Westminster conference of 1866, at which the Confederating partners

133

had agreed on what became the British North America Act. On 8 July 1867 Monck, on Macdonald's advice, appointed Major-General Henry William Stisted Lieutenant Governor of the new Province of Ontario. Stisted, again on Macdonald's advice, asked John Sandfield Macdonald to form a provincial government. On 20 July 1867 Sandfield Macdonald took office as Ontario's first Premier, with a cabinet made up of himself, the brewer John Carling, Stephen Richards, the "Tory of Tories" Matthew Crooks Cameron, and Edmund Burke Wood, an old Clear Grit stalwart.

Sandfield Macdonald saw his government as a "Patent Combination", designed "to complete the constitutional superstructure which must precede ordinary legislation". He took it to face the people in an election that lasted for six weeks in August and September 1867, chose members for both provincial and federal legislatures and was administered by John A. Macdonald. Sandfield Macdonald and John A. Macdonald campaigned together in Ontario – known in the press of the day as "the two Macdonalds ... hunting in pairs". Their theme was that the new goverments in both Ontario and Canada at large were seeking office as bipartisan coalitions that would preside over the founding of the new Confederation. "Party", John A. Macdonald declared, "is merely a struggle for office; the madness of many for the gain of a few."

Determined to stand up for the two-party system (and the rights of Upper Canada), George Brown tried to organize his old Canada West Reformers into an effective oppositon. But when the election was over the two Macdonalds had triumphed. When the first Legislative Assembly of Ontario met at the old Front Street Parliament Buildings in Toronto on 27 December 1867, Sandfield Macdonald's government could count on the support of almost fifty members in an eighty-two member house.

Though they had been partisan opponents in United Canada, Sandfield Macdonald had come to share John A. Macdonald's view of the new Confederaton. Sandfield Macdonald had not supported the project at first. Despite his own failure to make it work in the early 1860s, he had continued to urge the ideal of a French and English United Province with a Double Majority constitution. When

The Denison family, on the steps of "Rusholme" in Toronto, 1871: surviving High Tories and supporters of the South in the American Civil War. In the generation after Confederation they remained influential socially and economically (and in federal politics). But a different political vision would dominate the provincial government of Ontario.

Confederation became inevitable, however, he found himself in essential agreement with the other Macdonald on what it should be. As under the Act of Union, there would be only one real Government of Canada. The work of the provincial legislature would resemble that of "a glorified county council", best handled by some form of non-party administration. Though the Patent Combination had its shaky moments, it survived intact until 1871 largely because it genuinely was a non-party administration. But its conception of the limited scope of the new provincial government was not shared by the more partisan Reformers in opposition, who were encouraged by Brown and *The Globe* and who found an articulate leader in Edward Blake. Only thirty-four years old, he was already the leading Chancery lawyer in Upper Canada.

As the good will of the early Confederation period faded, Sandfield Macdonald began to seem to many what George Brown and Edward Blake said he was: John A. Macdonald's "Man Friday" – a vehicle for the perpetuation of the Macdonald-Cartier tyranny against Upper Canada that had led to political deadlock in the old United Province. Sandfield Macdonald's decision to spend $120,000 on a new Government House (official residence of the Lieutenant-Governor of Ontario) played into the hands of critics who claimed he was only a tool of the reactionary Tories in Ottawa. The gritty farmers of Upper Canada, living in houses typically worth no more than $1,000, were advised that no less than $7,000 was to be spent on housing the Lieutenant-Governor's horses.

The case that Blake and the new "Reformers of Ontario" steadily built was somewhat unfair to Sandfield Macdonald, who presided over the formative first four years of the provincial government in a fundamentally high-minded and bipartisan spirit. But his view of the Ontario future would prove no more realistic than his Double Majority view of United Canada. Following the second provincial general election in 1871, Edward Blake became the second Premier of Ontario. Four years after Confederation, Reform had finally won decisive power in the old Upper Canada. The Reform Party that George Brown had willed to the new province began a regional regime that would last for thirty-four consecutive years.

The Early 1870s: Ontario and the West

Edward Blake himself would remain Premier of Ontario for less than one year. Though he made his political name in Canada's most populous province, it was Canadian federal politics that interested him. Even this would prove ultimately unsatisfying, and he ended his career as an Irish Nationalist member of the British House of Commons.

During his brief tenure, however, Blake and his first Reform government made two decisions for Ontario that would echo into the future. One involved an Act which abolished dual representation in the provincial and federal legislatures. Since 1867 several members, including Blake, had held seats in both the Ontario and federal parliaments. At one point even John A. Macdonald had contemplated taking a seat in "the local legislature". But to Ontario Reformers this was a device which only invited federal domination of provincial politics. As one of its final deeds, Blake's government ended any connection which might have existed between the provincial and federal houses.

Blake's other historic decision involved a controversy surrounding the establishment of the new province of Manitoba. At the time, there were two main elements in the Manitoba population, both with links to Ontario history. One was Louis Riel's Métis – polyethnic descendants of the Canadian fur trade, with their earliest roots in the wilderness romance of French and Indian Ontario but now linked more closely with the French Catholic mainstream of Quebec. The other was an advance party of the North American agrarian frontier, with its closest Canadian links to the English Protestant mainstream of nineteenth-century Ontario.

In 1870 Riel, as leader of the provisional government in Manitoba, had impulsively executed an Ontario Orangeman, Thomas Scott, for "insubordination" during the aftermath of the Red River Rebellion. This aroused widespread indignation in Scott's home province. Blake and the Ontario Reformers had used the incident in the provincial election of 1871, charging the two Macdonalds with failure to bring Riel to justice as a result of "the French interest at Ottawa". Shortly after Blake took office early in 1872, the Ontario Government offered a $5,000 reward "for the apprehension of Riel".

Louis Riel remains an object of controversy in Canadian history, as does Ontario's role in the events surrounding the creation of the Province of Manitoba. In offering the $5,000 reward, undoubtedly Blake was pandering to a popular Ontario prejudice (which he himself shared). But the Ontario Orangemen are only part of the story. The Orangemen, far from a majority in the region, were "the storm troopers of the Tories", not the Reformers. In the old world, Blake would go on to become an Irish Nationalist, not an Ulster Loyalist.

Perhaps the ultimate Ontario prejudice at work was captured by the English novelist, Anthony Trollope, on a visit to the United Province of Canada in the early 1860s:

> The streets in Toronto are framed in wood, or rather planked, as are those of Montreal and Quebec; but they are kept in better order. I should say that the planks are first used at Toronto, then sent down by the lake to Montreal, and when all but rotted out, are again floated off by the St. Lawrence to be used in the throughfares of the old French capital.

To the people of Blake and George Brown, the issue at stake in Riel's Red River Rebellion was who would lead in the development of western Canada: the Indian, French, and Scottish heirs of the North West Company along with the traditional "Priestocracy" of Quebec; or the Anglo-American agrarian frontier, with its roots in the "progressive, well-farmed country" north of the Great Lakes?

As elsewhere in North America, there seems a harsh inevitability to the ultimate triumph of the frontier. The newer nineteenth-century English Canadian experience that old Ontario residents took west, however, would develop along different lines from the experience that stayed behind. George Brown's vision of the new Confederation would reach its greatest height in the later history of western Canada. Ontario would fall under the spell of another kind of Reform politician.

Oliver Mowat's Political Base

On Blake's departure for Ottawa, Oliver Mowat (a lawyer and then a judge, who "sat at God's right hand") became Ontario's third Premier in October 1872 at the age of fifty-two. He had been Brown's nominee in the Sandfield Macdonald-Dorion government of 1863-64 and had participated in the early Confederation debates. But unlike both Brown and Blake, he was no ideologue. Mowat was even more determined to assert Ontario's provincial rights. But like John A. Macdonald, he had grown up in the loyal old town of Kingston, and he had a larger sympathy for the traditional society of French Catholic Canada. As a result of migrations from Quebec, Ontario's own historic French minority had already increased from about 2½ per cent of the total population in 1861 to more than 4½ per cent by 1871. Under Mowat's leadership it would rise to almost 7½ per cent in 1901.

Though no one seems to have envisioned such success at the time of his appointment, Mowat would remain Premier of Ontario without interruption for almost a quarter of a century, a record in the history of parliamentary democracy. Mowat personified Ontario's particular variation on the agrarian tradition of hard work and earnest sobriety. But he was also "a Mameluke when roused". When he first entered public life in the mid-1850s, he had declared his intention to speak for "the views which become a Christian politician" – a phrase, his first biographer would later note, "often afterwards applied to Mr. Mowat, not always in the kindliest spirit".

To Reform partisans, the longevity of the late nineteenth-century "Ontario Great Reform Government" simply proved that their party was indeed the true voice of Upper Canada. The hard political facts were not so clear. In the provincial election of 1871 the Reformers did take an unambiguous majority of the popular vote (about fifty-one per cent). But in the four subsequent elections the division of the popular vote between Reformers and Tories (or Liberals and Conservatives) was very close – approximately forty-eight per cent to forty-seven per cent in each case, with the balance going to independents and early minor third-party candidates.

The single member[2] constituency system of parliamentary democracy that both Ontario and Canada had inherited from the United Kingdom, however, placed a premium not on winning shares of the popular vote but on winning a large number of local, geographically-defined seats in the legislature. This in turn placed a premium on the arts and crafts of democratic political management. And the Christian politician proved to be a gifted political manager.

Despite their slim edge in popular vote, Mowat's Reformers won comfortable majorities of seats in the Ontario Legislative Assembly in each of the provincial elections of 1875, 1879, 1883, and 1886. The 1879 election, which saw a deftly managed forty-eight per cent of the popular vote win the Great Reform Government almost two-thirds of the seats, was perhaps Mowat's most striking political achievement. The electoral geography of the victory sheds light on Ontario's two-party system in its prime. There were twenty-four provincial seats in the traditional Tory stronghold of eastern Ontario, and in 1879 the Conservatives under the new leadership of William Ralph Meredith took two-thirds of them. But Mowat's Liberal Reformers took two-thirds of the eighteen seats in the central area from Toronto east to Hastings County, three-quarters of the forty-four seats west of Toronto, and both of the two northern seats of the day, Algoma and Muskoka-Parry Sound.

The Conservatives' one consolation for the more distant future was that they had taken four of the Province's five largest cities (Kingston, London, Ottawa, and Toronto). Part of the explanation was that in federal politics John A. Macdonald's "National Policy" of protective tariffs on imported manufactured goods spoke to the employees as well as to the vested interests of the emerging Canadian manufacturing sector, while his Trade Unions Act of 1872 had made labour unions legal in Canada.

Despite the abolition of dual representation, there remained important connections between federal and provincial politics in Ontario. But the late 1870s marked the beginning of a much observed and almost systematic tendency for the majority of the Ontario electorate to support one party in provincial elections and the other party

Oliver Mowat, once George Brown's lieutenant and guiding light of the Ontario Great Reform Government for almost a quarter of a century. "There are difficulties in everything," Mowat declared in later life, and "though a Christian may not be perfect, his efforts are in the direction of perfection."

federally. The provincial triumph of Reform in 1871 had carried over into the federal elections of 1872 and 1874, when Ontario sent Liberal majorities to Ottawa. But Ontario elected majorities of federal Conservatives in the 1880s and 1890s. This trend continued until Laurier's Liberal victory in 1896, when Ontario sent equal numbers of Liberals and Conservatives to Ottawa.

Part of the explanation for the Ontario electorate's federal-provincial split allegiance in the late nineteenth century was that John A. Macdonald was at least as gifted a political manager federally as Oliver Mowat was provincially. Furthermore, after the mid-1870s an average of ten per cent more eligible Ontario voters took part in federal than in provincial elections. And a substantial majority of the extra federal votes went Conservative. The strategic Conservative voters who gave Macdonald his Ontario federal majorities in the 1880s and 1890s, it might be said, took his views on the insignificance of provincial politics to heart and declined to vote in provincial elections.

Beyond his skills as a political manager, Mowat's record quarter century as provincial Premier also owed much to his capacity for empathizing with the genuine depth of conservative sentiment in the province. Though a staunch partisan of what was increasingly known as the Liberal Party, he commanded a regime that was, according to his modern biographer Margaret Evans, a "blend of conservatism and reform, of caution and advancement". Unlike George Brown, Mowat saw the intrinsic diversity and factionalism of Ontario society as something to be managed and contained, not polarized in the hope of securing a final victory for one dominant faction.

After fifty years of recurrent political strife, this approach brought Ontario stable democratic government and a new degree of social unity, but at the price of a certain dullness on the surface of public life. When Oliver Mowat was introduced to a prominent English statesman he was greeted with the comment: "Have you no public opinion in that province?" Mowat might have replied that he had been Premier for so long because he took such pains to know exactly what public opinion in his province was and then act accordingly.

The New Democracy and the Great Reform Machine

At Confederation, the qualifications for voting even in Canadian federal elections were the same as those for provincial elections in the province in question – a mark of regional control that belied John A. Macdonald's centralist image of the new constitution. In Ontario, the old Upper Canadian freeholder's franchise gave the vote to virtually all heads of family farm households and perhaps most "middle class" heads of households in urban areas.

Sandfield Macdonald had begun the process of extending the Ontario franchise with the Election Act of 1868, which gave the vote to male British subjects twenty-one years of age and older who "owned, rented or occupied" real estate worth at least $400 in cities, $300 in towns, and $200 in villages and townships[3]. In 1874 Mowat added to the list similar persons with an annual income of at least $400 without regard to real estate and a new category of "enfranchised Indians". The process of gradual expansion continued until the Manhood Suffrage Act of 1888, which gave the vote to all adult male British subjects, "except unenfranchised Indians living on reservations".

Women, still subject to a more general inferiority of legal status, would not join the new democracy in Ontario for another generation. But the struggle for women's rights had started, and the Great Reformers at least began the slow march of progress. In 1884 acts were passed enabling married women to hold property and enabling widows and unmarried women to vote in municipal elections, provided they met the property qualifications that would also apply to men in municipal elections until the second half of the twentieth century.

In the mid-1870s the Great Reform Government reorganized the region's system of state-supported mass education in a more general way. Education was an unambiguous provincial responsibility under the British North America Act, except for a federal power to protect the rights of denominational schools in place at the time of Confederation. Before 1876 both public and separate local school boards in Ontario had been loosely accountable to a provincially-appointed Council of Public Instruction (whose last chairman was Goldwin Smith). In 1876 the local systems were made accountable to a new Department

143

of Education under the direction of a provincial cabinet minister[4].

Adam Crooks became the first Ontario Minister of Education in 1877. In 1883 he was succeeded by George Ross, who later became Premier, establishing a recurrent though not inevitable link between the two offices that has echoed down to the present. When the new department was proposed, it was criticized for a perceived tendency to place dangerous powers of patronage in the hands of the government. This tendency did not prove decisive. But the new arrangements did enhance tendencies toward rigorous centralization and standardization, which under Egerton Ryerson had already in the minds of some "brought the school system of Ontario ... too close to the Prussian bureaucratic system". By the late nineteenth century, state-supported mass education had settled into efforts to mold a common social character for the region, that would not be seriously challenged until the middle of the twentieth century.

It used to be an Ontario prejudice that the traditional British forms of its political life helped prevent the worst excesses of the democratic machine politics which developed in the new industrial areas of the United States during the later nineteenth century. Ontario produced no one comparable to Boss Tweed in New York. Yet Oliver Mowat did perfect a meticulous regional tradition of robust political management. "Everything else being equal", he once explained, "no administration" is "in the habit of preferring their opponents to their friends".

Ontario had received a generous financial settlement from the federal government not long after Confederation, producing healthy surpluses in the provincial budgets of the late 1860s and early 1870s. To no small extent, this reflected John A. Macdonald's determination to provide John Sandfield Macdonald with some practical means of winning support for the "national" view of the new federal system in Ontario. But the federal Macdonald later complained that the provincial Macdonald lacked the right touch.

Oliver Mowat did not. When he took office the provincial budget was still in surplus by some $4 million. He quickly set in motion a process by which the money was

Ontario elementary school students, about 1872. Progress brings its own problems. In the later twentieth century, the Ontario mass education system born in the nineteenth century has become an object of controversy and discontent. In the later nineteenth and earlier twentieth centuries, it perhaps seemed more of an unqualified success.

gradually used to discharge debts contracted by many Ontario municipalities through rash investments in railway development during the heyday of Francis Hincks' Municipal Loan Fund. The scheme helped consolidate support for the new Great Reform regime and gave Mowat a portfolio of political credits in many different parts of the province.

Mowat's style of political management had a more garish side, epitomized by his notorious "Liquor Licence System". By an Act passed in 1875, tavern operators in Ontario were required to obtain renewable licences from local boards of commissioners, appointed by the provincial government largely from among "pronounced partisans" of the Reform Party. The Act had been passed in response to an early regional case of the North American temperance agitation, that would only reach its largest influence almost fifty years later. It was characteristic of Mowat to turn such good works to his political advantage. P.B. Waite has observed one side effect of promoting temperance in this way:

> It was dangerous for a tavern licenceholder to be an active Conservative in provincial politics. Inactivity was tolerated; some display of zeal for the Mowat government was likely to assure the renewal of the licence.

This side of Mowat's politcal style helps account for the unkind twist that sometimes accompanied references to his Christianity. But genuine religious convictions and exemplary personal habits at least helped him practise an especially aggressive and systematic political control of government patronage without ever being touched by any serious hint of scandal.

Mowat's personal vision of the Christian politician was rooted in convictions about the need for a particular blend of morality and deceit in public life. The blend was illustrated in an exchange that took place in the Ontario legislature during the late 1870s. The Tory leader of the day, Matthew Crooks Cameron, had protested a proposal to begin each daily session of Assembly with prayers. The "honourable members", Cameron observed, "were sent to

146

the House to support one party or the other". They "did so without any reference to the nature of the measures introduced". To offer prayers for "Divine direction" in the business of the day could only "bring discredit upon religion".

The Premier rose to reply. He was "surprised and disappointed" by Cameron's protest. He himself did not believe "that members voted for bad measures for party reasons". But "if there were men in the House who so acted, there was all the more necessity for prayer, for Divine blessing and guidance, to prevent such wickedness in the future". What "a world this would be", Mowat remarked on another occasion, "if the Christian Ideal of character and conduct should be generally realized...."

> All men loving one another as brothers love, as sisters love; and notwithstanding diversity of condition, or culture, or color, or race. No wars ... no hostile tariffs. All men just and true in politics, in business.... No bribing or misleading of voters.... No false weights and measures.... All husbands loving their wives; all wives loving their husbands; all children dutiful and affectionate to their parents.

But that would be "the Kingdom of Heaven upon earth". And it had not come yet.

8

Economy and Society
in Transition

The territory that became the Province of Ontario in 1867 was dramatically different from the territory that had become the Province of Upper Canada in 1791. In most of southern Ontario the virgin forest had been largely replaced by geometrically precise plots of cleared farmland. Five cities had more than 10,000 people each, and several others were approaching the mark. Even the old mid-northern fur trading outposts at Sault Ste. Marie and Fort William had begun their earliest development as modern urban centres (though the far north remained much the same and remnants of the fur trade continued on Hudson Bay).

The pace of growth in Ontario during the first generation of Confederation, however, slowed significantly. The population of the region increased by scarcely half a million in the 1870s and 1880s, compared with just under one million in the 1840s and 1850s. In the 1890s the population hardly increased at all. Many people from Ontario were among the one million Canadians who emigrated to the United States during the period. As elsewhere in Canada, the three decades after Confederation were an era of increasing hard times, with only brief, intermittent periods of real prosperity. Yet it would be misleading to exaggerate the extent of hard times in Ontario during the later nineteenth century. They were accompanied by a growing sophistication in the region's economic base. As in

Canada at large, there was strong political leadership and a determination to surmount obstacles. A generation of slow growth helped bring stability and coherence to a regional society that was still in an adolescent stage of development.

Ontario and the Canadian "Arduous Destiny"

The regional economy of Oliver Mowat's Ontario was shaped, as in the past, by national and international economic trends. The provincial government itself could not have much direct impact on these trends or on policies to manage them devised by the federal government. But the provincial government did not hesitate to voice concerns over the impact of forces beyond its control on behalf of particular regional economic interests.

The half dozen years immediately following Confederation had brought a new wave of economic optimism north of the Great Lakes. By 1873 the Dominion of Canada had spread "from sea to sea". The federal government headquartered at the Ontario lumbering centre of Ottawa had purchased the old northwest territories of the Hudson's Bay Company. A new Province of Manitoba had been created to the west of Ontario. The Pacific coast colony of British Columbia and the Atlantic coast colony of Prince Edward Island had joined the Confederation. Work had begun on a transcontinental railway. The sheer geographic extent of the new Dominion seemed to promise Canada's most populous province (with almost forty-five per cent of the total population) an expansive future.

In September 1873, however, a new financial crisis swept through New York City. The "Panic of 1873" precipitated a five-year depression that became a psychological watershed throughout North America. Some part of the continent's unbridled optimism disappeared forever. By 1878 prosperity had begun to return in many parts of the United States. But the economy in Canada would not fully recover until the last years of the nineteenth century.

To the regional Reform Party that would govern the Province of Ontario without interruption from 1871 to 1905, the fundamental reason for Canada's failure to join in on the economic recovery of the late 1870s was the Canadian federal government's failure to re-negotiate the

Reciprocity Treaty of the 1850s and 1860s with the United States. There were three somewhat different versions of Canadian-American reciprocity in the Ontario debate of the later nineteenth century. "Restricted reciprocity" meant free trade in natural products only. "Unrestricted reciprocity", the policy endorsed by the Ontario government, meant free trade in both natural and manufactured products, but with Canada retaining its own tariff for countries other than the United States. "Commercial union", which meant that Canada would simply become part of the American tariff structure, was often viewed as a disloyal first step toward the eventual political annexation of Canada to the United States. Yet throughout the period the American federal government would only consider commercial union and was unenthusiastic even about that. To the political leaders south of the Great Lakes, the boundary between Canada and the United States was an "unnatural division". Political union with the American republic was Canada's "manifest destiny". A "principal objection urged in the United States against reciprocity", Premier Mowat himself observed in the early 1890s, "is that it would prevent political union".[1]

As an alternative to the apparently impossible ideal of reciprocity, John A. Macdonald introduced a new Canadian development strategy dubbed the "National Policy", which was given much credit for a major Conservative victory in the federal election of 1878. One ingredient of this strategy was fresh government aid for the construction of the Canadian transcontinental railway that British Columbia had demanded as its price for entering Confederation. But the key was a high protective tariff, designed to foster the growth of the regional manufacturing sector that had begun to develop in the pre-Confederation era, largely in Ontario and Quebec. In spite of tariffs and government trade policies, Ontario's links with the larger North American economy would remain strong, particularly in the forest industries and later in mining. It seems that one conscious objective of Macdonald's National Policy was to lure industrial jobs in the branch plants of American manufacturers north of the border. High American tariffs prompted a few Canadian manufacturers to establish branch plants in the United States. But the National Policy did foster industrial growth inside Canada, and much of

this growth gravitated toward the Dominion's most populous province.

Macdonald's policy, however, never enjoyed wide
popularity among the mass of Ontario farmers. More
important (as the Liberal Reformers who continued to support the ideal of reciprocity liked to point out), the
National Policy did not in fact bring a notable return of
prosperity north of the Great Lakes in the 1880s and
1890s. Above all else, the "Canadian market", which even
in 1901 comprised less than 5½ million people spread
across a vast territory, was simply too small to support a
vigorous regional manufacturing base. The growth of the
aggressive and expanding Massey farm machinery enterprise, which moved from Newcastle to Toronto in 1879,
illustrated the ultimate Canadian alternative to the unob-
tainable reciprocity with the United States. In 1887 the
Massey Manufacturing Company catalogue boasted:

> In England, Scotland, Ireland, France, Germany, Bel-
> gium, Russia, Asia Minor, South Africa, South Amer-
> ica, the West Indies, Australia, our machines are at
> work.

In the same year, the firm opened branches in London,
England and Adelaide, Australia. More generally, by the
start of the twentieth century Canadian industry (and
Canadian agriculture) had reembraced the international
commerce of the British Empire, that had been so important in its development before the great boom of the 1850s.

This final ingredient in the new alternative development strategy was confirmed by a new "Imperial Preference" in Canada, arranged by Prime Minister Wilfrid
Laurier's federal Liberal government in 1897. British
manufacturers could flood the small Canadian market as
easily as American manufacturers. The manufacturers of
central Canada did not support imperial free trade, but
only imperial preference – a reduction in the Canadian
tariff on British goods – intended as a gesture of goodwill
that would promote a parallel degree of special status for
Canadian products in the markets of the Empire.

Mowat's Great Reformers would continue to press for
the impossible ideal of reciprocity with the United States,
and by the 1890s this had become the declared policy of

Laurier's federal Liberals as well. But, for the moment at least, the ideal would remain an impossibility. The Ontario regional economy entered the twentieth century in the context of a national development strategy that stressed the domestic Canadian market and new links with the commerce of the United Kingdom.

The Movement from Farm to City

Despite slow growth, the generation after Confederation was a time of important poplulation change for Ontario. In 1871 about seventy-eight per cent of the people in the province still lived in rural areas; by 1901 the proportion was down to fifty-seven per cent. Part of the force behind the movement to the city involved change in the agrarian society itself. The frontier in southern Ontario had reached the rocky limits of the Canadian Shield not long after Confederation. It was not until the discovery of a northern Clay Belt in 1900 that new (and somewhat false) hopes would be raised for a second agricultural settlement frontier in northern or New Ontario. In the 1870s, 1880s, and 1890s, not all the children of the farmers of southern Ontario could themselves become farmers unless they left the province – which many did.

Increasingly, the family farmers who left took the commercial wheat economy with them. The largest wheat crop in Ontario history, 40.9 million bushels, was harvested in 1882. But like the fur trade before, the wheat economy was migrating to the more economical spaces of the western prairie, at first in the United States and then later in Manitoba and the Northwest Territories. The decline of the wheat harvest in the later 1880s marked a major transition in Ontario agriculture. As in the neighbouring American states, the family farm in the region gradually shifted toward a more diversified production of food for expanding urban centres, with corn (the old staple of the Ontario Iroquois) ultimately becoming the principle field crop. The agrarian society would remain the life of the Ontario majority until the early twentieth century. But the depression of the 1870s signalled the start of a long decline in its relative size and political influence.

The movement to the city north of the Great Lakes was also part of a larger international trend, often linked at the time with the new mass education and the new railways. By the 1890s a substantial majority of Ontario children were attending elementary school, and by provincial law virtually all of them were supposed to be. With the help of British capital looking for an outlet during the depression years of the 1870s and 1880s in the United Kingdom, the regional railways of the 1850s had expanded dramatically by the end of the nineteenth century. In the early 1890s Goldwin Smith noted: "Ontario is a network of railways; probably she has more miles of them in proportion to her population than any other district in the world."

Macdonald's National Policy played some part in providing jobs for the new migrants to Ontario cities. Without it, at least some would no doubt have become migrants to the United States. The Imperial Oil Company, headquartered in London, Ontario began under the umbrella of the National Policy in 1880. It was a successful effort to pick up the pieces into which the southwestern Ontario oil industry that started in the 1850s had been shattered by the depression of the 1870s. In the 1880s and 1890s Hamilton, an earlier centre of the Ontario wheat economy, started a Canadian steel industry, based on American coal imported via the Welland Canal.

By the mid-1880s there were ten Ontario urban centres with more than 10,000 people each[2]. But some smaller towns and villages were losing population. The outstanding development was the growth of Toronto – from about 50,000 people at the time of Confederation to more than 200,000 people at the turn of the twentieth century. In the 1880s alone, the city's population grew by nearly 100,000. Toronto's status as capital city for the new Province of Ontario played some role in its growth during the later nineteenth century. Even more important, in the three decades after Confederation Toronto became the financial capital of Ontario. This achievement was accompanied by a bitter struggle with the merchants of Montreal. But Montreal's ambitions for control of the new Canadian banking system were thwarted by political pressure from Ontario banking interests, expressed in the federal Banking Act of 1871. Two new Toronto banks, the Dominion and the Imperial, were established in the early 1870s, lending additional weight to the earlier Canadian Bank of Commerce and Bank of Toronto. Though Montreal remained somewhat larger (about 265,000 people in 1901), by the end of the century Toronto had asserted commercial primacy in its own province.

In the wider Canadian setting, grain shipments had begun to travel Toronto's combined water and rail route to western Canada by the late 1870s. Yet the western Canadian wheat boom would not arrive until the early twentieth century. The transcontinental Canadian Pacific Railway, completed in 1885, avoided Toronto, following instead the route of the historic economy of the north – from Montreal and then up the Ottawa River. In 1869, however, Timothy Eaton had moved from St. Mary's in western Ontario to the provincial capital, where he began what would become Canada's largest chain of retail department stores. The first Eaton's mail-order catalogue (dubbed "the farmer's bible") appeared in 1884. When a party of some 2,000 English immigrants settled near what subsequently became the border between Alberta and Saskatchewan in 1903, Eaton's agents would deliver catalogues to their tents.

Much of the new manufacturing employment gravitated toward economies of scale in Toronto. But manufacturing was not all a Toronto monopoly. In 1881 some fifty per cent of the work force in Hamilton was classified as "industrial", compared with forty-four per cent in Toronto, thirty-eight per cent in Kingston, and thirty-two per cent in Ottawa. Yet by 1890 Toronto's new position as the commercial and financial metropolis of Ontario was reflected in a re-arranged railway network focused on the provincial capital city. Montreal was still the economic capital of Canada, but not as it had been in the 1820s and 1830s.

Light at the End of the Tunnel

Ontario reached the bottom of its post-Confederation decline in another international depression – the Great Panic of 1893. This time, however, Canada at large was a

154

Eaton's operations in Toronto, at about the turn of the century. Electric streetcars were in full flower, but the automobile had yet to make its mark.

full partner in the wider economic recovery that took place in the later 1890s.

The urban development that had established itself during the hard times of the 1870s and 1880s helped poise Ontario to take advantage of the economic recovery. Macdonald's National Policy deserves at least some credit in this context. But contemporary supporters of the ideal of reciprocity pointed to the growth of Buffalo and Detroit, each of which was larger than either Toronto or Montreal by 1900.

There were also other developments that helped poise Ontario for new growth in the earlier twentieth century. Internationally, the period after the American Civil War was a time of great inventions which quickly became part of the new life in the cities. It is sometimes said that the telephone was invented in Boston. According to his own account, however, the Scotsman Alexander Graham Bell discovered "the principle of the telephone" in 1874 at his parents' house in Brantford, Ontario. The first long distance call in the world took place between Brantford and the neighbouring town of Paris, Ontario in 1876.

Electricity had arrived in Ontario cities by the 1880s. By the early 1890s the streets of Toronto were, in the words of Goldwin Smith, "a maze of wires, telegraphic and telephonic, and the chief throughfares ... lit with electric light". The lumbering centre of Peterborough at the edge of the southern extension of the Shield was electrified in 1891. The electric streetcar, "family chariot of democracy", made possible the first suburban real estate developments in the larger cities. By the 1890s the prospect of using Ontario's abundant water resources to generate hydroelectricity on a massive scale (especially at Niagara Falls) was under discussion.

The North American assault on the Canadian forest had continued throughout the hard times after 1873. The sale of timber rights on Crown land gave Ontario a stronger public revenue than its slow population growth alone could have supported. Sawn timber had been supplemented by pulp and paper by the 1870s. In 1888 J.R. Barber of Georgetown, Ontario became the first paper-maker in North America to use hydroelectic power. In the 1890s Francis Clergue pioneered the joint development

156

of a pulp and paper mill and a hydroelectric project in the Sault Ste. Marie area.

The Canadian Pacific Railway that was completed in 1885 was Montreal's not Toronto's route to western Canada. But as construction made its way through northern Ontario, it gave a strategic push to the mining industry that had been struggling to gain a foothold on the Canadian Shield since the middle of the nineteenth century. The CPR track from Montreal reached the north shore of Lake Nipissing in 1882. By the later 1880s a Grand Trunk line had linked Toronto with the area which became North Bay in 1891. Sudbury was created by CPR work crews in 1883. Nickel was discovered during construction on the rail line. The first nickel smelter was "blown in" at Copper Cliff in 1888, and the International Nickel Company was formed in 1902. In 1897 iron was discovered in the Michipicoten area north of Sault Ste. Marie while silver was discovered in the Cobalt area north of North Bay in 1903. By the turn of the twentieth century, a new northern resource frontier was ready to provide the stimulus for a new "Empire Ontario".

The Sage of the Grange on Ontario Society

If there is such a thing as an Ontario character, it both crystallized and reached its zenith in the later nineteenth century. In 1871 about seventy per cent of the region's population had been born in the province. By 1901 the proportion had reached a historic high of eighty-two per cent. Through the slow growth and hard times of the 1870s, 1880s, and 1890s, Ontario society acquired a degree of homogeneity that it had lacked before and that would start to fade again with the new growth of the twentieth century.

The society saw itself more as English Canadian than Ontarian (a word that has never quite graduated into popular usage). And the best contemporary writing on this "Ontario ... better designated as British Canada" was that of an English immigrant who greatly admired the democratic ideals of the American republic. Goldwin Smith, an old world intellectual adrift in late nineteenth-century Canada, had been Regius Professor of Modern History at

Oxford University in the 1850s and 1860s. A family tragedy prompted him to move to Cornell University in upstate New York in 1868. In 1871, at the age of forty-eight, he settled in Toronto where he lived as a political journalist of independent means – popularly known as "the Sage of the Grange" – until his death in 1910.

Though he disagreed with Ontario's dominant leadership on the importance of the British Empire in Canadian development, Goldwin Smith saw the world through the same nineteenth-century British liberal prejudices that George Brown had brought to the voice of Upper Canada in the pre-Confederation era. A sketch of the province he prepared in the early 1890s characterizes the society of "Old Ontario" on the eve of the twentieth century.

An attraction to Smith was that "At present the great industry of Ontario is farming ... in spite of the desperate efforts of protectionist legislators to force her to become a manufacturing country without coal." The "basis of society", as in the United States, was the "yeoman proprietor of one or two hundred acres" – a species of humanity quite different from the European "peasant characters of Zola". This "Canadian farmer" was "altogether a moral man and a good citizen, honest, albeit close, as he needs to be, in his dealings", who "supports his minister and his schoolmaster, though both perhaps on a rather slender pittance."

With some regret, Smith allowed that "of late" there had been "a great rush of population to the cities". Toronto especially had "grown with astonishing rapidity at the expense of the smaller towns and villages". He noted as well that the new "tendency to city life is universal" (by which he meant it was evident in both western Europe and North America). In Ontario cities where the protected manufacturing sector had begun to settle, "Industrial questions, trade unionism ... its conflict with capital ... are the same ... as in the United States and England."

Society north of the lakes was "equally commercial" as to the south. Though the scale of the new business civilization in the growing metropolis of Toronto "is smaller than that of Wall Street the strain is almost as great". Not surprisingly, there was less new wealth in Ontario than in

William P. Hubbard, first elected as a Toronto alderman in 1894, and a prominent local politician in Ontario's capital city in the subsequent two decades: an Ontario Black who did well, "in spite of the obstacles".

the American republic. "Of the leaders of society", Smith went on to suggest, "some are English by birth, and all of them keep up the connection by going a good deal to England."

Yet in both the city and the country, beyond "the special connection of a limited circle with the Old Country" Ontario was "a new and crude democracy", like the neighbouring states of the republic. "In everything the pleasure and convenience of the masses are consulted", Cricket and other "English games" were "kept up in the face of great difficulties" among a minority, "as indeed they are among the young men of wealth in the United States." But baseball was "the game of the continent". Lacrosse, "Indian in its origin", was "called the Canadian game."

Like George Brown, Goldwin Smith tended to see the future of both Canada and the United States as part of some wider future of the Anglo-Saxon or "English-speaking race". But he was too careful an observer to ignore the cultural diversity that continued to mark Ontario society. Though "the voice of God is still the general foundation of Canadian morality", among the Protestant churches "dogmatic differences are softened or forgotten". Orangeism "in Canada ... is a bulwark not of Protestantism, but of a Tory" political party. Yet there remained important differences between Protestants at large and the "Church of Rome", in "Ontario ... mainly the church of the Irish".

There were also "Scotch-Irish" in the region, and "a settlement of Germans in Waterloo County who remain German, and make excellent farmers and citizens." In some "Highland settlements ... Gaelic is still spoken." Canada had once been "the asylum of the fugitive slave", and there were still "a number of negroes, of whom some have done well, in spite of the obstacles." In the cities Jews had begun to appear in some numbers, and there were "scatterings of other races, the last arrival being the Italian". A "French settlement" survived "beside the Detroit River, a relic of the era of old French fur-trading and adventure". In the "Eastern part of the Province" the "French population of Quebec ... has already in two or three counties almost supplanted the British."

160

In some ways, Ontario at large remained "British". In "all Canadian courts ... Justice ... keeps her gown though not her whig, while in the United States the gown is worn by the judges of the Supreme Court only." Of the regional literature that had begun to appear, "a kind critic might say that it still retains something of the old English sobriety of style, and is comparatively free from the straining for effect which is the bane of the best literature of the United States."

In other ways, "Ontario is an American State of the Northern type". The "reforming and philanthropic movements, such as the Temperance movement, the Women's Rights movement, and the Labour movements" had continental connections. The regional press was "in the main, American not English in its character. It aims at the lightness, smartness, and crispness of New York journalism rather than at the solidity of the London *Times*." And in "the use of agricultural machinery the Province ... believes herself to have outrun the mother country."

In several respects, Goldwin Smith spoke for an Ontario society that had more to do with the nineteenth century than it would with the twentieth century that lay ahead. The voice of the majority in his Ontario was still the voice of the family farm, with strong memories of the pre-Confederation frontier. Yet the provincial government that spoke politically for this majority (and for its companion interests in the world of commerce) would persist until 1905. And it left a political legacy that would thrive in full vigour until the middle of the twentieth century.

9

The Regional State

Mowat's Great Reform regime involved more than mere skill in political management and a willingness to compromise with the genuinely conservative side of late nineteenth-century Ontario. There was an important sense in which Mowat himself was, according to historian W.S. Wallace:

> ... an incorrigible Reformer ... inspired with the modern idea that it is the duty of a legislature to legislate; and that the more it legislates, the better it is performing its duty.

This was something of a departure from the Reformism of William Lyon Mackenzie, who had arrived in Upper Canada in the same year that Oliver Mowat was born. As in the neighbouring states of the American republic, progressive sentiment in the early nineteenth century had tended to see government as an instrument by which conservative elites tried to oppress the mass of the people. But here as elsewhere, the American Civil War had been a great watershed.

By the end of the century, progressive government had become an instrument through which the democratic majority could expand its opportunities and try to protect itself from a new and often predatory corporate enterprise in transportation and industry. Such regional corporate entrepreneurs as William McMaster and Timothy Eaton were themselves supporters of Mowat's Reform Party. But

162

as the Conservative Adam Beck would show in the early twentieth century, there was a side to the Ontario business community that also looked to government for support against Carnegie, Morgan, Rockefeller, and other "Robber Barons" to the south. Mowat was "glad to believe there is little antagonism between the different classes in this glorious Province." Unlike the Conservatives, however, "if there is antagonism, my sympathy and that of my colleagues is with the masses rather than with the classes."

At the same time, Liberal Reform in Ontario retained much of its earlier enthusiasm for economy and efficiency in public administration. During the Great Reformers thirty-four consecutive years in power, the provincial Conservatives periodically tried to win votes by attacking the extravagance of the government. But in Mowat's last election in 1894, the government could boast in its campaign rhetoric that despite "many progressive measures affecting the general interests of the community ... Mr. Mowat is still able to show a comfortable surplus."

Mowat's enthusiasm for government activity was qualified as well by a somewhat different attraction to the traditions of the past. In the late nineteenth century, Canadian liberals largely retained a historic decentralist vision of democratic federalism, which progressive sentiment in the American republic was abandoning. In the 1870s, 1880s, and 1890s, the Ontario Great Reformers were still standing up for the ideals of de Tocqueville's *Democracy in America* in the 1830s, stressing the "necessity of examining the condition of the states before that of the union at large." On the eve of the First World War, W.S. Wallace could write:

> In the United States the tendency since 1867 has been toward strengthening the federal government; in Canada it has been, thanks to Sir Oliver Mowat and the liberal party, toward weakening the federal and strengthening the provincial government.

Ontario and the Revolt of the Provinces

Ontario's quest for provincial rights in the new Canadian Confederation was in part an early variation on a recurrent

163

theme in Canadian economic development, much later characterized as "province building". Political conflict between the Premier of Ontario Oliver Mowat and the Prime Minister of Canada John A. Macdonald in some degree reflected the late nineteenth-century economic conflict between the merchants of Toronto (especially those who looked first to New York) and the merchants of Montreal. The Reformers of Ontario could not deliver reciprocity with the United States. But in one sense provincial rights was their alternative to Macdonald's National Policy – lending the weight of regional government to Toronto's quest for commercial primacy in its own province.

For most Ontario voters, the height of Mowat's achievement in the struggle for provincial rights was his victory at the British Empire's highest court in the Ontario Boundary case of 1884. Having won his case, the Premier returned from England via New York. When he crossed into Ontario from Buffalo, he was greeted by a torchlight parade. When he finally arrived at the provincial capital in Toronto, he was met by a crowd of nearly 50,000 people. A public tribute from the "Reformers of Ontario" to the man who had "worn the white flower of a blameless life" was read by William McMaster.

The Ontario Great Reformers' support for provincial rights also had more philosophical roots. In the Confederation debates of the mid-1860s, Mowat's own interest had focused on the structures and powers of the provincial governments. Like the old Upper Canada Clear Grit William McDougall, he had supported a failed proposal for an elected Canadian Senate to reflect regional interests in the structure of the new federal state[1]. Mowat believed in decentralization for all parts of Canada, not just Ontario. In 1880 he wrote to John Thompson of Nova Scotia, urging that "the Provincial Governments of all parties should always diligently watch over and maintain the rights of the Provinces".

The major centre of federal-provincial struggle in the later nineteenth century (following precedents set by the American republic) was the courts – ultimately the British Judicial Committee of the Privy Council at Westminster. In the 1870s and 1880s Ontario won four key cases at the

Privy Council, that subsequently enhanced provincial powers under the British North America Act. The Judicial Committee of the Privy Council went on to establish a decentralist judicial interpretation of the Act, stressing the general provincial responsibility for "property and civil rights" (and confining the federal government's clear power to disallow provincial legislation to "emergency situations").

The Judicial Committee of the Privy Council was also the setting for Mowat's ultimate triumph in the Ontario boundary dispute. At the time of Confederation, Ontario's boundaries were declared to be those of the old Province of Upper Canada, which had never been systmatically defined to the north and west. The issue became significant when the Government of Canada purchased the Hudson's Bay Company lands in 1869. A process to settle the matter was set in motion. And by the late 1870s a well-defined dispute had developed, pitting Macdonald and the federal government against Mowat and the provincial government.

For Macdonald, Ontario's northern boundary was the height of land that marked the Hudson Bay watershed, while its western boundary ended some half a dozen miles west of Fort William. For Mowat, Ontario ended at James Bay and the Albany River in the north and at the Lake of the Woods in the west, giving a total geographic area for the province about twice as large as the boundaries envisioned by Macdonald[2]. In 1881 Macdonald implicated Manitoba in the issue by declaring that its boundaries extended to include the disputed area claimed by Ontario between Fort William and the Lake of the Woods.

By the summer of 1883, Manitoba and Ontario had established competing police forces in what is now Kenora, Ontario. An impasse had been reached. Macdonald had been encouraging Manitoba to press its case. But Manitoba had its own provincial complaints about Macdonald's federal government. The *Free Press* in Winnipeg declared that the new western province in fact had "a common interest" with the old Upper Canada "in opposing the centralizing proclivities of the Macdonald clique".

In 1884 the dispute was taken to the Judicial Committee of the Privy Council at Westminster, which decided in

Map: The Province of Ontario, about 1905, after the boundary dispute of the 1880s, but before the modern boundaries of 1912. The map was prepared for the Ontario Forestry Commission, and the more northerly area bounded by the heavy line marks those parts of the province still "Predominantly Forest" at the turn of the century.

166

favour of Ontario's claim. Ontario, Mowat declared, had resisted Macdonald's conspiracy to make her "one of the least of the great provinces' (the other "great provinces" of the day being Quebec and British Columbia). Ontario now had "an extent of country ample enough to admit of its development, so that, as the other provinces develope, Ontario should develope also."

Mowat's strongest ally in the provincial rights struggle of the 1880s was Honoré Mercier, Premier of Quebec. In 1887 Mercier convened an Interprovincial Conference at Quebec City – marking the origins of what would later become another important instrument of federal-provincial conflict in Canada. Mowat was elected chairman of the Interprovincial Conference of 1887. Nova Scotia, New Brunswick, and Manitoba were represented, along with Ontario and Quebec. Prince Edward Island, British Columbia, and the federal government did not attend. The Conference was no more than a strong protest against the centralizing proclivities of the Macdonald clique. But it established precedents in the political life of the Con-federation. Ontario suspected any grand proposal to raid the federal treasury (to which the most populous province contributed so much). Nonetheless, the Conference passed twenty-three unanimous resolutions urging improved federal-provincial financial arrangements and constitu-tional reforms to enhance the status of the provinces. One resolution, "drafted by Mr. Mowat and his colleagues from Ontario", was an attack on Macdonald's National Policy and later became a troublesome plank in the election plat-form of Laurier's federal Liberal Party. It urged:

> a fair measure, providing, under proper conditions, for unrestricted reciprocal trade relations between the Dominion and the United States ... would be of advantage to all the provinces of the Dominion.

The Great Reform Programme

The new late nineteenth-century progressivism, reflected in Mowat's activist attitude toward government, also helped enhance provincial status in the developing Canadian Confederation. It implied that governments should actively intervene to promote social and economic welfare among the mass of population.

In mid-nineteenth-century Canada, the more conservative alliance of Macdonald and Cartier had not seen the public welfare responsibilities of government as important, and they had largely been given to the provinces under the British North America Act. Thus, it was the provincial Great Reform government, not the federal government at Ottawa, that brought the early modest beginnings of the modern "welfare state" to Ontario. And in the hard times and slow growth of the 1870s, 1880s, and 1890s, the new progressive regional state had an inevitable underlying concern with economic development.

Agriculture and resources were at the centre of the Ontario Great Reformers' regional economic policy. Mowat was particularly attentive to the needs of the family farmers who dominated the Reform electorate. Ontario farmers also faced increasingly higher American tariff barriers in the later nineteenth century, which helps explain part of the Reform passion for unrestricted reciprocity. It also suggests another ingredient in the enthusiasm for imperial preference in the 1890s. By the end of the nineteenth century, some eighty-five per cent of Ontario's export surplus of agricultural produce was being sent to the United Kingdom.

Mowat's government took steps as well to help the family farm adjust to the new, more diversified, and less dominant agriculture signalled by the decline of the regional wheat economy in the 1880s. A provincial commission on agriculture reported in 1881, and the following year a Bureau of Industries was established to collect statistics (especially agricultural statistics) under the Commissioner of Agriculture and Public Works. A separate provincial Department of Agriculture was established in 1888, and Charles Drury became the first full-time Minister of Agriculture.

Sandfield Macdonald had made fresh efforts to promote a new northern agricultural frontier with the Free Homestead Act of 1868. Despite continued promotion, farming on the thin soil of the Shield was proving little more than a transient phenomenon, which followed the lumber camps engaged in the increasingly northward assault on the Canadian forest.

Regional strains of a new North American conservation movement attacked the short-sightedness of an Ontario forestry policy that simply surveyed huge tracts of Crown land and then leased timber rights to the highest bidder. The defence was that a "business first" approach ensured needed public revenue and economic activity in hard times. Nonetheless, in response to the new conservation pressures, Algonquin Park in the northern Shield country of southern Ontario was established in 1893 as a provincial "forest reserve" (which would eventually help provide the region's growing urban population with at least a tourist's experience of the Ontario wilderness).

The Great Reformers also took steps to promote the new mining industry that was starting to take root on the northern Ontario Shield. A provincial mining commission reported in 1891, and a Bureau of Mines, later affiliated with Queen's University, was established in 1893. In 1895 the provincial government ran summer schools for "young miners and prospectors" at Sudbury, Sault Ste. Marie, Port Arthur, and Kenora.

Provincial government subsidization of railway development was the leading theme of Ontario regional industrial policy in the later nineteenth century. But by the 1890s the Great Reformers could also boast a substantial body of labour legislation, addressed to characteristic vices of the new industrial civilization that was establishing itself in the province's larger urban areas. In 1894 the Woodstock Knights of Labour praised Mowat for "legislation passed under your premiership, which especially affects the interests of workingmen."

The list included a (not too rigorously enforced) Factories Act, designed to protect working women and children and to ensure "proper sanitary condition of factories". Among other laws cited by the Woodstock Knights were a Mechanics' Lien Act, a Mining Operations Act, and a Work and Wages Act. A provincial Co-operative Associations Act, designed "to facilitate agreements between masters and workmen for participation in profits", held out a noble but largely idealistic vision for the development of the new industrialism.

169

By the late nineteenth century, much of the agrarian society had turned its back on the earlier "too free use of ardent spirits" as a matter of principle. But, as on the old agrarian frontier, alcohol was the characteristic refuge from the often harsh pressures of the new urban life – at least for those who could not find complete solace in the teetotaling Christianity promoted by the Premier of Ontario. As early as the late 1860s, a *Globe* reporter had toured "the slums" of Toronto, where he found "a drunken brute of a father" beating "a half-frozen six-year-old girl" and in "one delapidated house after another ... amid poverty and dirt ... drunken women of all ages." [3]

As elsewhere, experiences of this sort led many public-spirited people to see alcohol itself as the region's crucial social problem. By the 1890s "Prohibition" had replaced "Temperance" as the leading issue in what might be called early regional social policy. The Christian politician appreciated the potential divisiveness of the issue and adopted delaying tactics. In this particular case, Mowat suggested, it may in fact be the federal government that had the appropriate constitutional authority. The Judicial Committee of the Privy Council would be queried on the matter. Meanwhile, a plebiscite held in 1894 showed a clear majority of the active electorate favouring some form of legislation that would "prohibit the sale of spiritous liquors".

In 1892 a progressively graded system of succession duties (or taxes on inherited property) helped strengthen a more enduring form of social policy in Ontario. By statute, the proceeds of the duties were "to be applied to pay the expense incurred by the province in support of asylums for the insane and idiots, institutions for the care of the deaf and dumb, hospitals, and other charities."

By the 1890s the pace of French Catholic immigration from Quebec had also confronted the Ontario Great Reformers with the thorny problems of Canadian social diversity. Mowat, like George Brown, had not supported Catholic separate schools in Ontario before Confederation. But the Confederation bargain of 1867 had guaranteed the limited system of Ontario separate schools bequeathed by the old United Province of Canada. This guarantee was not supported by many staunch Protestant

PROHIBITION PLEBISCITE !

CONVENTION

——FOR THE——

COUNTY OF YORK.

All prohibitionists and friends of temperance in general in the County of York, are requested to meet in the

Mechanics' Hall, Aurora,

——ON——

TUESDAY 31ST OCT.

For the purpose of organizing in connection with the plebiscite for prohibition and endeavoring to get out the largest vote possible on the 1st of JANUARY, 1894.

The Convention will commence at 10 o'clock, and let each municipality in the County be fully represented.

A MASS MEETING !

WILL BE HELD

IN THE EVENING.

Chair taken at 8 o'clock.   Collection taken up to defray expenses.

Let all friends of temperance rally and work for "God, Home and Country"

REV. H. S. MATTHEWS,

COUNTY CONVENER.

Aurora, October 24th 1893.   Aurora Banner Print.

Poster advertising Prohibition Meeting, 1893.

partisans in late nineteenth-century Ontario or by others who believed that state-supported mass education in the region should be rigorously secular. But as Premier of Ontario, Mowat had no doubts that it must be honoured, as a symbol of commitment to the larger public life of the Dominion.

Catholic separate schools benefitted Irish immigrants to Ontario as well as French Canadian migrants from Quebec. Yet influenced perhaps by his partnership with Honoré Mercier in the struggle for provincial rights, Mowat had also come to believe that the language of French Catholic Canada had at least limited claims on a degree of special status in the Province of Ontario. This belief was even less universally shared in the old upper country. In 1889 newspapers like the Tory *Mail and Empire* in Toronto and the *Orange Sentinel* had begun to express alarm that Mowat and his Minister of Education George Ross had struck a "bargain with the Romish hierarchy and clergy" to promote "the use of the French language in some of the public schools of the province".

Mowat appointed a commission to look into the matter. It reported that some French textbooks were being used along with English textbooks in 98 of some 6,000 Ontario public schools, especially in the counties of Essex and Kent as well as Prescott and Russell. As Minister of Education, George Ross felt obliged to make clear that English was to be the prime language in Ontario schools. But Mowat himself summarized the "proper policy" suggested by the commission's work:

> Now ... English is the language of the immense majority in this province ... it is on that account in the interest of the French population in Ontario to learn English.... There is no danger of the French language taking the place of English....
>
> French-Canadians cherish their own language lovingly; they wish their children to love it and be educated in it; but they know it will be for their interest to be familiar with English also, and to be educated in English as well as French.... Permit their own tongue to receive attention, and they are glad to have their children learn English.

172

It would be some three-quarters of a century before any Ontario provincial government would begin to live up to the full implications of this "proper policy". Yet as Ontario's leading modern French Canadian historian Robert Choquette has put it: "Mowat et son gouvernement se montrèrent plus ouvert aux droits de la minorité franco-ontarienne que les gouvernements subséquents".

Winds of Political Change

The Great Reformers won a comfortable majority in the Ontario general election of 1890. But they came out of the election of 1894, Mowat's last contest in provincial politics, with what was technically a minority government. This marked not a new surge of Conservative strength but the earliest beginnings of a regional three-party political system that would gradually develop during the twentieth century. By the 1890s the political implications of the new industrialization in the region had made a first appearance.

The growth of organized industrial labour was the most obvious implication. A typographers' union had flourished in Toronto since the 1830s, and by the 1860s a regional labour movement was gaining momentum in Hamilton, Toronto, and other urban centres. Following Macdonald's federal Trade Unions Act of 1872, Toronto labour leaders tried to establish a national Canadian labour organization. But the Depression of the later 1870s had cast the effort adrift.

By the early 1880s branches of the Holy and Noble Order of the Knights of Labour (founded at Philadelphia in 1868) had appeared in Ontario. A Trades and Labour Congress of Canada met in Toronto in 1886 to start a national labour organization that would remain intact until it became the Canadian Labour Congress in the mid-twentieth century. But modern collective bargaining in industrial wage settlements made scant progress. In 1885 a "first class artisan" was earning from $6 to $7 for a 58-hour week.

173

In 1894 Labour Day (the first Monday in September) became a national holiday in Canada, as in the United States, in the wake of unrest brought on by the financial Panic of 1893. To some extent, Mowat's labour legislation was a response to the early growth of labour organizations in Ontario. An avowed "socialist" had briefly sat as an Independent in the provincial Legislative Assembly during the mid-1870s, and "Labour" candidates first ran in a provincial general election in 1883. Yet it was the early beginnings of organized agriculture, not organized industrial labour, that launched a significant political challenge to the regional dominance of the Ontario Great Reformers in the 1890s.

The new industrialization threatened the traditional agrarian society of the family farm as much as the earlier world of the independent mechanic. In both cases, the response was a quest for power through mass organization. The "Grange movement", voice of a new North American agrarianism founded at Washington in 1867, had reached Ontario by the mid-1870s. And organized agriculture, with its roots in what was still the single largest economic sector of the region, made more rapid progress in developing an effective political arm than organized labour.

In the late 1880s branches of the "Patrons of Industry", an agrarian political party that had originated in Michigan, began to form in Ontario – a regional variation on a new wave of progressive "populism" in the midwestern, western, and southern parts of North America at large. In the election of 1894 the Ontario Patrons took seventeen of the ninety-four seats then in the provincial Legislative Assembly. Mowat's Liberal Reformers took forty-six seats; the Conservatives, twenty-eight; a short-lived minor party called the Protestant Protective Association, two; and there was one Independent.

Mowat took the attitude that in Ontario the Patrons were simply "reformers in a hurry". In effect, they were a revival of the old radical Clear Grits, and the Liberal Reformers formed what amounted to a coalition government with them. Mowat had already done much for agriculture in Ontario, and he was prepared to do a little more. The isolation of farm life in comparison with the new life in the cities was a great cause of complaint. The railways

174

had given the cities a new mobility that the farms still lacked. An Ontario Good Roads Act was passed in 1894, and a Good Roads Branch was established in the Department of Agriculture in 1896.

Economic life in all sectors had begun to improve by the later 1890s. The election of 1894, on the heels of the Panic of 1893, marked the height of the Patrons' success. They would never again win seats in the Ontario legislature. But they had begun a new, more radical progressive politics in the province, that would grow much larger in the earlier twentieth century.

A revival of a quite different kind of earlier political tradition north of the Great Lakes had more immediate significance. The publication of Egerton Ryerson's *The Loyalists of America and Their Times* in 1880 marked a starting point. The formation of the United Empire Loyalists Association of Ontario in 1896 was a culmination, confirmed by the most enthusiastic young members of Ontario militia regiments who went off to the South African War in 1899.

The United States was building its industrial base through a rigorous policy of high tariffs. And beyond its general impact on agriculture and labour, the new industrialization in Ontario was strengthening the region's particular links to the British Empire. In the United Kingdom, an Imperial Federation League and Joseph Chamberlain's Tariff Reform League helped to revive the "British connexion". Industrialization in late nineteenth-century Canada helped give many Canadians new economic as well as old sentimental interests in the global civilization of the British Empire on which the sun never set.

Mowat himself showed his respect for shifts in public opinion by accepting the offer of a British title in 1892. This was an honour traditionally embraced by such Canadian Conservative politicians as Sir John A. Macdonald and Sir Georges Etienne Cartier. But earlier Reform stalwarts like George Brown and Edward Blake had refused such tokens of an outdated European aristocracy. Mowat thought up appropriate excuses. Like earlier Reformers, at bottom he continued to see the link with the British Empire as a shield for a nascent New World patriotism in Canada, rather than an end in itself. The provinces, he declared in the early 1890s "are not yet sufficiently

175

Officers of the Third Dragoons militia regiment at Belleville summer camp, 1898. Several thousand young men from Ontario would fight for the Empire in the Boer or South African War that broke out just over a year later. On the last day of December in 1900, an audience at Massey Hall in Toronto heard a report on the war from Winston Churchill, described by the Globe *as "an extremely young-looking man, with a boyish face, fine features and a good voice". (Churchill had just turned twenty-six). At one point in the talk, "a large map of South Africa was thrown on the screen. 'Take a good look at it,' said Mr. Churchill. 'It belongs to us.'"*

welded together to form Canada into an independent nation ... the strongest tie which up to this moment binds the provinces together is their common British connection."

By the early 1890s some two decades of frustratingly slow regional growth, right beside the expanding and aggressive new American union that had come out of the Civil War, were placing strong pressures on the unity of the Canadian Confederation. The old cry for annexation to the American republic was being raised in some quarters once again. In the same year that he became "Sir Oliver Mowat", the Premier of Ontario had dismissed the provincially-appointed Attorney of Dufferin County "for the public expression of annexationist sentiments".

Like Mowat, the main body of Great Reformers in Ontario believed in a separate political destiny for Canada in the northern part of North America. But by the end of the nineteenth century, it seemed clear that the fledgling Canadian Confederation could only escape the Manifest Destiny of the American republic by remaining a staunch supporter of the British Empire. Even Mowat's resolution at the Interprovincial Conference of 1887 had explicitly linked provincial aspirations for unrestricted reciprocity in Canadian-American trade with an earnest expression of "fervent loyalty to Her Majesty the Queen".

"Remember Ross.... He is Building up New Ontario"

In June 1896 Wilfrid Laurier led the federal Liberal Party to power in Ottawa, breaking the eighteen-year dominance of the federal Conservatives and becoming the first French Canadian Prime Minister of the Dominion of Canada. Shortly afterwards, Oliver Mowat accepted an invitation to serve in Laurier's cabinet, along with W.S. Fielding (the former Premier of Nova Scotia), A.G. Blair (the former Premier of New Brunswick), and Clifford Sifton (the former Attorney-General of Manitoba).

Mowat was seventy-six years old at the time and had agreed to enter Laurier's cabinet largely as a symbolic gesture. He remained for only a year. In November 1897 Laurier appointed him Lieutenant-Governor of Ontario, a post which he held until 1902. When Mowat left Ottawa, he had expressed a desire for "liberty to choose my own subjects for study and work". In 1898 he published a pamphlet entitled *Christianity and its Influence*.

On Mowat's departure from provincial politics in 1896, Arthur Sturgis Hardy, who had served in the cabinet since 1877 – first as Provincial Secretary, then as Commissioner of Crown Lands – became Premier of Ontario. Hardy led the twenty-seven year old Great Reform regime to a majority of only a few seats in the provincial election of 1898. The Patrons of Industry's show of strength in 1894 proved transient or at least premature. But the Conservative opposition under the new leadership of James P. Whitney actually polled a slightly larger share of the popular vote than the Liberals.

In 1899 Hardy felt compelled to resign as a result of poor health. He was succeeded by George Ross, the former Minister of Education. Ross later wrote: "though greatly honoured I felt my tenure of office would not last long." To the surprise of many, he managed to hang on with a very slim majority of two or three seats in the provincial election of 1902; all told, he would remain Premier of Ontario for half a dozen years.

The new economic prosperity that began in the late 1890s no doubt helped the Great Reformers preserve a skillful but precarious hold on power after Mowat's departure from active provincial politics. The leading theme in the "late Reform" programme was the promotion of development in the "New Ontario" north of the French River, that the Canadian Pacific Railway and the Ontario boundary dispute had helped open up in the mid-1880s.

John Dryden, who became Minister of Agriculture under Mowat in 1890 and remained in office under both Hardy and Ross, led a new drive to promote agricultural settlement in the north. In both the northeast and the northwest, there was some land suited to farming (though nothing like the western prairie). The discovery of a "Little Clay Belt" north of North Bay in 1900 seemed to bear out Dryden's faith in a new northern frontier similar to that of the south. Enthusiasm grew with the subsequent announcement of a Great Clay Belt, a stretch of some 25,000 square miles extending westward from the Ontario-Quebec boundary into the district of Thunder Bay.

In 1902 Ross' government began work on the Temiskaming and Northern Ontario Railway, the first railway owned by a Canadian province, to promote settlement on the Little Clay Belt. It started at North Bay on the CPR line and had reached Englehart some 140 miles to the north by 1904. Settlement proceeded slowly. But the line proved fortuitous when silver was discovered along the route at Cobalt in 1903. Many of the new settlers in northeastern Ontario were French Canadian migrants from Quebec. And in 1904 Ross appointed Ontario's first French Canadian cabinet minister – Albert Evanturel from the Ottawa valley riding of Prescott, who served as a Minister without Portfolio.

Despite energy and political skill, however, Ross was in an increasingly untenable position. The new prosperity was enlarging the cities and diminishing the agrarian society that had been the vital base of Reform politics since Mackenzie and the Baldwins. By 1905 the urban and rural population in Ontario was about evenly split. With Mowat gone, the Great Reform Government seemed more and more like a well-oiled political machine that had lost its purpose and its heart.

The new Conservative leader James P. Whitney gained ground with attacks on the corruption of a tired regime that lacked the defences once provided by the blameless posture of the Christian politician. The Great Reform machine itself seemed to be losing its sense of proportion. In the election of 1902, the pulp and paper pioneer and staunch government supporter Francis Clergue had brought a trainload of visitors from Michigan, well supplied with liquor and other refreshments, to vote at several polls in Sault Ste. Marie. This lent credibility to the equally fraudulent stunt of the Conservative Robert Gamey, who early in 1903 rose in the house, and displaying $3,000 in bank bills, avowed that he had been given them by the government as the price of his political support.

To make matters worse, Mowat's delaying tactics on the Prohibition issue had returned to haunt his former Minister of Education. In 1901 the British Privy Council finally offered a definitive response to Mowat's earlier query on the constitutionality of provincial legislation prohibiting the sale of liquor; in the Judicial Committee of the Privy Council's view, this too was a provincial right. Like Mowat, Ross had come to believe that even with the support of a majority of the active electorate, Prohibition would be a mistake. His solution was to hold another referendum, in December 1902, requiring a two-thirds majority. Under these rules, Prohibition was defeated. But again, a simple majority had voted in favour. Many felt betrayed by George Ross, regarded as "one of the idols of the temperance party".

Ross became entangled as well in a controversy over hydroelectricity at Niagara Falls. A coal strike in Pennsylvania during the summer of 1902 had prompted new enthusiasm among Ontario industrialists and municipal officials for the "white coal of Niagara". At the same time, even Conservatives like Adam Beck were expressing fears about domination of hydroelectric development in the province by large American corporations. Ross created the Ontario Power Commission in 1903 to safeguard provincial interests and promoted development on the Canadian side of Niagara Falls by a private Canadian firm. But he was skeptical about the demand for "public power" raised by Beck and his supporters. A small provincially-owned northern railway fit with Reform philosophy on the need for active government. The concept of a major provincially-owned hydroelectric system seemed quite different.

By 1904 conflict of all kinds was placing strains on the government's slim majority in the legislature. Hoping to improve his position, the Premier called a general election for 25 January 1905. On the day before polling, the front page of *The Globe* urged its readers: "Remember Ross.... He is Building up New Ontario." But the newspaper that George Brown had founded was "the voice of Upper Canada" no longer. James P. Whitney's Conservatives took fifty-three per cent of the popular vote and sixty-nine seats. Ross and the Liberal Reformers were reduced to forty-five per cent of the vote and a mere twenty-eight seats. The regional state that the Great Reform Government had created would survive. But the triumph of Reform in Ontario had come to an end.

Part Four

New Frontier, 1905-1943

"The Dutch may have their Holland, the Spaniard have his
Spain,
The Yankee to the south of us must south of us remain;
For not a man dare lift a hand against the men who brag
That they were born in Canada beneath the British flag."
Tekahionwake (Pauline Johnson)

"An honest attempt to enumerate the points on which our
Canadian civilization differs from that of the United States
is apt to be almost as brief as the famous essay upon snakes in
Ireland...."

... The thing which is most impressive to anyone who really
tries to make himself acquainted with American civilization
is the extraordinary variety of American cultural expression,
and the extraordinary variety of self-criticism within the
American community."
Frank Underhill

A shipment of silver bars at Cobalt in "New Ontario": enough to put a smile on anyone's face. Mining at Cobalt is said to have begun when a blacksmith threw a hammer at a fox in 1903. The hammer missed the fox, but hit a rock and exposed a vein of silver. Mining in the north would help stimulate new urban growth in the south, especially in the rising financial centre of Toronto.

10

New Industrialism
and New Northwest

The return of prosperity in the early twentieth century was accompanied by a significant increase in Ontario's population – from 2.2 million in 1901 to 3.4 million in 1931. The buoyant times were interrupted by two rather serious recessions immediately before and after the First World War. But compared with the prolonged economic doldrums of the last three decades of the previous century, the first three decades of the twentieth century were a boom period. Even during the Great Depression of the 1930s, some 356,000 people were added to the province's population (an increase of more than ten per cent).

Several broader developments were linked with the better times that the earlier twentieth century brought to the region. One was a consolidation of the share in the North American manufacturing production that urban southern Ontario had acquired in the later nineteenth century. Another was a major expansion in the new mining and forestry frontiers of northern Ontario. Still another was (at last) a vigorous wave of mass settlement on the new agrarian frontier of the western Canadian prairie – the "last best west" of North America. The more southerly part of the old Northwest Territories became the provinces of Alberta and Saskatchewan in 1905, the same year the T.Eaton Company of Toronto opened a major new department store and catalogue operation in Winnipeg, Manitoba.

Reciprocity, National Policy, and Imperial Preference

By the turn of the twentieth century, the alternative to the impossible ideal of reciprocity with the United States – Macdonald's National Policy and Laurier's imperial preference – had left significant marks on the Canadian economy as a whole and on the Ontario regional economy in particular. Increasingly, the flow of Canada's international trade had assumed a transcontinental and transatlantic character. In 1870 fifty-one per cent of all Canadian exports had been going to the United States and only thirty-eight per cent to the United Kingdom. By 1916, sixty-one per cent of all Canadian exports were going to the United Kingdom, and only twenty-seven per cent to the United States. And Montreal's commercial empire of the St. Lawerence was once again a dominant force in Candian economic life.

As in the past, the empire of the St. Lawrence leaned on an east-west transportation network, now featuring the Canadian Pacific Railroad headquartered in Montreal. The farmers of Ontario were still sceptical about the "protected" commerce of Montreal. But those parts of the Toronto business community that had acquired strong interests in national trade and finance – for example, Eaton's and the Canadian Bank of Commerce – were now prepared, for the time being at least, to acquiesce in the status of junior partner to Montreal. Moreover, much of the industrial manufacturing that had developed in urban southern Ontario since the later nineteenth century had also acquired very specific interests in the National Policy and imperial preference.

These changes in the Ontario economy appeared in bold relief when in 1911 President William Howard Taft of the United States suddenly offered practically free trade in "farm, forest, and fish products", in an effort to enhance US access to Canada's burgeoning western grain and northern resource frontiers. Prime Minister Laurier called a federal election on the issue for 21 September 1911. Laurier and the Liberals at last stood up for the old impossible ideal of reciprocity with the United States, imagining at first that they had stumbled on a major stroke of good fortune. But the federal Conservatives, led by Robert Borden of Nova Scotia, opposed President Taft's offer on a

185

platform that appealed to British Canadian patriotism as well as economic interests in central Canada. Eighteen Toronto Liberals prominent in trade and finance deserted Laurier. In the end, Borden won the election, thanks in large part to a massive victory in Ontario, where the Conservatives took seventy-three federal seats to the Liberal's thirteen.

As historian Frank Underhill saw it,

> In 1911 Canadian capitalism celebrated its coming of age. The dream of the Montreal merchants of one hundred years before had at last come true.... Toronto capitalists, who at times had shown some inclination to challenge the position of the senior metropolis, were now working hand in hand with it.

Despite the election of 1911, in the strategic Ontario industrial sector of agricultural implements, reciprocity was in fact achieved gradually, through the complete abolition of the American tariff in 1913 and a slow reduction in the Canadian tariff culminating with virtual Canadian-American free trade in the sector by 1944. Anticipating a victory for the forces of reciprocity in the election of 1911, the Massey-Harris farm machinery enterprise of Toronto purchased its first branch plant in the United States.

Similarly, the new forestry and mining industries that were making crucial contributions to Ontario's growth (and in the case of mining, to Toronto's increasing importance as a financial centre) were promoting north-south trading relationships between Canada and the United States. The share of all Canadian exports going to the United Kingdom fell from sixty-one per cent in 1916 to twenty-nine per cent in 1932. During the same period the share going to the United States rose from twenty-seven per cent to forty-three per cent. There was a brief resurgence of imperial trade during the 1930s Great Depression. But even in 1937 some forty-one per cent of Canadian exports were going to the United States compared with thirty-eight per cent to the United Kingdom.

Throughout the 1920s and 1930s the old National Policy and imperial prefence remained important for much of the Ontario regional economy. But new more "continental" trading interests were taking root. By the

Tekahionwake in concert: "born in Canada beneath the British flag". Pauline Johnson was the daughter of a Six Nations Iroquois chief (and his English wife), descended from an adopted son of William Johnson of the Mohawks, who had made peace with Pontiac for the British in 1766. Born in Brant County, Ontario in 1862, she became a figure in the Canadian popular culture of the late nineteenth and early twentieth centuries. She travelled much of the country, giving dramatic readings of her verse, and eventually settled in British Columbia, where she died in 1913.

later 1930s Canada and the United States had negotiated trade agreements that owed much to the spirit of the reciprocity agreement proposed in 1911. In 1935, for the first time in a generation, the Ontario electorate sent a majority of Liberals to the federal parliament at Ottawa. Since 1919 the federal Liberal Party had been led by William Lyon Mackenzie King – a loyal Laurier Liberal, grandson of William Lyon Mackenzie, a former employee of the Rockefeller family in the United States, and someone who believed that Canada's economic future was tied not to the British Empire but to the North American continent. The Ontario electorate would send a majority of Mackenzie King's Liberals to the federal parliament at Ottawa once again in 1940. Two years before Harold Innis had observed:

> Canada is facing to an increasing extent the effects of contrast between two systems. An old system linked her to Europe by a geographic background dominated by the St. Lawrence.... The new system links Canada to the United States and is evident in the increasing exports from Canada to the United States, such as pulp and minerals, and in the rapid spread of inventions from the United States to Canada.

Manufacturing and the New Service Sector

By the early twentieth century southern Ontario and an adjacent comparatively small part of Quebec in the vicinity of Montreal had become the industrial heartland of Canada. At the end of the First World War, Ontario had only about one-third of the total Canadian population but almost half the country's total manufacturing employment. Statistics of this sort can give a misleading impression of the importance of manufacturing in the region. The story of Ontario secondary industry in the early twentieth century was less about expansion and more about a struggle to retain the industrial base acquired in the later nineteenth century. Internationally, a new "second industrial revolution" was underway by the early 1900s. Technology advanced, firms became larger, and there were fewer of them. But the proportion of the Ontario labour force in manufacturing in 1921 was almost exactly what it had been in 1881 – just over twenty-five per cent.

The one dramatic success was in agricultural implements. By the 1920s Massey-Harris, with head offices in Toronto and plants in Toronto and Brantford (and with the Massey family now virtually retired from active involvement in the business), was on its way to becoming Ontario's one home-grown multinational corporation, with branch plants in the United States and elsewhere. It had never been a technological innovator. But it produced, up-to-date, durable, and dependable farm machinery, and it finally penetrated the American market as well as markets in Europe and the British Empire.

Moore Business Forms of Toronto, a development of the regional pulp and printing industries, was another Ontario enterprise that successfully penetrated the US market. Beyond this and a few other exceptions (and beyond such supporting primary industries as oil, steel, and hydroelecticity), the manufacturing sector in the region had two main elements: a group of domestically-owned smaller companies producing textiles and other consumer goods largely for the Canadian market under the shelter of the National Policy; and a group of much-discussed branch plants of large American industrial corporations, attracted by both the National Policy and trading advantages brought about by imperial preference.

In fact, the Ontario manufacturing sector that secured its positon in the early twentieth century was largely a northern extension of the "manufacturing belt" in the northeastern United States. Canadian federal, provincial, and municipal governments in Ontario encouraged the branch-plant syndrome as one of the few available alternatives for keeping manufacturing jobs in the region. And the Canadian automobile industry became the syndrome's highest expression.

By the late nineteenth century Dickson Carriage Works in Toronto was producing an electric carriage, and the Good Brothers in what was then Berlin, Ontario were producing an early gasoline-powered automobile known as the Le Roy. In the earlier twentieth century many strictly Canadian products, such as the Russell, the Frontenac, and the Iroquois, appeared briefly. But a thirty-five per cent tariff on imported American autos was not enough to shelter small Canadian producers from their much larger competitors south of the border. A much higher tariff would have put the automobile beyond the reach of the emerging mass market in Canada.

The characteristic Canadian compromise began in 1904 when entrepreneurs in Windsor made arrangements with Henry Ford to produce Ford cars for the Canadian and British Empire markets. In 1908 the McLaughlin Carriage Company in Oshawa began to produce Buick automobiles under similar circumstances, making way for the creation of General Motors of Canada in 1918. Chrysler Motors, founded by the great grandson of the first resident of Chatham, Ontario had a Canadian plant at Windsor by 1924.

By 1923 the branch-plant Canadian automobile industry centred in Ontario was producing 147,000 vehicles annually, almost half of which were exported – principally to Australia, the United Kingdom, New Zealand, India, and Argentina. In 1929 the industry produced a record 262,000 vehicles, making Canada the second largest automobile producer in the world (after the United States). In the wake of the depression of the 1930s, the 1929 production levels would not be reached again until the late 1940s. But the automotive sector had settled in as a vital part of Ontario's industrial base.

Manufacturing was not the ultimate key to continuing urbanization in early twentieth-century Ontario. By 1911 about fifty-three per cent of the region's population was living in organized urban areas, and the proportion had risen to more than sixty per cent by the 1930s. But the striking difference between the late nineteenth and earlier twentieth centuries was that population had shifted not from the farms to the factories but from the farms to the stores and offices of an expanding regional "service sector". In 1881 about half the Ontario labour force had been employed in agriculture and resources, just over a quarter in manufacturing, and about one-sixth in trade and services. By 1921 less than thirty per cent of the regional labour force was employed in agriculture and resources, just over twenty-five per cent in manufacturing, and somewhat more than thirty per cent in trade and services.

190

"The Chatham," about 1905-1910. Built by the Chatham Motor Car Company of Chatham, Ontario — some 70 kilometres (or about 45 miles) east of the border city of Windsor, where the branch plant auto sector first took root.

191

Manufacturing was comparatively "footloose". It helped stimulate growth in such smaller centres as Windsor, St. Catharines, Berlin (which became Kitchener during the First World War), Oshawa, Peterborough, and Belleville. The expansion of the service sector was concentrated in the largest centres. Toronto and Hamilton – which both profitted from manufacturing as well – doubled their populations in the first fifteen years of the twentieth century. By 1925 Toronto had just over half a million people and Hamilton almost 125,000 people. The next two largest centres were Ottawa (almost 120,000 people) and London (about 65,000 people).

Eaton's department stores and local mail order offices dominated much of the Ontario retail service sector, though they were rivalled by the Robert Simpson Company headquartered across the street from Eaton's in Toronto. Eaton's also had a strong base in western Canada and opened a store in Montreal in 1925. It was a representative Canadian enterprise of the era, imbued with a high-minded paternalism toward its employees, a fondness for the symbolism of the British Empire, and aggressive instincts for the new mass markets in the cities as well as its traditional catalogue customers among Canadian farmers.

Toronto banks and insurance companies dominated the "higher order" end of the emerging Ontario service sector. Although its total population remained somewhat smaller, by 1911 Toronto had a somewhat larger number of employees in trade and finance than Montreal. Canada's two largest banks were headquartered in Montreal. But Toronto's Canadian Bank of Commerce had absorbed the Bank of British Columbia in 1901. By the 1930s it owned two banks in California. Like the Montreal banks (and the Bank of Nova Scotia[1], with large Toronto administrative offices erected as early as 1904), it had begun to expand into the British West Indies.

The northern Ontario mining boom that brought Toronto new stature as a financial centre in the early twentieth century also helped the city weather the hard times that set in after the Great Crash of 1929 in New York. The Standard Stock and Mining Exchange had been incorporated in 1908. In 1934 it amalgamated with the earlier Toronto Stock Exchange (created at the height of the nineteenth-century wheat economy), giving Toronto the largest exchange in Canada and one of the largest on the continent. The new Stock Exchange was located on Bay Street near the Canadian Bank of Commerce, which had recently erected the tallest building in the British Empire. After some recovery in the mid-1930s, prices on the Toronto Stock Exchange slumped again in the later 1930s and early 1940s. But a new recovery began in 1943, and prices reached a historic high in 1945. The depression of the 1930s had not exactly helped Toronto. But it had not hurt it to the same extent that it had hurt Montreal.

New and Old Frontiers

Perhaps above all else, the first three decades of the twentieth century in Ontario mark the era of expansion on the new regional frontier of the north. In 1891 there had been just over 75,000 people living north of the French River – about 3½ per cent of the province's total population. By 1931 more than 11 per cent of the total population was living in "New Ontario" – about 385,000 people.

In 1912 the province arrived at its present boundaries when the Candian federal government formally assigned that part of the old Northwest Territories between the Albany River and Hudson Bay to the Government of Ontario. A northern branch of the Ontario steel industry had taken root in Sault Ste. Marie. By 1925 both northern centres of Sault Ste. Marie and Fort William were among Ontario's ten largest cities.

Northeastern Ontario had more than twice the population of northwestern Ontario in 1931 and was different in other ways as well. The northeast had been attracting French Candian migrants from the adjacent province of Quebec since the later nineteenth century, and French Canadians would become as important a minority there as they were in the most easterly counties of the south. The northwest attracted a population more like that of the adjacent western Canadian prairie, with substantial numbers of "other Europeans" who were neither French nor English.

Until the 1930s (and except for a few years after the First World War), the buoyant enthusiasm for agricultural settlement in the north, stimulated by the discovery of the

193

clay belts in the early 1900s, remained official provincial government policy. But climate and drainage on the surrounding mass of the Canadian Shield made the new agricultural frontier in the north more arduous, heartbreaking, and unrewarding than the frontier in the south. Geographic constraints on agricultural settlement would finally limit the extent of northern population growth.

New Ontario, however, played a more important role in the development of the province at large than its ultimate population weight might suggest. Railways – the two new Canadian transcontinental lines along with the Algoma Central (which ran from Sault Ste. Marie to Hearst in 1914) and the Temiskaming and Northern Ontario (which finally reached James Bay in 1932)[2] – helped open up what has in many ways remained Ontario's vast expanse of haunting northern wilderness. By the late 1920s the bush pilot and the small "seaplane" could penetrate where the railways did not.

In the 1820s and 1830s the emerging economic base in southern Ontario had been dominated by wheat and lumber. A century later, the wheat economy had migrated to the prairie of western Canada, and lumber had largely moved to northern Ontario. Hydroelectricity and pulp and paper were at the leading edge of the twentieth-century forest industry. Northern Ontario produced the newsprint for the new mass daily press in much of the northeastern United States.

Even more important, mining on the Canadian Shield, that had gained momentum in the late nineteenth century, gave the Ontario business community focused on Toronto access to resources of global consequence. The Shield proved to be a repository for virtually every known economic mineral except coal and tin. By the First World War, Ontario was by far the world's greatest supplier of nickel.

As nickel mining showed most clearly, Ontario's mineral resources (like its older forest resources) were significant enough to attract aggressive American business interests. The struggle to create local employment by promoting the processing of Ontario resources within the province, rather than merely exporting raw materials, became a leading, if typically difficult, theme in regional economic policy.

Northern development also helped revive something of the pioneering spirit in Ontario at large. In the north itself, the new frontier was rough and rugged, like the old frontier in the south. Improvements in transportation and communications technology worked to relieve some of the isolation of the earlier frontier. But a new tyranny of distance in a much larger geographic setting worked in the opposite direction. As on the old frontier, Indians were a more visible presence in New Ontario than elsewhere in the province (and this remains true in northern Ontario today).

If agriculture in the north never lived up to the hopes bred by official enthusiasm, the depression of the 1930s did bring a brief revival of the old agrarian society in the south. Some saw the depression as a sign that the new industrialism in the cities was not working out. A few others moved "back to the land" simply to grow food. Ontario agriculture did not suffer from the droughts that spread grim tragedy on many parts of the new western Canadian frontier in the 1930s. Farm prices fell as much as fifty per cent, and financial difficulties forced some established operators off the land. But in the depression, the family farm in southern Ontario also became something of a refuge from harsher economic realities faced by many in large urban centres.

The movement back to the land was far from dramatic. Statistically, it was only a stall in the long relative decline in the size of the rural population that had begun in a serious way in the 1870s. (And even this had some deceptive "suburban" elements). Ontario's rural population declined from some fifty-seven per cent of the total in 1901 to about thirty-eight per cent in 1941. In absolute terms, the number of rural dwellers rose from 1.2 million in 1921 to 1.4 million in 1941[3].

Total improved farm acreage in Ontario increased slightly between 1931 and 1941. But the number of owner-occupied farms decreased, reflecting an increase in average farm size and in the number of farms run by tenants or professional managers. The total value of farm products in the three prairie provinces of western Canada had exceeded that in Ontario by the 1920s. Yet even in 1940 Ontario accounted for about thirty per cent of the total value of farm products in all of Canada.

195

A settler's first log cabin on the new agricultural frontier in the Cochrane area. Unlike the old frontier in the south, Ontario's northern frontier was captured in photographs.

By the early twentieth century, rural living standards, as measured by such variables as average family income, electrification, indoor plumbing, and access to schools, shopping, and entertainment, had fallen below those in urban centres. Rural mail delivery, however, began in 1908. The period that ended with the Second World War saw the final high tide of the railway age in Ontario. Farmers had the same interest as the new automobile owners in good roads. Both the automobile and the early beginnings of the modern provincial highway system in the 1920s made a start on bringing rural life closer to the standards that had been set by the new life in the cities.

The Anglo Mass Society North of the Lakes

Overseas immigration from the United Kingdom once again played an important role in Ontario growth during the early twentieth century. But this time people from the crowded urban areas of England were dominant not the old dislocated peasantries of Ireland and Scotland. By 1931 about seventy-two per cent of the people living in Ontario had been born there. Almost exactly ten per cent had been born in England, about 3½ per cent in Scotland, and about 1½ per cent in Ireland. Another two per cent had been born in the United States. About twenty-two per cent of the population reported itself as Roman Catholic, and less than two per cent as Jewish, with the great bulk of the remainder claiming some form of Protestant affiliation. Only 3,418 people or 0.1 per cent claimed to have "no religion" at all.

The new wave of immigration from the old mother country strengthened the sense of a white Anglo-Saxon Protestant mainstream in the region. But in this respect the "British connexion" was only Ontario's particular variation on a wider North American theme. Rudyard Kipling had published "The White Man's Burden" in 1899 and declared that it was addressed to the people of the United States. In 1903 the father of John Dos Passos, the American radical novelist of the 1920s and 1930s, had published a book on *The Anglo-Saxon Century and the Unification of the English-Speaking People*.

197

At the same time, traces of Ontario's cultural diversity remained, and there were early signs of a later expansion. The Black children of the fugitive slaves had become a very small and, to many, barely visible minority. But in 1931 there were some 30,000 "registered" Indians in the region, somewhat more than there had been in the middle of the eighteenth century. Nearly nine per cent of the population reported its "racial origin" as French (and just under three per cent had been born in the province of Quebec). About five per cent reported German origins, about two per cent Dutch, and a similar percentage Italian. A little over one per cent of the population had been born in Poland, and some 6,500 people (0.2 per cent) had been born in China.

The later 1920s and earlier 1930s did mark the last great burst of popular enthusiasm for British Loyalism. And the region's anglified social elite attracted new wealth. In the earlier twentieth century, Henry Pellat (later Sir Henry) made a modest fortune selling land in western Canada as well as electricity and streetcar transportation in Toronto. Echoing the much earlier career of Allan Mac-Nab and "Dundurn Castle" in Hamilton, he then cultivated a Kiplingesque appearance, became a generous patron of the Queen's Own Rifles militia regiment, and lost his fortune building "Casa Loma" in Toronto.

Unlike the United States, Canada joined France and the United Kingdom from start to finish in the First World War (and the Second World War as well). But conscription for military service was almost as contentious an issue among the Canadian farmers of Ontario as it was in Quebec. Travel to Europe during the First World War also showed many among the mass of "English Canadians" that they were unlike their fellow subjects in Great Britain. The period after the war saw the rise of the new North American mass culture of the movie, the phonograph record, and the radio. As Harold Innis put it, "Radio crosses boundaries which stopped the press" (a phenomenon also noted by Ontario's Loyal Tory Premier of the 1920s, G. Howard Ferguson).

"Americanization" is something of a misnomer. To no small extent, the new mass culture reflected mores and aspirations that Ontario and other parts of Canada shared with the United States. Mary Pickford and Walter Huston became Ontario's two early contributions to Hollywood. Guy Lombardo and the Royal Canadians, a "regional band" from southwestern Ontario, became a New York-based fixture on the English-language airwaves of North America for more than a generation. Glen Gray's Casa Loma Orchestra, on some accounts the first white jazz band, took its name from the Toronto hotel that Henry Pellat's castle had become by the late 1920s.

By the late nineteenth century, the "Canadian game" was not so much lacrosse as ice hockey. In the new century hockey became Canada's contribution to the North American mass culture of spectator sport. Kingston, Montreal, and Halifax have all laid claims as the site of the first hockey game. But in 1891 the Ontario Hockey Association had become the first organized league promoting hockey as a spectator sport. The OHA eventually became a training ground for many professional hockey players who went on to compete in the National Hockey League after it was formed in 1917. By the early 1930s the Toronto St. Patricks had moved into a new arena known as Maple Leaf Gardens. The team was renamed the Toronto Maple Leafs, and its exploits were chronicled for a generation by the radio broadcasts of Foster Hewitt.

The 1920s and 1930s marked the serious beginnings of regional scientific and artistic expression as well. In 1912 Stephen Leacock, by then a professor at McGill University in Montreal, published *Sunshine Sketches of a Little Town* – a gently critical portrait of small-town Ontario on the eve of the First World War. In 1920 the Group of Seven held the first public exhibition of its innovative paintings of the wild Canadian Shield. Though not well received at first, a later critic would declare that they showed "this isn't Europe, but it's interesting". In 1921 Frederick Banting from Alliston, Ontario was a principal member of the University of Toronto research team that discovered insulin – a treatment for diabetes.

In 1923 Ernest Hemingway from Chicago was working as a reporter for *The Daily Star* in Toronto, on his way to literary fame in Paris, France. He encouraged the writing career of the Toronto Irish Catholic Morley Callaghan. In 1928 Callaghan published *Strange Fugitive*, said to be the first of the gangster novels, and the first of half a dozen books in which he captured something of the anonymous, bittersweet quality of the new urban life.

In 1935 the federal government at Ottawa established the Canadian Broadcasting Corporation, with its French language radio broadcasting services based in Montreal and its English language services based in Toronto. To some extent, the Corporation was modelled on the public British Broadcasting Corporation rather than the private commercial radio networks that had quickly sprung up in the United States. In 1937, however, Harold Innis (a Baptist farmer's son from Oxford County) became the first Canadian-born Chairman of the department that taught politics, economics and commerce and finance at the University of Toronto – traditionally a refuge for British academics.

As elsewhere, women in Ontario entered the urban labour force in numbers during the First World War. The experience would be repeated in the Second World War. In 1917 women won the right to vote in provincial elections and in 1918 in federal elections. In 1921 Agnes Macphail from Grey County became the first woman elected to the Canadian federal parliament. By the 1920s the labour-saving devices of a new "consumer society" in the cities had begun to transform earlier traditions of housework. The depression of the 1930s slowed the pace of change in many aspects of life. Much of the older world of the nineteenth century hung on. But society in Ontario, as in other places, had begun to move in new directions.

11

Empire Ontario
and its Opponents

The Whitney Conservative government that won provincial power in Ontario early in 1905 did not make abrupt changes in the policies which the Liberal Great Reformers had pursued for more than a generation. Just as Mowat had tempered his Reformism with respect for conservative sentiment in the region, James P. Whitney was (on the testimony of an observer of the day) "in no sense a conservative".

Whitney's party still ran under the Liberal Conservative banner that John A. Macdonald had devised half a century before. Whitney himself had been a protege of William Ralph Meredith, who in the 1880s had tried to attack Mowat from the left, as an advocate of the "Tory Democracy" represented by Benjamin Disraeli and Randolph Churchill in the United Kingdom.

Whitney adopted the northern development programme of George Ross and John Dryden as his own. And he bettered the Great Reformers' activist approach to government by establishing the Hydro-Electric Power Commission of Ontario, which would operate the world's first publicly-owned power system. At the same time, Whitney's Conservatives had their deepest roots in the new cities of the south (and the new frontier of the north), rather than the old agrarian society that had remained at the centre of Mowat's Reformism. Whitney's regime also had more in common with the revived empire of the St. Lawrence in the early decades of the new century.

Though he was born in Kingston, Mowat had moved to Toronto early in his legal career. As Premier he represented the southwestern riding of North Oxford in the legislature. Whitney was a lifelong resident of the village of Morrisburg on the upper St. Lawrence, about midway between Kingston and Montreal. As Premier he represented the riding of Dundas in the traditional Loyalist Tory stronghold of the southeast, a part of Ontario that still tended to see Montreal as the unquestioned economic capital of the British Dominion of Canada.

Mowat's Ontario Great Reformers (like the later Laurier Liberals federally) had tended to see the British Empire as a cocoon for the evolution of a new Canadian nationality. The Ontario Conservatives who took office in 1905 tended to see the Empire as a more permanent feature of Canada's political destiny. Ontario in the nineteenth century had no official motto. But in 1909 Whitney gave it one: "Ut incepit fidelis sic permanet" – "Loyal she began, loyal she remains." If antagonism arose, Mowat's Reformers were at least rhetorically prepared to side "with the masses rather than with the classes". Like the Tories of an earlier era, Whitney's Conservatives were more inclined to hold the classes up as a model for the masses to emulate.

In some ways, the new regime that Whitney established was an early anticipation of the progressive conservatism that would dominate Ontario provincial politics after the Second World War. In other ways, it was Tory enough in an older sense to meet defeat in 1919 on the first major wave of popular political protest in the region since Confederation.

The Loyal Regional State

Despite the revival of Montreal's economic empire of the St. Lawrence, James P. Whitney proved to be as careful a guardian of provincial rights as Oliver Mowat ever was. So long as Toronto remained a junior partner to Montreal, co-operation between Canada's two largest centres of commerce and finance did not imply co-operation between the Canadian federal government and the provincial government of Ontario. An account of Ontario government

202

James P. Whitney, the Province of Ontario's sixth Premier. Hold-
ing office continuously from 1905 to his death in 1914, Whitney
became the second longest-lived Premier, next to Oliver Mowat.
Not until the early 1960s would Leslie Frost set a new record (and
William Davis would then surpass Frost's record in the 1980s).

organization published in 1914 began with the declaration: "Within the limits prescribed by the British North America Act the Province of Ontario is a sovereign state."

The major achievement of Whitney's regional state was the Hydro-Electric Power Commission of Ontario. Practically, Whitney's own role in bringing "the people's power" to the region was largely confined to supporting the work of Adam Beck. Beck was a public-spirited, irascible (and somewhat dictatorial) local box manufacturer and former Mayor of London, Ontario. By the early 1900s he had placed himself at the head of a provincial movement for inexpensive, publicly-provided hydro-electric power – rooted in support among municipal officials and regional manufacturers, but with a significant popular base as well. The power movement was centered in the newly industrialized central and southwestern parts of the province, within a reasonable distance of Niagara Falls. It was a protest against both American-dominated private power companies and such Toronto "plutocrats" as Henry Pellat, with connections in the international financial capital of London, England.

Beck was elected as a Conservative provincially in 1902 and became Minister without Portfolio in Whitney's first cabinet in 1905. What was at first popularly known as HEPC (officially renamed "Ontario Hydro" in 1974) began in 1906, with Beck as Chairman. It started delivering power to its member municipalities in 1910.

The first power plants on the Canadian side of the Niagara River were built by private interests, as George Ross had arranged. Initially, Beck's new public commission simply secured control over hydro rates by building transmission lines. Ross' Reform government had been unwilling to push "socialistic" government intervention quite as far. But in the election of 1905 Whitney's Conservatives had sensed a popular issue. They were more open to the argument that an independent business community in Canada presupposed a unique role for government north of the Great Lakes. And HEPC could be fitted into a regional Tory tradition that reached back at least to the Welland Canal in the first half of the nineteenth century.

Adam Beck would remain Chairman of Ontario's hydro-electric commission until the mid-1920s, and he became an important political power in his own right. Another key figure in Whitney's cabinet was "Silent" Frank Cochrane, who managed northern development. Whitney's regime continued to promote agricultural settlement in the north. In 1911 Whitney himself anticipated that soon enough there would be as many as a million people living north of the French River (an objective that, even today, remains unrealized). But it was significant that Dryden, who had managed Ross' New Ontario policy, had been Minister of Agriculture. Silent Frank Cochrane was Minister of Lands, Forests, and Mines.

Cochrane had been raised in northern Ontario and made a name for himself as a hardware merchant and local political magnate in Sudbury during the earliest phases of the mining boom. But with his first real success in private life, he moved his family to the less rough and rugged ambience of the new Rosedale district in Toronto. His taciturn image as a man of the new north won many admirers, and Borden lured him into a career in federal politics after the reciprocity election of 1911.

Whitney's declared policy on resource development was to "enlarge the people's share". Cochrane had a local businessman's sensitivity to the somewhat contradictory needs of attracting capital to the northern mines and forests, much of which came from the United States. In the aftermath of the failed reciprocity discussions of 1911, however, a new Canadian determination to export processed pulp and newsprint rather than raw pulp logs was rewarded by the abolition of all American tariffs on Canadian pulp and newsprint in 1913. This helped prompt the establishment of several American-owned pulp and paper mills, providing jobs for Ontario workers. Some new mills were in the north. Others, like Ontario Paper (owned by the *Chicago Tribune*) in the Niagara region, were in the south. A parallel strategy in mining would not produce results for three more years. But Cochrane at least organized an efficient public system for the sale of private mining rights.

Whitney once declared: "Ontario does not think I am a great man."[1] His governments were more collegial than Mowat's had been, with strong ministers like Beck, Cochrane, and the Provincial Secretary, W.J. Hanna, sharing the political limelight. They included Ontario's second French Canadian cabinet minister, Joseph Reaume, from Essex North. And they were very popular. All told, Whitney won four elections (in 1905, 1908, 1911, and 1914), each with a clear majority of the popular vote (from fifty-three to fifty-five per cent). The provincial Liberals – still often described as the Reformers of Ontario – entered a political wilderness from which they would not emerge until the 1930s.

Until 1911 Conservative provincial governments in Ontario faced Liberal federal governments at Ottawa. But with only one exception (in 1921), Ontario itself would send solid Conservative majorities to the federal parliament from 1900 to 1935. Except for the early 1920s, the first three decades of the twentieth century marked the triumphant era of "Tory Ontario".

Whitney had come to power in 1905 as a critic of corrupt patronage under the late Reform regime, and he made some effort to restrain the particular regional tradition of machine politics perfected by Mowat. In 1908 it became illegal to use government vehicles to transport voters to the polls. Skill in political management, however, remained an important part of governing Ontario. In 1914 a text on the subject noted that liquor licence boards were established "within each riding of the province". Members were appointed "by the government on the nomination of the local member, or, in cases where the sitting member is not a follower of the government, by the defeated candidate at the last election."

Whitney, who was sixty-one years old when he became Premier, had only limited sympathy with the early social policy and labour legislation that had appeared in the later years of the Mowat era. Yet in other ways he was a somewhat more ardent advocate of active government. A revision of Mowat's Workmen's Compensation legislation was his one concession to the industrial labour force. But his regime reorganized the University of Toronto (including the School of Practical Science established in the later nineteenth century), raised the salaries of elementary and secondary school teachers, lowered the price of school books, and established the Ontario College of Art and the Royal Ontario Museum. The Conservative governments of the early twentieth century also presided over the first major expansion in the size of the Ontario public service. Under the Great Reformers, the service had risen from a few hundred employees inherited from the old United Province at Confederation to just over 700 in 1904. But there were more than 4,000 employees when the Conservatives were suddenly thrown from office in 1919.

Problems of Empire

By the start of the second decade of the twentieth century, a new "empire Ontario" had left the slow growth and hard times of the generation after 1867 well behind. With vigorous mass settlement on the western Canadian prairie and new immigration to Ontario itself, Macdonald's National Policy of the later nineteenth century had at last begun to show results. In the federal reciprocity election of 1911, majorities of the electorate in Prince Edward Island, Ontario, Manitoba, and British Columbia had voted, as Frank Underhill would put it, "to remain loyal subjects of St. James and King Streets".

The newly prosperous empire, however, did not appeal to everyone in Canada at large or even in Ontario. A new agrarian radicalism developed among the western prairie wheat farmers. It took an attitude toward the new plutocrats of Montreal and Toronto similar to that which the old agrarian radicalism of the wheat economy in Upper Canada had once taken toward the British Canadian merchants of Montreal. And as John Bartlett Brebner later observed, the underlying conflicts were similar to those which also bred populist agrarian radicalism in the republic to the south:

> The American cartoonist's cow that stood on a map of
> the United States, eating corn in Kansas and being
> milked on Wall Street, had close Canadian analogies.

The prosperity of the early twentieth century also encouraged a new French Canadian nationalism, led by Henri Bourrassa – a liberal but committed Catholic and a friend of Goldwin Smith in his declining years. The rights of the French-speaking minority in Ontario, bolstered by

207

more recent migrations from Quebec, became a test of the new nationalism's strength beyond the banks of the lower St. Lawrence River. In 1910 the Association Canadienne-Française d'Education d'Ontario (ACFEO) was established to promote improved French language education for the children of Ontario's more than 200,000 French Canadians. Like the French-speaking population itself, support for ACFEO was concentrated in the east. But the organization's first president was Napoleon Belcourt, who had been born in Toronto (though he became best known as a Liberal Senator in Ottawa).

Mowat's Great Reform vision of the Ontario future had at least implicitly left room for the gradual development of an indigenous Canadianism that acknowledged the region's historic French roots. Even with Joseph Reaume in the Cabinet, the Conservatism that Whitney brought to power saw both Ontario and Canada as fundamentally "British" and French language education as a privilege confined to the Province of Quebec.

Urged on by popular pressure led by Howard Ferguson, an eastern Ontario Orangeman and prominent Conservative backbencher, Whitney's Minister of Education, R.A. Pyne, promulgated "Regulation 17" in 1912. This decreed that all Ontario children were to be educated in English, and that French as a "language of instruction and communication" was "in no case to continue beyond" the third year of elementary school. An extended crisis over bilingual education in Ontario, that would not be resolved until the late 1920s, had begun.

"Empire Ontario" was also developing opponents among the province's English-speaking majority. In 1911 just under half of Ontario's population still lived in rural areas, and perhaps two-thirds of the rural labour force still worked in agriculture. Ontario's agrarian society was older and more established than that on the last frontier of western Canada. But it was still vigorous and sensitive about its declining prospects under the new urban-dominated order that Whitney's regime seemed to speak for.

The Patrons of Industry, who had led the region's first wave of agrarian revolt in the 1890s, had virtually disappeared by the early 1900s. But the Ontario Farmers'

Association began in 1902, and it prospered under such leaders as J.J. Morrison and E.C. Drury. In 1914 regional farm leaders formed the United Farmers of Ontario, modelled on the earlier United Farmers of Alberta.

Even in the industrial cities there was a growing political constituency that Whitney's Conservatives were ignoring. In 1913 when the provincial Liberal leader Newton Rowell urged that the time had come to strengthen Mowat's Factory Act of the later nineteenth century, Whitney declared: "I don't care whether our Act is up to date with other countries." If a working man wanted to improve his lot in life, he could work harder and get a better job.

In a by-election held in 1906, however, Allan Studholme in Hamilton East had become the first elected Labour member of the Ontario Legislative Assembly. And he was re-elected in 1908, 1911, and 1914. A loosely organized "Independent Labour Party", modelled on the Independent Labour Party in the United Kingdom, had begun to put down roots in Ontario[2].

The Northern Premier and the First World War

Whitney died in office, not long after his final victory in the election of 1914. In October 1914, William H. Hearst from Sault Ste. Marie, who had earlier replaced Frank Cochrane as Minister of Lands, Forests and Mines (and manager of northern development), became the new Conservative Premier of Ontario.

In the early 1900s, the French political writer, André Seigfried, had observed that Canadian politics were customarily characterized as "American actors on an English stage". This was in some ways a uniquely apt description of the Ontario Conservative Party that Hearst inherited from Whitney. In the United States the populism of William Jennings Bryan had been brought into the increasingly urbanized political mainstream by the "progressive" Republican Theodore Roosevelt. Despite Whitney's Loyalist enthusiasm for the Tory imagery of the British Empire, there was much in the rhetoric of "the people's power" and "enlarging the people's share" that matched the politics of progressive Republicanism south of the border. (And Theodore Roosevelt himself was something of a

209

Kiplingesque figure). After 1914 the Conservatives under Hearst were, if anything, more progressive than they had been under Whitney. Among other things, the growing prospect of an organized Labour vote threatened the Conservatives' new stronghold in the cities.

Hearst's most immediate problem, however, was the First World War. Formally, it began on 4 August 1914 when George v declared war against Germany in defence of Belgian neutrality. Alone among the British Dominions, which by this time included Australia, New Zealand, and South Africa, the Canadian federal Parliament at Ottawa made at least a gesture toward an independent declaration of war to show that, while Canada had every intention of coming to the aid of the Empire, it was still something more than a British colony.

Hearst and the Liberal leader Newton Rowell adopted a bi-partisan policy in support of Ontario's war effort and toured the province together to promote enlistment in the Canadian forces that were sent overseas. In the end, more than 240,000 Ontario men and women (almost ten per cent of the total population) would be in uniform, and some 68,000 were among the "killed, wounded, or missing". Ontario's soldiers included a "coloured regiment" of some 350 men and specially organized units of the old Indian allies of the Crown, who enlisted in proportionately much higher numbers than the white population. But the province's farm community especially objected to conscription when it was imposed in 1917.

In the region itself, the war helped make possible things that had not seemed possible before. Popular support for Prohibition – part of the "social gospel" and "moral uplift" mixed in with the progressive impulse – had strengthened. Like Mowat and Ross, Whitney had remained sceptical about the issue. But in March 1916 some 10,000 demonstrators carried a Prohibition petition with more than 825,000 signatures to Queen's Park in Toronto. Shortly thereafter, the Hearst government made the sale of liquor illegal in Ontario, except for "medical, mechanical, scientific and sacramental purposes". The new law was introduced as a measure of wartime discipline, with the promise of a referendum on the issue when the war had ended.

Men of the 119th Algoma Battalion: part of Ontario's contribution to the war in Europe. The writer, Robert Graves, a British captain in the war, attended a dinner of fellow officers where it was unanimously agreed that the Canadians were the roughest and most aggressive of all the soldiers of the Empire.

The war also helped secure the kind of enlargement of the people's share in mining that had been won for pulp and newsprint in 1913. The American-owned International Nickel Company had obtained generous mining rights in the Sudbury area at a time when the crudest of economic development priorities were still being emphasized by the Great Reformers. For almost fifteen years the company had been sending raw Ontario nickel ore to refineries in the United States. In 1916, however, concern about shipments of Ontario nickel to the German enemies of the British Empire helped the Canadian federal government and Hearst's Minister of Lands, Forests and Mines, Howard Ferguson, pressure the company into refining locally as the International Nickel Company of Canada. Ferguson declared that all mineral rights on Crown land would subsequently be sold "subject to a requirement that the mineral be refined in Ontario."

The struggle for women's rights that had begun in the later nineteenth century was another strand in the strengthening progressive impulse. And the role of women in the wartime economy helped convince many of their claims to full citizenship in the new democracy that Mowat had confirmed with the Manhood Suffrage Act of 1888. In 1917 the Hearst government conceded the vote to women in both provincial and municipal elections. As the First World War ended, Hearst also took steps toward moving forward with the social policy and labour legislation that had appeared during the later years of the Mowat era. Legislation for a mother's allowance and a minimum wage for women was prepared (though not enacted). Legislation for a new Minister of Labour was enacted (though a minister not yet appointed).

With what one observer of the day described as such "huge concessions to socialism" in the wings, Hearst went to face the voters in the provincial general election of October 1919. Hearst himself and many others were confident of Conservative success. But the war and its immediate aftermath had helped move the progressive impulse in Ontario farther than "progressive conservatism" could contain. In 1918 the United Farmers had decided to run candidates in the imminent provincial election. Perhaps the most progressive of the Conservatives,

212

Adam Beck had fallen out with the government over its efforts to control the burgeoning empire of HEPC. In 1919 he ran against a Labour candidate in London as an Independent.

When the election results came in, the United Farmers of Ontario, which had not even existed as an organized political party in the election of 1914, had won forty-five seats. The Liberals had twenty-eight seats, and the Conservatives, twenty-five. Labour, which had earlier managed to win only Allan Studholme's seat in Hamilton East, now had eleven seats. The new, rigorously progressive "Farmer-Labour"forces combined had won only thirty-four per cent of the popular vote. But they took office on 14 November 1919 as Ontario's first (and as yet only) third-party government, proclaiming a "new order of things" north of the Great Lakes, and an end to"the old game of politics."

The Light that Failed

The provincial election of 1919 is the one point in Ontario history from 1867 to the present when genuinely spontaneous mass protest might be said to have played a decisive role in regional politics. The Farmer-Labour members who suddenly found themselves with a bare majority of seats in the Legislative Assembly in the last days of October had not expected to do at all as well as they did. And despite their bold rhetoric, they were unprepared for victory.

Neither the United Farmers nor the Labour faction had an acknowledged leader. Significant numbers of the Farmers were declared opponents of traditional parliamentary institutions who supported new "group government" concepts advanced by Henry Wise Wood in western Canada and Mary Parker Follet in the United States. This amounted to an untested form of democratic politics organized around economic sectors, somewhat analogous to the "guild socialism" of G.D.H. Cole in the United Kingdom or to what was known as "syndicalism" in France.

The Ontario Independent Labour Party was vaguely attracted to the parliamentary British socialism of Keir Hardie and Ramsay Macdonald. But Tim Buck, a British immigrant who later won fame as Canada's best-known Communist, noted that early Labour activists in Ontario "made a shibboleth of their independence, so much so that the Independent Labour Parties in London, Hamilton, and Toronto couldn't get together."

For a brief time, the prospect of Adam Beck as leader of the new Farmer-Labour government was raised. Though Beck had been defeated by the Labour candidate Hugh Stevenson in London, he retained some credibility as a progressive figure. In the end, however, the premiership settled on the farm leader E.C. Drury from Simcoe county. Drury was the son of Mowat's first Minister of Agriculture. He had won earlier attention as an unrepentant supporter of rigorous free trade and reciprocity principles which he saw Laurier's Liberals as having abandoned. He believed that Ontario's variation on the North American agrarian society was part of "the finest yeomanry that civilization has yet produced"; and he was convinced that this achievement was threatened by the particular vision of the new industrialism promoted by the plutocrats and "the exploiting classes".

Perhaps what Drury and the other Farmer-Labour leaders lacked most was practical political experience and skill – the sense, so highly developed in Oliver Mowat, of how to deal with the wickedness of the kingdom on earth. They came to power as a reforming movement without any coherent programme or unified organization. And they governed in the period of international economic and political stress that followed the First World War (and the Russian Revolution of 1917). Nonetheless, they remained in office for some 3½ years. In at least a few (sometimes ironic) ways, they were apostles of a new, more genuinely progressive Ontario society that would take root after the Second World War.

The social welfare and labour side of the Drury government's policy did little more than rapidly accelerate implementation of the "socialistic" measures that Hearst had prepared on the eve of the 1919 election. A mother's allowance was introduced, and a minimum wage for women became law. Walter Rollo from Hamilton became Ontario's first Minister of Labour. Drury also created separate Mines and Lands and Forests ministries in an effort to bring both mainstays of the New Ontario economy under more scrupulous public oversight.

The Farmer-Labour government of 1919-1923 was also an heir of the nineteenth-century tradition of "the farmers and mechanics of Upper Canada", that the Liberal Party seemed to have forgotten. It retained something of the earlier agrarian enthusiasm for economy and efficiency in public adminstration. To support new progressive programmes, the provincial budget doubled from about $19 million in 1919 to almost $40 million in 1923. But the size of the public service was reduced between 1921 and 1922. An unsuccessful attempt was made to close the Lieutenant-Governor's official residence in the "Government House" at Chorley Park – viewed by agrarian radicals as a symbol of British colonial dependence, aristocratic Tory extravagance, and Toronto's "nice sensible plutocracy".

With four times more seats than Labour had, the United Farmers were dominant in the coalition. Drury's regime assiduously pursued the "Good Roads" policy that Mowat had begun in response to the earlier agrarian revolt of the Patrons of Industry. Here again, Hearst had made a beginning, with the appointment of Ontario's first Minister of Highways in 1914 (combined with the earlier portfolio of Public Works). But under Frank E. Biggs, the Drury government began the first aggressive phase of modern public highway development in Ontario.

Adam Beck remained Hydro Chairman, but not as a minister of the government. Drury admired Beck and supported the Hydro Commission's first major "Chippawa" generating station that opened at Niagara Falls in 1922. Yet Beck also wanted HEPC to construct and operate a system of radial electric railways around the cities of central and southwestern Ontario. Labour tended to support this extension of the old "chariot of democracy", that had brought the workingman decent housing in the earlier streetcar suburbs. The Farmers did not, and Drury saw to it that Beck's radial railways proposal was shunted aside. Drury was also "progressive" in the sense that he understood how the dominant mass transportation of the future would centre on the highway and the private automobile.

Drury tried to shape the Farmer-Labour coaliton into a more broadly based "People's Party". This looked to James B. Weaver's People's Party of the 1890s in the

Yonge Street, north of Newmarket, before and after surfacing,
1921. In Ontario, the United Farmers helped make way for the
automobile age.

United States and to a new Progressive Party that won some twenty-three per cent of the popular vote in the Canadian federal election of 1921 (and that came to power under John Bracken in Manitoba in 1923). But the United Farmers, under the spell of J.J. Morrison, group government, and the need for co-operative economic institutions, repudiated the broadening-out policy[3]. The urban trade union activists of the Independent Labour Party, who included many British and other immigrants from the cities of Europe, were different from the old independent mechanics of nineteenth-century Ontario. In the day-to-day working world, the Farmer and Labour sides of the coalition faced quite different economic realities, and serious conflicts developed between them.

Labour, for instance, tended to be "wet"; the Farmers tended to be "dry". Prohibition had been ratified by a provincial referendum, held during the 1919 election. Under Attorney-General W.E. Raney, the Drury regime became strongly identified with strident efforts to strengthen and rigorously enforce Hearst's Ontario Temperance Act of 1916. The Ontario Provincial Police were reorganized to meet the task. But as Mowat, Ross, and Whitney had long suspected, this aspect of progressive "moral uplift" helped prompt second thoughts about both Prohibition and the government of the day among the mass of the electorate.

As the 1920s set in, a more general reaction against postwar radicalism, bolstered by a "Red Scare" that looked with alarm at the recent rise to power of revolutionary communism in Russia, gathered strength throughout "capitalist" North America. By 1922 the new mass production of the automobile had begun a dynamic seven-year economic boom in the United States.

Drury called an election for June 1923, hoping for the best and standing on the government's record. When the results came in, the Conservatives under the new leadership of Howard Ferguson had won fifty per cent of the popular vote and seventy-five seats. The United Farmers had seventeen seats, the Liberals fourteen, and Labour only four. Adam Beck had run again as a Conservative in London and won handily. The brief experiment with a "new order of things" in Ontario had ended. The region returned to the "old game of politics" that Drury had denounced when he first took office.

217

12

Last Hurrahs

The years from 1923 to 1943 in Ontario were shaped by final blazes of the stridently partisan Tory and Reform traditions that had begun to develop in the Upper Canada of a century before. The period is dominated by two strong political personalities who, whatever else might be said about them, are perhaps the two most colourful Premiers in Ontario history – personifications of elements in the region's past that would start to fade quickly with the changes brought on by the Second World War.

The first is the Conservative G. Howard Ferguson, a "small-town lawyer" and authentic Orangeman from the southeast, a fervent British Empire Loyalist, and the last genuine "Ontario Tory" in an old sense of the term. The second is the Liberal Mitch Hepburn, a family farmer from the southwest, sometimes described as "Canada's Huey Long" in the press of the day, and the last successful exponent of the old "Ontario Grit" politics of the agrarian society north of the Great Lakes.

Though the Drury regime had seemed to show that third-party forces were not yet ready to govern Ontario, the period from 1923 to 1943 also saw fresh developments in this direction. By the early 1930s Labour and socialist activists and a few United Farmers had re-grouped as the Co-operative Commonwealth Federation (a name which echoed the title of a book by Laurence Gronlund, an American radical writer of the 1880s).

Like the earlier United Farmers, The Ontario CCF was a regional variation on a political movement which had its birthplace in western Canada. In Saskatchewan the CCF would succeed in forging an "agrarian socialism" that blended the traditional populist radicalism of North America with the more cosmopolitan themes of the new industrialism. But in Ontario, where industrial manufacturing had made much stronger inroads, the CCF became more narrowly attracted to the ideals of the British Labour Party that formed its first government in 1923.

Despite Drury's failure to create an Ontario People's Party, many among the United Farmers who remained active in provincial politics after 1923 had become attached to the Canadian Progressive movement of the later 1920s. Reaching out to the Progressives became a key ingredient in Mitch Hepburn's strategy for rejuvenating the Ontario Liberals in the 1930s. This was a tactic pursued earlier by Mowat in his dealings with the Patrons of Industry. Harry Nixon from Brant County, who served as Provincial Secretary in both the Drury and Hepburn cabinets, personified the trend[1].

By the early 1940s, the progressive impulse in the region had shifted once again. In the wartime election of 1943, the Ontario CCF came as close as it ever would to duplicating the Farmer-Labour success of 1919. But the accession of the Progressive Premier of Manitoba, John Bracken, to the leadership of what had become the National Conservative Party helped set the stage for a new "Progressive Conservatism", that would dominate Ontario politics after the Second World War. The amorphous, centrist political tradition of Whitney and Hearst in the early twentieth century, not the more fundamentalist traditions of Howard Ferguson or Mitch Hepburn (or the new, socialistic CCF), would become the ultimate wave of the Ontario future.

Howard Ferguson's Loyalist Normalcy

Howard Ferguson came to the Premiership of Ontario in 1923 as a robust and seasoned party politician. In many ways he was the exact opposite of the defeated leader of moral uplift and the social gospel, E.C. Drury, who had rebelled against "the old game of politics". Popularly

219

known as "Fergie", Ferguson had first been elected as member for the traditionally Conservative southeastern riding of Grenville in Whitney's sweep of 1905. Though never in Whitney's cabinet, he developed a reputation as a rambunctious but able backbencher and a stout advocate of old Tory ideals. Nevertheless, as Premier in the election of 1926, he felt it necessary to deny publicly a rumour that he was "the grandson of the Orange Lodge's founder".

In 1914 Ferguson had become Hearst's Minister of Lands, Forests, and Mines. His career as a cabinet minister was touched with broad hints of scandal over the sale of timber rights. But when Hearst was defeated in 1919, many Tory activists concluded that it was "because he was not a Conservative but an undisciplined theorist." Ferguson had ability and was clearly a disciplined Conservative, so he replaced Hearst as party leader. As a journalist of the day saw it, Fergie was ready to bring back "the old-time political religion ... take the Conservative harps off the willows and give the boys some political jazz. They've had about enough moping by the waters of Babylon". '

Ferguson won elections in 1923, 1926, and 1929 with a majority of the popular vote. But, whereas seventy-four per cent of the registered electorate had turned out to vote in 1919, only fifty-six per cent turned out in 1923 and in 1929, and sixty-four per cent in 1926. Ferguson's greatest victory was in 1929, when the Tories took 92 seats in a 112-seat legislature. Only four and a half years later, however, Mitch Hepburn would win an almost equally dramatic victory for the Liberals, and the Conservatives would be reduced to seventeen seats.

In one important way, Ferguson's regime was up to date, if not progressive in the old sense. "Thru business, properly conceived, managed, and conducted", the American writer Edward Earl Purinton had declared in 1921, "the human race is finally to be redeemed." In 1923 the Conservative George Oakley won the Toronto riding of Riverdale (which the United Farmers had taken in 1919), by running as "a successful businessman who will help to make a success of the business of this Province." In 1926 a leading theme of the province-wide Conservative campaign was "Business Methods in Administration". Though often draped in traditional anti-American rhetoric,

Ferguson's old Ontario Toryism embraced "the new American religion" of the business civilization that the 1920s brought to influence in the United States under the conservative Republicans Warren Harding and Calvin Coolidge.

This side of Ferguson's regime was reflected in its approach to northern development. The crux of Tory policy was enunciated by Charles McCrea from Sudbury, Minister of Mines, shortly after Ferguson's government took office:"The thing of initial importance is to give confidence to the practical mining man and the investor.... A sympathetic government policy will encourage capital."

American markets and American capital were vital parts of the business of mining and forestry. Without much success, Ferguson also tried to keep faith with Macdonald's National Policy. He urged cheap freight rates for Alberta coal coming to Ontario. And he supported plans for a St. Lawrence Seaway development that would give Great Lakes shipping more direct access to the old markets of the United Kingdom. At the same time, he continued Mowat's quest for provincial rights, and he stood up for Toronto mining interests in disputes with Montreal and the federal government over railroad development along the northern border between Ontario and Quebec.

Philosophically, Ferguson was an advocate of "the limited state", who took pride in opposition complaints that he never really had a legislative programme. It fit with this philosophy that he had ended Prohibition in Ontario by 1927. Yet he also enjoyed Mowat's kind of political skill (though the preferred comparison was with John A. Macdonald), and he pursued the defeat of Prohibition gradually and with caution. From 1923 to 1926 his first Attorney-General, W.F. Nickle, administered the Ontario Temperance Act with almost as much rectitude as W.E. Raney, while a beer with limited alcoholic content – popularly known as"Fergie's Foam" – was introduced for public sale. As elsewhere in English-speaking Canada, when Prohibition finally ended[2], it was replaced by a draconian system of government-controlled distribution of alcoholic beverages, that (in a milder form) has survived to the present.

Despite his disdain for the progressive functions of government, Ferguson continued to support HEPC and was

221

shrewd enough to accommodate at least the minimum demands for public action that seemed built into the development of democracy in the region. Especially after Adam Beck's death in 1925, HEPC took a growing interest in parts of the province away from Niagara Falls, notably in Ferguson's home territory of the southeast and in the north where hydroelectricity was crucial for pulp and paper development. Official enthusiasm for agricultural settlement in the north was revived, after languishing briefly under the Farmer-Labour government. Ferguson took political steps to ease growing northern resentment over southern domination by appointing a Legislative Secretary for Northern Ontario, who served from 1923 to 1926. A new agency for northern development channelled assistance to immigrant farmers, undertook drainage projects, and built colonization roads. Ferguson also appointed Ontario's first Minister of Health in 1924 (though until 1930 the Health and Labour portfolios were held by one minister, Ferguson's crony Forbes E. Godfrey). At almost the end of his career as Premier in 1930, he appointed Ontario's first Minister of Public Welfare, partly in response to the initial shock of the Great Crash of 1929.

After its brief decline under the Drury regime, the size of the Ontario public service continued to increase, reaching some 7,000 employees by the later 1920s. Ferguson insisted that his senior appointments were made strictly on the basis of merit. But in keeping with long-standing regional traditions of political management, he took it for granted that lower level positions in the service normally would go to Conservatives. According to one story, Ferguson was once bitterly attacked in the legislature for dismissing a large group of civil servants who were not known Tories, except for one lone Grit. In reply, the Premier rose, took his pen from his pocket, apologized, and requested the name of the Grit so the mistake could be corrected.

For all his right-wing rambunctiousness and public image as "a village cut-up", there was a side to Ferguson that reflected the old high-minded Upper Canadian Toryism of John Beverly Robinson. Above all else, he believed that the highest function of government was to

The hamlet of Balderson in Lanark County in the mid-1920s. Part of the traditionally Tory loyal southeast in which Howard Ferguson, like James P. Whitney, made his home. Hydroelectricity had arrived, but the roads still left much to be desired.

mold social character and create worthy citizens. In deference to the belief, he served as his own Minister of Education.

Ferguson's most ironic achievement as Minister of Education was to end the Ontario bilingual schools crisis, that he himself had played so important a part in starting, with the agitation which led to the "English-only" Regulation 17 in 1912. On some accounts, he was motivated in part by an arrangement with Premier Alexandre Taschereau of Quebec, through which Ontario also acquired rights to purchase excess hydroelectricity from private power companies east of the Ottawa River. The enobling influence of high office may have been equally significant. For whatever exact reasons, by 1927 French Canadians in Ontario had acquired what amounted to legal status for French-language elementary schools where large numbers warranted. French education rights in Ontario were still significantly weaker than English education rights in Quebec. But a start had been made on the conception of "proper policy", tentatively advanced by Mowat in the later nineteenth century.

Technical education in Ontario was strengthened as well during the 1920s. But increased emphasis on the virtues of the British imperial civilization that Howard Ferguson held in such high esteem was even more important. The *Ontario Reader (Third Book)*, authorized by the Minister of Education in 1925, started with a colour print of the Union Jack and the motto "One Flag, One Fleet, One Throne". The Minister began by thanking such writers as Rudyard Kipling, Sir Arthur Conan Doyle, John Masefield, and Alfred Lord Tennyson for permission to put their thoughts at the disposal of the students of Ontario. This was followed by a homily on Empire Day by Earl Grey, Governor General of Canada, urging students to remember

> that a special responsibility rests with you individually
> to be true to the traditions and to the mission of your
> race ... to remember that one day Canada will become,
> if her people are faithful to their high British traditions, the most powerful of all the self-governing
> nations, not excluding the people of the United Kingdom, which make up the British Empire....

224

End of Old Empires ... New Hard Times

Howard Ferguson's final electoral triumph in 1929 took place only days after the "Black Thursday" Great Crash in New York City, that later came to symbolize the start of the Great Depression of the 1930s. Ferguson remained Premier for almost a year. But in late July of 1930 the federal Conservatives came to power in Ottawa under R.B. Bennett. Ferguson had played a prominent role in the federal campaign. Commonly known as "the high priest of Canadian Toryism", by December 1930 he had resigned his provincial office to become Canadian High Commissioner to the United Kingdom in London, England. On Ferguson's recommendation, the "capable" member for York East and former Minister of Public Works and Highways, George S. Henry, became Premier of Ontario.

The office of High Commissioner to the United Kingdom was a traditional ambassadorial post, designed to provide official Canadian representation in the imperial metropolis. Part of the logic behind Ferguson's appointment was what would prove an excessively rosy Conservative belief in closer imperial economic ties as an approach to the new troubles brought on by the stock market crash and a new wave of American protectionist sentiment. Perhaps Howard Ferguson's most enduring legacy to Canadian public life, however, culminated in 1931 as a result of imperial political developments.

At an Imperial Conference in 1926, it had been explicitly conceded that Canada and the other self-governing dominions (Australia, New Zealand, and South Africa) were autonomous states within a British Commonwealth of Nations – not mere colonies of the British Empire. At another conference in October and November 1930, which Ferguson attended as an informal advisor to Bennett, the details of the new dominion status were formally negotiated and legally enshrined in the Statute of Westminster of 1931.

As part of the new arrangements, the power to amend Dominion constitutions was to be transferred from the British to the respective Dominion parliaments. In Canada's case, this would have meant that the Canadian federal parliament alone had the power to amend the British North America Act, without provincial consent. In defence of the quest for provincial rights begun by Mowat more than half a century before, Howard Ferguson had led provincial objections when the matter was first raised in the late 1920s, and his position won particular support from Quebec, Saskatchewan, and British Columbia. In the end, section 7 of the Statute of Westminster left the power to amend the Canadian constitution in the hands of the British Parliament until Canadian federal and provincial governments could agree on an appropriate amending formula – an event which would not take place for another half century.

In the Ontario where Ferguson seems to have more than once wished he had remained, George Henry was having trouble with the first four leanest and most unsettling years of the 1930s depression. For some, the new industrialism and the new consumer society of the 1920s meant that economic hard times brought on greater social dislocation than when the old agrarian society had been stronger. By 1933 as many as 400,000 people in Ontario (about twelve per cent of the total population) were eking out a bare existence on direct public relief. For the majority, living standards fell significantly. The urban job market tightened dramatically in the south. In the north, the lumber and pulp and paper industries went into shock. Despite some movement back to rural areas, financial crisis was pushing some established farmers off their land.

Henry's Tory government coped as best it could. Parsimonious (and quite repressive) direct relief programmes were organized with federal, provincial, and municipal funds. An Ontario Marketing Board for farm products was established in 1931. In 1932 the Temiskaming and Northern Ontario Railroad was pushed to James Bay, largely as a job creation measure. Some 40,000 men worked on public road building projects. But Henry, a wealthy farmer, dairy operator, and insurance investor, could not face up to the broader implications of the new urban-industrial wave of hard times in the region. Above all else, he was irritated by the depression and lacked sympathy with those whom fate had caused to suffer more than himself.

For others in Ontario, hard times were a call to new kinds of action. The labour movement, which had

Haliburton County Relief Road Camp in the 1930s. Many among "the four-fifths of the labour force who remained employed during those disastrous years," the social policy analyst, Albert Rose, has suggested, "were critical of what they considered to be wasteful measures of assistance to many persons whom they considered to be lazy and indolent."

struggled through a series of ups and downs since the late nineteenth century, would finally acquire a new strength and legitimacy in the 1930s. Canadian-American industry often implied Canadian-American labour as well. Though an All-Canadian Labour Congress that resisted the trend had formed in 1926, the more established Trades and Labour Congress of Canada supported international unionism. As the decade wore on, labour in Ontario was bolstered by a growing radicalism among manufacturing workers in both Canada and the United States, mobilized by the formation of John L. Lewis' Committee (later Congress) for Industrial Organizations in 1935.

In the fall of 1933 Henry's government had used tanks and machine guns to break up a strike of furniture workers at Stratford. But following American precedents, the dominant regional labour unions were at first sceptical about the new Ontario CCF that had taken its first steps by the end of 1932. The CCF's most prominent early leaders in the region were not union leaders, but such people as Ontario's early female political activist, Agnes Macphail, who had ties with what remained of the United Farmers, and Elmore Philpott, a former Liberal.

The new party, however, won the support of some old Labour activists and old progressive middle-class professionals with a new faith in "social democracy". Unlike the Farmer-Labour coalition of 1919-1923, it was an avowedly socialist organization that believed in government intervention and systematic public ownership as solutions to the woes of the depression. To Premier Henry, it advocated a programme "that might have been framed in Russia". He supported periodic police efforts to suppress CCF outdoor meetings. But in fact, even the early CCF was not in any sense "communistic".

For the moment, the most potent challenge to the faltering Ontario Tory regime came from more traditional quarters. In 1930 Mitch Hepburn, a prosperous farmer from Yarmouth Township in southwestern Ontario, former supporter of the United Farmers, and a federal member of parliament, had become the new leader of the Ontario Liberal Party. What Ferguson was to the region's old tradition of Toryism, Hepburn was to the old tradition of agrarian Reform. Beyond this, he brought the instincts of a North American populist demagogue to bear on the

228

problems of the Great Depression. He was for "the little man", against the Lieutenant-Governor's mansion at Chorley Park, for bringing all of "the left" together – "Liberal, Progressive, and Labour" – against the limousines of Tory cabinet ministers, and for "a complete re-alignment of political thought in this country".

George Henry had other problems. Arrangements for the purchase of Quebec hydro power from the Montreal "power barons" made by Ferguson in the late 1920s were proving expensive and unnecessary in the early 1930s. Ferguson's recognition of French elementary schools had helped revive old complaints that Ontario's non-French Catholic separate schools were not publicly supported through to the end of the secondary or high school level. Henry dithered on the issue and offended an influential group of English-speaking Catholic laymen led by an Ottawa lawyer, Martin Quinn. Without making specific commitments, Hepburn, a Protestant, declared his deep belief in "fairness to our Catholic friends".

At last Premier Henry called an election for 19 June 1934. As an economy measure, the number of seats in the legislature was reduced from 112 to 90. The Tories tried to brand Hepburn's old populist rhetoric as "Red" radicalism, warning that if the Liberals were elected, British institutions would topple and property would be confiscated.

Some seventy-three per cent of the registered electorate turned out to vote, matching the high turnout of 1919. Hepburn's Liberals won sixty-six seats to seventeen for the Conservatives. There were four Liberal-Progressives (who would sit with the Liberals), one United Farmer (the Grey County "orator" Farquhar Oliver, who would later become a Liberal cabinet minister), one CCF, and one Independent. After an absence of almost thirty years, the Ontario Grits had returned to power.

The Boy from Yarmouth Gets a Chance

Like Howard Ferguson, Mitch Hepburn had roots in an older Ontario society that was being transformed by the twentieth century. Yet it was Mackenzie King in Ottawa (back in power himself by 1935) who most faithfully carried on the legacy of Oliver Mowat's moderate and politically adroit Great Reformism. Hepburn stood for the more radical and untamed "Clear Grit" tradition of the Great Lakes Peninsula. He was the last flower of an Ontario agrarian democracy that instinctively detested Toryism and admired oratory. The spirit of his world is captured in the often-told story of the southwestern Grit farmer who noticed a large pile of manure in the village square, jumped on top of it, and began an impromptu political speech with elaborate apologies for speaking from the Tory platform[3].

It is tempting to suggest that Mitch Hepburn's career as Premier of Ontario ultimately showed the limitations of the old agrarian radicalism in meeting the challenges of a new century. Yet this may discount too much Hepburn's peculiar personality. Though his formal education had ended with two years of high school, he had great native intellectual capacity and a folksy brilliance in political debate. He was a big man physically but high-strung, with weak health, and a mercurial temperament. A promising political career for his father (the original "boy from Yarmouth") had been cut short by a local scandal involving women and liquor. Mitch Hepburn's wife bravely held together a conventional family life for him. But one of his own cronies once wrote to another: "If you hear anything break regarding Hepburn and women you'll know it's probably true." An Indian band that made Hepburn an honourary chief gave him a name that translates into English as "Turbulent Waters".

Hepburn would serve as Premier longer than any of his predecessors except Mowat and Whitney. But he won only two provincial elections – in 1934 and 1937. In both cases voter turnout was high (over seventy per cent), and Hepburn's supporters won at least a bare majority of the popular vote and an overwhelming majority of seats in the legislature[4]. The first government, from 1934 to 1937, was in many ways genuinely progressive, and it even had its radical moments. By 1937, however, Hepburn's regime had begun to lose its sense of direction. It equivocated on its earlier radicalisms, turned its back on its earlier labour support, and began a series of often wild political lurchings that culminated in "the phantom government" of the early 1940s. If nothing else, Hepburn's career does suggest the extent of regional political confusion brought on by the national and international pressures that marked the years immediately before the Second World War.

Hepburn had rejuvenated the Ontario Liberal Party in the earlier 1930s by reaching out to what remained of the Farmer-Labour coalition of 1919-1923. And he made an unsuccessful bid for alliance with the new CCF. His first cabinet included Harry Nixon, who had been a United Farmer in Drury's cabinet, and Peter Heenan, who had won Kenora as a Labour member in 1919. It also included two prominent left-wing Liberals: Arthur Roebuck, a Toronto radical noted for his habit of wearing formal wing-tip collars; and David Croll, a former Mayor of Windsor who swore the oath of office on the Torah. Roebuck served as Attorney-General and, for a time, as Minister of Labour. Croll was Minister of Welfare, also for a time Minister of Labour, and Minister of Municipal Affairs – a new department established in 1935 to help municipalities that went bankrupt in the depression and to support municipal relief programmes.

From the start, there was a demagogic or strictly symbolic dimension to Hepburn's re-alignment of political thought. On one level, he was simply an old radical Grit who had successfully blamed the Tories for the depression and was determined to put them in their place. His regime began with an auction of government limousines at Varsity Stadium in Toronto. By 1938 he had realized Drury's earlier ambition of selling the Lieutenant-Governor's colonial Government House at Chorley Park, "a haven for broken-down English aristocrats who should be paying for their rooms at the hotels." And he declared the wild trillium Ontario's official flower, an alternative symbol to the Tory coat of arms and Loyalist motto devised earlier by Whitney.

Following the instincts of the Farmer-Labour coalition, Hepburn put an end to official enthusiasm for agricultural settlement in northern Ontario. And like Drury's regime, Hepburn's government also inherited the old agrarian enthusiasm for economy and efficiency in public administration. While campaign rhetoric about firing half the Tory civil service was ignored, its size did decline from more than 7,700 employees in 1932 to less than 7,000 in 1937. Hepburn served as his own Provincial Treasurer and

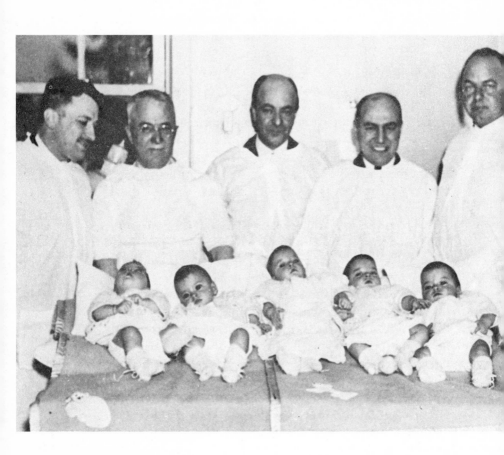

*David Croll (extreme left) and Mitch Hepburn (extreme right)
with the Dionne Quintuplets. On 28 May 1934 Oliva Dionne
gave birth to the world's first surviving quintuplets (five girls), in
the village of Callander, Ontario. "The Quints" were front-page
news from New York to Hong Kong. Hepburn, who swept to office
just three weeks after they were born, was not averse to sharing the
limelight, with his Minister of Public Welfare.*

proudly pointed to "the first provincial budget surplus in years" as evidence of sound financial management.

Hepburn's two most radical acts took place during his first government, and both would later be abandoned. The first was a repudiation of the Quebec hydro-power contracts that Ferguson's government had signed with the power barons of Montreal, orchestrated by Attorney-General Arthur Roebuck. This amounted to a declaration that duly elected governments could renege on public financial commitments to private corporations and greatly disturbed the Montreal and Toronto business communities. It ran into trouble in the courts, and by the later 1930s Ontario actually did need extra hydroelectric power. In the end, Hepburn's government simply renegotiated the original contracts at reduced prices.

The second radical act was legislation that for the first time since the early 1860s significantly enriched the tax base for Ontario's separate schools and envisioned a complete publicly-supported Catholic high school system in the province. Paul Leduc, Minister of Mines, represented French Catholics in Hepburn's cabinet. Peter Heenan, Minister of Lands and Forests, represented English-speaking Catholics. Maurice Duplessis, who became Premier of Quebec in 1936, became one of Hepburn's great political friends, recalling the "Mowat-Mercier Concordat" of the late nineteenth century. And Martin Quinn's English-speaking Catholic laymen had helped the Ontario Liberals come to power in 1934.

Hepburn, who could be a courageous man of principle, stood up for his separate schools legislation in the face of enormous popular opposition from Ontario's Protestant majority, and he almost ruined his health unsuccessfully fighting an eastern Ontario by-election on the issue. But Quinn tried to push the Catholic victory too far too fast in a period of hard times and psychological unrest. The issue became extremely divisive, and Hepburn finally acceded to a Conservative motion abandoning the legislation. At the same time, he had broken the ice on an ancient point of contention. For the most part, Ontario's Catholic community – French and English – continued to respect his efforts on its behalf.

233

As in Drury's Farmer-Labour coalition, farmers had a stronger voice in Hepburn's government than labour, and it was the increasingly important issue of labour relations that finally stalled the progressive momentum of the Hepburn regime. Hepburn's empathy for "the little man on the back concessions" was not exactly matched by a parallel empathy for the little man in the factory, whose situation was remote from the Premier's personal experience. As owner himself of a 1,200 acre family farm, Hepburn was also vulnerable to flattery from such new cronies in business as the youthful mining investor and newspaper owner George McCullagh (who merged the old Liberal *Globe* and the old Tory *Mail and Empire* to form the modern *Globe and Mail*), the Toronto distiller Larry McGuiness, and the New York financier "Sell Em" Ben Smith.

Hepburn did have some commitment to the workingman. Arthur Roebuck had guided a notably pro-labour Industrial Disputes Act through the legislature in 1934, and in 1937 David Croll announced Ontario's first minimum wage for men. But when Canadian locals of the United Auto Workers, helped by John L. Lewis' "Red" Congress of Industrial Organization, began to organize illegal sit-down strikes in Ontario early in 1937, Hepburn put his foot down against "John L. Lewis' paid agitators in Canada", American domination of Canadian trade unions, and "Communism in general". Matters came to a head with a strike at General Motors of Canada in Oshawa, that Hepburn repressed with a specially-organized police force quickly dubbed "Hepburn's Hussars".

In the end the strike at Oshawa was settled, and a collective agreement between General Motors of Canada and its workers was signed. But Hepburn had taken a (quite popular) stand against John L. Lewis' aggressive new kind of unionism north of the Great Lakes. The All-Canadian Congress of Labour supported the Premier's efforts to maintain Canadian unions free from foreign domination. At the Premier's request, however, Croll and Roebuck (who had wavered in their support for the Premier on the Oshawa strike) resigned from the cabinet in April 1937, and Hepburn's regime took a turn to the right.

Hepburn's rightward shift after 1937 was neither systematic nor particularly consistent. In the election of that year, a leading Liberal theme was the need to plug old Tory loopholes in the collection of succession duties. Though out of the cabinet over disagreements on labour policy, Croll and Roebuck ran again as Liberals who supported the government's "generally good record" – reduced taxes and hydro rates, new municipal subsidies, a new pension for the blind, improvement in the provincial highway system, and a surplus in the provincial budget.

Moreover, by the end of his regime Hepburn was moving to the left again. His largest budgetary surplus in 1941 owed much to a more than twofold increase in corporation taxes. One of his last public appearances as Premier in the fall of 1942 was on a platform with Tim Buck at a rally in Toronto urging the federal government to lift its wartime ban on the activities of the Communist Party of Canada. Throughout the lurchings of the late 1930s and early 1940s Hepburn remained loyal as well to a diffuse, depression-era populism, also popular elsewhere in Canada and the United States. There were some similarities between Hepburn and Huey Long in Louisiana (or Upton Sinclair's failed "End Poverty in California" movement). In 1938 the Montreal lawyer and CCF publicist, Frank Scott, conceded that Mitch Hepburn in Ontario, Maurice Duplessis in Quebec, and "Bible Bill" Aberhart in Alberta "provide the only vigorous – if erratic – leadership to be found in Canadian politics today."

Nonetheless, in the confused years of the later 1930s and early 1940s Hepburn did seem to lose what philosophic bearings he had. For a time, he became convinced that communism was a great threat to Ontario society. Though his government held some three-quarters of the seats in the legislature, to resist communist influence he toyed with the idea of forming a "Union government" with the Conservative George Drew – a rival to the new Tory leader Earl Rowe and a future Tory leader himself. For a time, Hepburn channelled his radical instincts about the depression toward a vague interest in the inflationist schemes for monetary reform advocated by William Aberhart's Social Credit movement in Alberta. He carefully

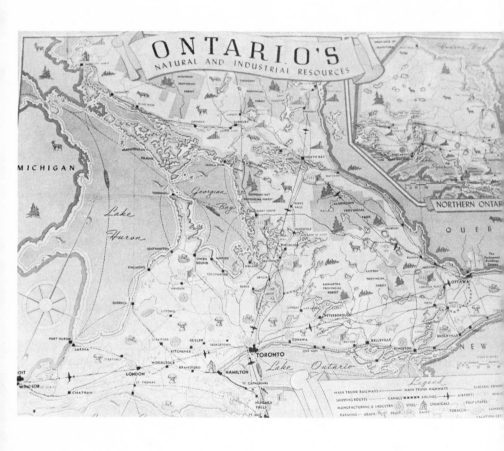

Map: Ontario in the 1940s. Prepared for a statistical handbook published by the King's Printer.

studied pamphlets sent along by the Alberta Premier, who unsuccessfully urged Hepburn to take the lead in organizing an "All-Canada" party, that would "get the country moving again"[5].

Yet, according to his first biographer, there remained at least one steady theme in Hepburn's career – the Premier's consistent championing of provincial rights. In part, this was encouraged by a feud between the dramatically different personalities and political styles of Hepburn and Mackenzie King in Ottawa, that Hepburn pursued with increasing animosity in the later 1930s and early 1940s. But it also reflected a faithful pursuit of the claims of the Ontario regional state advanced by Mowat in the later nineteenth century and continued by virtually every other Ontario premier since then.

Hepburn's conflicts with Ottawa were stimulated by such specific issues as hydro development and St. Lawrence Seaway plans, income taxation, and the federal government's reluctance to increase its contribution to direct relief programmes. They were focused in a more general way by the federal Rowell-Sirois Commission, involving a former Ontario Liberal leader. The Commission was appointed to study the broader questions of strains and regional tensions in Canadian Confederation, brought into harsh light by the depression. Like Mowat, Hepburn stood for the Ontario Reformer's traditional belief in a decentralized Confederation. When the Commission's work pointed toward recommendations for greater federal power, Hepburn declared: "we are a stupid people if we imagine ourselves immune to the consequences of concentrating power ... were the men of 1837 to take stock of our politics in 1938, they would find little left of the ideals on which they placed such store."

Hepburn's views on federal-provincial relations implied as well a lack of sympathy for provinces less fortunate than Ontario and (somewhat ironically) even a defence of the "empire Ontario" that had set down roots in the earlier twentieth century. In 1934 Harold Innis, born like Hepburn on a farm in the southwestern Great Lakes Peninsula, had written:

The elasticity of the economy of Ontario has been based on a wealth of developed natural resources and has been obtained in part through inelastic developments which bear with undue weight on less favoured areas of the Dominion. The strength of Ontario may emphasize the weakness of the federation. An empire has its obligations as well as its opportunities.

The Rowell-Sirois Commission's approach to the problem was increased federal grants, designed to "equalize" the capacity of all provincial governments to provide a basic level of services to their citizens. To Hepburn, this implied "a raid on Ontario's treasury". He insisted: "Equality between the provinces is impossible." If some provinces were too small to handle their constitutional responsibilities adequately, "the remedy that first suggests itself is amalgamation."

A federal-provincial conference was held on the Commission's final report at Ottawa early in 1941. Hepburn declared Ontario "would stand solidly beside Quebec if at any time her minority rights are threatened." If the centralizing philosophy of the Rowell-Sirois Report were implemented, "Quebec and the rest of us will have to agree to a surrender to the central authority of rights and privileges granted by the North America Act." John Bracken, the Progressive Premier of Manitoba, was among the most ardent provincial supporters of the Rowell-Sirois recommendations. But Ontario's rejection of the report was strongly seconded by Alberta and British Columbia, and the federal-provincial conference of 1941 broke up without taking action.

To no small extent, however, what Mackenzie King and the federal government at Ottawa could not win through the Rowell-Sirois Report, it won in the end through the emergency circumstances of the Second World War. Early in 1939, a trip to Australia, where fears of Japanese invasion were gathering strength, helped convince Hepburn that "fascism" in Germany, Italy, and Japan was the ultimate menace: "three nations have agreed on a conquest of the world and the rest of us must stand together and resist the inroads of dictators." Hepburn's traditional anti-Tory Ontario Grittism did not imply any empathy with isolationist sentiment in the United States.

His quarrel with Mackenzie King over the Second World War was that the federal government was not prosecuting Canada's war effort aggressively enough.

The federal parliament at Ottawa declared war on Germany on 10 September 1939, a full seven days after the United Kingdom as an unmistakable gesture of Canadian independence[6]. Fewer Canadians would die overseas than in the First World War. But in support, first of the British and then the allied struggle in Europe, the Canadian federal government gradually took command of a vigorous wartime economy, that finally pulled Ontario and Canada at large out of the 1930s depression. Something similar had happened during the First World War, but in a much milder way. By 1941 the federal government was administering a national unemployment insurance scheme. By early 1942 Ontario had transferred its constitutional jurisdiction over corporation and income taxes to Ottawa for the duration of the war in exchange for federal grants.

As a staunch supporter of the war effort, Hepburn did not protest, although he regretted that for the time being the Ontario legislature had been reduced to the status of the "glorified county council" envisioned by John A. Macdonald and John Sandfield Macdonald in 1867. And the stage was set for the boy from Yarmouth's somewhat bizzare demise.

Hepburn's last real enthusiasm in Ontario politics had been a successful struggle to make the pasteurization of milk compulsory during the later 1930s in an effort to reduce tuberculosis. By 1942 he was neglecting even his routine duties at Queen's Park for a more intriguing social life at his King Edward Hotel suite in Toronto. The new Conservative Opposition leader George Drew was bemoaning the "phantom government" of Ontario. Finally, on 21 October 1942, Hepburn resigned as Premier. He appointed Gordon Conant, member for Oshawa and a longtime Hepburn loyalist, as his successor. Until March 1943 Hepburn continued as provincial Treasurer and also continued his personal feud with Mackenzie King in Ottawa.

By April 1943 a convention of the Ontario Liberal Party had replaced Conant as Premier with Harry Nixon, the former United Farmer, Progressive, and Liberal-

239

Progressive, who had retained a loyal respect for the federal party leader Mackenzie King in the course of Hepburn's private feud. Premier Nixon called a provincial election for 3 August 1943, which proved a disaster for the Liberals. George Drew's newly rechristened "Progressive Conservatives" won thirty-eight seats. Though they had not won a single seat in the election of 1937, the CCF under the leadership of E.B. "Ted" Jolliffe, a thirty-three year-old lawyer and somewhat aristocratic looking "returned Rhodes scholar", won thirty-four seats. Only sixteen seats went to Harry Nixon's Liberals (one of which was still held by Hepburn). As the tide began to turn in the war in Europe, a new and seemingly quite confused era had begun in Ontario politics.

At the time, the sudden new strength of the socialistic CCF seemed the most important fact. Yet as events would unfold, the Progressive Conservatives had begun a regime that would last even longer than the Great Reform Government of the late nineteenth century.

Part Five

Canadian Region, 1943-1985

"During the war, when speaking in a hall in Montreal, I paid a warm tribute to the greatness of France, and a French Canadian woman, really moved, said 'Of course it is true, but that you, from Ontario, should say these things....' ... She was thinking that our province had a social pattern and that pattern had an articulate voice. Well the voice is still there and as articulate as ever, but the pattern was broken long ago. It was broken about 1837 at the time of the rebellion."
Morley Callaghan

"The world has changed. There are no more borders. You can't run home and be safe from the bomb, from the terrorists, from anything. We're all open to anything...."
Oscar Peterson

"Au revoir, mes amis, Canadiens. C'est toujours plaisir pour moi de faire séjour dans votre pays.... C'est un avenir splendide que vous attend demain."
Winston Churchill

Discover how much fun

YOU CAN PACK INTO A DAY IN

ONTARIO

Toronto, Ontario's capital city, is worth a place in every
vacation plan. Come in for the excitement of the Exhibition . . .
for the smart shops and restaurants . . . for the plays, the
ballet, the theatres, the museum. There's always something
going on. Get to **know** Toronto this 125th anniversary year.

Free Ontario Vacation Literature
write to Ontario Travel, 201 Parliament Bldgs., Toronto

KNOW ONTARIO BETTER

Ontario Department of Travel & Publicity. Hon. Bryan L. Cathcart, Minister

*Ontario Government tourism ad, prepared for a publication com-
memorating the 125th anniversary of the City of Toronto in 1959.
For some reason, the illustration in the bottom left hand corner
depicts Indian totem poles found only in British Columbia.*

243

13

A New Society

In Ontario as elsewhere, the end of the First World War had brought political radicalism and then economic hard times. As the Second World War moved to its conclusion, the CCF's performance in the provincial election of 1943 signalled more political radicalism. Conventional wisdom in the region anticipated that the end of the war would bring more economic hard times. In fact, just the opposite happened. The end of the Second World War at last brought an economic boom to Ontario that rivalled and in some ways surpassed the great boom of the early 1850s

There was a mild recession in the later 1950s and early 1960s. Unemployment in the region rose from an average of about 2½ per cent for the ten years from 1947 to 1956 to about 5 per cent for the five years from 1957 to 1961. But with such minor exceptions, the end of the Second World War brought a period of sustained growth that would last until the mid-1970s. The population of Ontario doubled, from just under 4.1 million people in 1946 to more than 8.2 million people in 1976.

A new generation of postwar prosperity brought improved economic circumstances to at least the large majority of the growing regional population. In round numbers, average non-farm wages in Ontario rose from about $50 a week in the earlier 1950s to $200 a week in the mid-1970s. Prices rose as well, but not by at all as much. Broadly, what $.60 would buy in the early 1950s, it took $1 to buy in the early 1970s (though, as a sign of new troubles ahead, $1.50 later in the decade). As elsewhere, the new prosperity was accompanied by a new wave in the spread of technological innovation, the exact implications of which remain a matter of great debate. But a few facts are clear.

In 1950 the horse still played some role in the Ontario transportation economy – in the countryside and the bush as well as in the province's largest city where it still pulled breadwagons and milkwagons. The triumph of the automobile and the truck, however, was complete by the 1960s. By the 1970s the passenger train's historic status as prime agent of regional mobility had been thoroughly usurped by the automobile and the superhighway.

The 1950s also saw the last age of the ocean-going passenger ship that had brought masses of people to Ontario for almost a century and a half. The long-distance airplane became the dominant vehicle of both immigration and travel abroad. The miracle of television (invented in the mid-1920s) began to reach the mass of the population by the 1950s. By the late 1970s only three per cent of all Ontario households did not have at least one television set.

By the later 1970s the boom was over. The 1980s began with the return of the kind of economic hard times that for a while some had imagined gone forever. In various shapes and sizes, major continuities with the past remained. But the long era of prosperity and innovation after the Second World War had left a virtually new society north of the Great Lakes.

The New North

As in the great boom of the early 1850s, the dynamic growth of the 1950s and 1960s was accompanied by increasingly stronger ties with the North American continental economy. Though this was a trend in Canada at large, it was especially pronounced in Ontario.

After the failure of the Conservative enthusiasm for revived British Empire trade in the early 1930s, a limited form of the Canadian-American reciprocity in natural products proposed in 1911 had been negotiated by the later 1930s. In manufacturing, virtual Canadian-American free trade in agricultural implements had arrived by 1944.

Twenty years later the Canada-us Auto Pact brought a regulated form of continental free trade in "road motor vehicles and parts". This led to a major restructuring of the Ontario automobile industry, which lost its earlier links to the old National Policy and imperial preference. North American automobile manufacturing became a continental industry, operating under an international agreement that ensured Canada a "fair share" of vehicle and parts production.

By the later 1940s just over half of Canada's exports were going to the United States (in fact, a return to the circumstances of 1870, just after Confederation). The proportion rose to about two-thirds in the early 1950s, fell just below sixty per cent in the 1960s, and was back to two-thirds by the later 1970s. In 1959, after some half a century of planning, debate, and negotiation, a Canadian-American St. Lawrence Seaway was finally completed. But it was more important for the hydroelectric projects that accompanied it than for any revival of Canadian trade with western Europe.

In Ontario alone, by the later 1970s some eighty per cent of all exports were going to the United States. Ontario's ten largest export customers beyond the U.S.A. were the United Kingdom, Venezuela, West Germany, Saudi Arabia, Australia, the Netherlands, Japan, Mexico, France, and Iran. About half of all Ontario exports involved road motor vehicles and parts, followed by newsprint, nickel, agricultural machinery, and office equipment. The region's ten largest import customers beyond the U.S.A. were the United Kingdom, Japan, West Germany, Italy, France, Taiwan, Hong Kong, the Netherlands, Switzerland, and South Korea. But about eighty-five per cent of all Ontario imports came from the United States.

As the Great Reformers of the nineteenth century had predicted, closer links with the North American economy did prove an effective strategy for the growth of Ontario's urban areas. After stalling somewhat in the 1930s, the relative size of the rural population resumed its earlier decline, falling to only eighteen per cent of the total in 1971 – an almost exact reverse of the urban/rural split of a century before. By 1981 about two-thirds of the

Ontario population lived in the province's ten largest metropolitan areas. Beyond Toronto, the list included two centres with more than half a million people each: Ottawa and Hamilton; four that hovered around the quarter million mark: St. Catharines-Niagara, Kitchener, London, and Windsor; and three centres with just over 100,000 people each: Oshawa, Sudbury, and Thunder Bay (an amalgamation of the earlier Port Arthur and Fort William).

The new urban growth was increasingly concentrated in the central part of southern Ontario, around the western end of Lake Ontario and north to Lake Simcoe (and including the area just west of the Niagara Escarpment). This area grew from just under 2½ million people in 1951 to more than 5½ million in 1981. During the same period, however, northern Ontario grew from just over half a million people to 820,000; the southeast from about 700,000 to almost 1.2 million (about forty-five per cent of whom were in the Ottawa area); and the southwest from some 850,000 to just under 1.3 million.

In absolute numbers, Ontario's 1981 rural population of more than 1½ million people was a little larger than it had been four decades earlier. In effect, the old agrarian society of rural Ontario had not so much declined as remained constant, while a new urban industrial world rose around it, building on the agricultural and resource base established by the gritty pioneers of the nineteenth century. By the later 1970s, rural population growth and growth in smaller urban areas had begun to show new strength.

As in earlier periods, the most striking feature of urbanization in the 1950s and 1960s was dramatic growth in Toronto and its surrounding region. The population of the greater metropolitan area was a little more than one million in the early 1950s, just under two million in the early 1960s, and about three million in the early 1980s. By the 1950s Toronto was again competing rather than co-operating with Montreal and no longer seeing itself as a junior partner. A publication commemorating the city's 125th birthday in 1959 declared that Toronto was now in fact "the economic capital of Canada". The publication noted:

Downtown Kitchener, 1951: known as Berlin before the First World War (Kitchener was the name of the leading British general during the war's early phases), and a centre for Ontario's historic German immigration of the late eighteenth and earlier nineteenth centuries. By the early 1980s the Kitchener census metropolitan area, with well over a quarter million people, was the fifth largest urban region in the province.

"Toronto is America's gateway to Canada," an editor from Montreal said this past winter. He thought that explained what was to him the unnatural pre-eminence of Toronto. But does it?

Nonetheless, it was allowed that Toronto had indeed become "Canada's bridge (not door) to the culture of the United States."

A new Quebec independence movement had also arisen by the later 1950s. It perhaps had much to do with a growing determination among Quebec's French-speaking majority to gain control over the regional economy in its own province. The trend gradually prompted some elements of the old English-speaking business community in Montreal to relocate in Toronto. But Toronto did not replace Montreal as Canada's most populous metropolis until the mid-1970s. By this time, the new merchants of Calgary and Vancouver had already begun to challenge Toronto's economic dominance, as Toronto had once begun to challenge Montreal.

Modern Toronto as a centre of regional capitalism is a favourite Canadian object of disdain both outside and inside Ontario. But in the early 1970s Jacob Spelt, a leading authority on Ontario urban development, perhaps expressed the crux of Canadian metropolitan growth after the Second World War: "Toronto's emergence as a worthy rival to Montreal destroyed the possibility of a truly primate centre in Canada."

The Newest Migrations

If postwar Toronto became Canada's bridge to the culture of the United States, Ontario's rapid population growth in the 1950s and 1960s was also shared by at least several other parts of a wider new north. Canada generally had an extremely high rate of population growth during the period, outstripping the United States and even the world at large. In Ontario, as elsewhere, part of the new population growth was the result of a striking rise in regional birth rates – the postwar "baby boom". Equally important, however, was a major new wave of immigration encouraged by

249

both federal and provincial government policy. From the later 1940s to the later 1970s, well over two million people born outside Canada came to live in Ontario.

Though in various senses Ontario had a long background of cultural heterogeneity, its overseas immigration had been dominated by the United Kingdom. Beyond the Indians and the handful of descendants of the Black fugitive slaves, Ontario society by the end of the Second World War had its broadest ancestral roots in western and central Europe. A few Italians and a handful of Chinese had arrived by the end of the nineteenth century, and the early twentieth century brought the early beginnings of a more cosmopolitan mix. Yet even by 1941, about ninety-five per cent of the Ontario population had been born in Canada, the United States, or the United Kingdom.

The change after the Second World War came in two major waves. The first brought large numbers of people from southern and eastern Europe. The second, starting in earnest in the 1960s, brought a still more diverse mixture from south and east Asia and the West Indies. The older patterns did not completely vanish. Even in 1981 about twenty-five per cent of Ontario's born-outside-Canada population had come from the United Kingdom. About thirteen per cent, however, had come from Italy. The next ten largest groups (each with from three to five per cent of the total) came from the United States, Portugal, Germany (East and West), the Netherlands, Poland, Yugoslavia, Jamaica, the Soviet Union, Greece, and India.

Largely as a result of immigration, Ontario's Catholic population had increased to thirty-five per cent of the total by the early 1980s (up from twenty-two per cent in the early 1930s). Hinduism and Islam had become new minority religions in the region, though more than seven per cent of the population indicated no religious preference.

As had also been true in the past, the new immigration was not uniformly distributed across the province. By 1981 about one in every four people in Ontario as a whole had been born outside Canada. But the proportion was four in every ten in Metropolitan Toronto and only one in every ten in the Algoma district of northern Ontario. "New Canadians" from the United Kingdom and Germany tended to be more evenly distributed. Those from Hong

Kong, Taiwan, Pakistan, and the Philippines tended to be most concentrated in the Toronto region.

Inter-provincial migration also played an increasingly important part in the development of Ontario after the Second World War. By 1981 one out of every ten Ontario residents had been born in Canada but outside the province itself. As a result of both migration and natural increase Ontario's French Canadian population peaked at about ten per cent of the total in the early 1960s. Afterwards, perhaps under the pressure of the independence movement in Quebec, it began to decline. In 1981 some 7½ per cent reported French "ethnic origins" (including just under 10,000 immigrants from France). As a different sign of French Canadian progress, however, in 1981 more than ten per cent of Ontario residents reported their "official language" as "both English and French".

Similarly, there were more than 75,000 "Registered Indians" in Ontario in the early 1980s, perhaps close to or even more than the total number of people living in the region when Europeans had first arrived in 1610. In 1980 the Ontario Métis and Non-Status Indian Association estimated that an additional 185,000 residents of the province had some form of unregistered ancestral attachment to Ontario's Indian peoples.

By 1981 one out of every ten Ontario residents had backgrounds that at least figuratively looked back to the polyethnic culture of the old Canadian fur trade: the region's "forgotten" French and Indian history of the seventeenth and earlier eighteenth centuries. At the same time, only fifty-three per cent of Ontario residents reported some form of "British" ethnic origins[1].

From Colony to Nation to Colony?

In 1945 Canadian historian Arthur Lower published a book entitled *Colony to Nation*, quietly celebrating Canada's role in the disappearance of the historic British Empire. After the Second World War both Ontario and Canada at large ceased to be a part of the Empire, if only because, like the other old European empires of France, Portugal, and the Netherlands, it ceased to exist. The transformation of what had once been "the greatest empire since Rome" into the modern Commonwealth of Nations had arguably begun with Canadian Confederation itself in 1867. It reached a first major turning point with the Statute of Westminster in 1931 and a second landmark when India – "jewel of the Empire" – became independent in 1947. In the early 1950s Vincent Massey, an heir to the old Ontario agricultural machinery fortune, became the first Canadian-born Governor General of Canada. By the later 1970s the Commonwealth of Nations had become a loosely-knit association of forty-nine member nation states.

In 1883 the Cambridge historian J.R.Seeley had published an influential set of lectures on *The Expansion of England*:

> If the United States and Russia hold together for another half century, they will, at the end of that time, completely dwarf such old European states as France and Germany, and depress them into the second class.... They will do the same to England if at that time England still thinks of herself as a European state.

By the end of the Second World War Seeley's prophecy had been fulfilled: the U.S.A. and the U.S.S.R. had become, in the English writer George Orwell's phrase, "the only two completely sovereign nations in the world." Like France, Germany, and Japan, the United Kingdom, which had grown into the world's first modern industrial society and leading international power by the middle of the nineteenth century, had been "dwarfed" into "the second class" on the world stage by the middle of the twentieth century.

Canada shared borders with both new superpowers, and it shared a continent, increasingly close economic ties, and a common New World culture with the United States. Since the American Declaration of Independence in 1776, an influential stream of opinion in the United States had envisioned annexation to the American republic as Canada's "manifest destiny". In the later 1940s, watching the rapid development of the Canadian-American economic relations that had begun their modern history after the First World War, Harold Innis quipped that

Canada was in imminent danger of sliding "from colony to nation to colony".

During the 1950s influential streams of opinion in both Ontario and Canada at large became increasingly concerned that some complete economic integration with the United States would indeed destroy Canada's prospects as an independent North American nation, with a respectable claim on at least the degree of international political sovereignty that was possible in an age of competing nuclear superpowers. Earlier in the decade, Canada had fought with the United States in the Korean War, as it had fought with the United Kingdom in the South African War a half century before. But in the 1960s Canada did not fight with the United States in Vietnam. Despite complaints from some quarters about "Canadian complicity", Ontario-born Lester Pearson, Prime Minister of Canada, and Nobel Peace Prize winner, publicly criticized the American role in Vietnam – an act which prompted President Lyndon Johnson, when the occasion arose, to seize Pearson "by the lapel of his coat, at the same time raising his other arm to the heavens". The new Canada would be America's "best friend in the world". But at least in its own mind, it resisted the status of a mere satellite.

In fulfillment of a promise made by Mackenzie King at the end of the Second World War, Pearson's regime at last replaced the Union Jack and the old British red ensign of Canada with a distinctive Canadian flag. The Ontario government, under the command of a nominally Tory regime throughout the period, retained at least a thin veneer of the old British Canada. Like neighbouring Manitoba, it adopted a variation on the British red ensign as a "provincial flag". Even in the early 1980s, the loyal militia regiments remained more popular in Toronto than in virtually any other part of Canada. But like the Orange Order, they had lost real influence in the wider society. Ontario's leading militia bandmaster had the very un-British name of Captain Gino Falconi. And in a revival of the tradition of federal-provincial split allegiance, it was the votes of the people of Ontario, almost as much as those of the people of Quebec, that kept the new nation-building Liberals of Lester Pearson and then Pierre Trudeau in office at Ottawa for more than twenty years[2].

Similarly, the Progressive Conservative government of Ontario became a staunch supporter of the Liberal government of Canada's nation-building acts. By the later 1970s an informal partnership between the two administrations had evolved, recalling the historic alliance of "the two Macdonalds" in the years immediately following Confederation. By the early 1980s the paradox of Ontario was that it was in some ways both the most American (or North American) province in Canada (though Alberta ran a very close second) and the province with the most developed commitment to the survival of Canada and its particular "arduous destiny".

The World has Changed

In many ways, the new society that arose in Ontario after the Second World War was transitional and without a finished shape. But some changes in the underlying economic base of the region were clear enough.

By the early 1970s the old gap between rural and urban living standards had virtually closed. Ontario still had the single largest agricultural labour force of any Canadian province. With improvements in agricultural technology, Ontario farmers produced almost 3½ times more corn, 2¼ times more apples, and one-third more cattle and calves in the late 1970s than they had produced in the early 1950s. But the less than thirty per cent of the regional labour force in agriculture and resources in the early 1920s had declined to less than fifteen per cent by the early 1950s, and it would decline again to less than five per cent by the early 1980s.

The mines and forests of the north were still crucial to the regional economy (though, like some farmers, both were hurt badly by the economic slowdown of the later 1970s). Yet even in the north, only a small minority of the new society remained directly employed in the agriculture and resource sectors that had occupied well over a majority of the work force at the time of Confederation.

The relative importance of the Ontario manufacturing sector as an employer peaked in the early 1950s, temporarily stimulated by the immense physical destruction of the Second World War in Europe (and Japan) and by the war itself. In 1951 almost thirty per cent of the regional labour force had jobs in manufacturing. But this had shrunk to a more traditional twenty-four per cent by the early 1980s. Parts of Ontario manufacturing (like domestic textiles and shoes) still depended on high tariffs inherited from the old National Policy. But these came under increasing pressure from the General Agreement on Tariffs and Trade (GATT) that emerged as a framework for international trade in the postwar era.

The Canada-US Auto Pact of the mid-1960s radically re-oriented the region's vital automotive (and automotive parts) manufacturing. The Massey-Harris agricultural machinery enterprise merged with a British firm in the late 1950s to become the Toronto-headquartered multinational corporation of Massey-Ferguson Limited.

In the mid-1970s more than fifty-five per cent of all goods manufactured in Ontario were shipped to points within the province itself. Another twenty-three per cent went to other parts of Canada, and just over twenty per cent were exported outside Canada. The old imperial preference was only a memory, with less than three per cent of all Ontario exports going to the United Kingdom in the later 1970s and an even smaller proportion to other parts of the Commonwealth of Nations.

Significant petrochemicals production remained as a legacy of the National Policy and the southwestern Ontario oil industry of the nineteenth century, though the centre of Canadian oil production had long since shifted to Alberta. Ontario was still the centre of Canadian steel production, especially in the Hamilton and Sault Ste. Marie areas. A new "high-tech" microelectronic mini-sector had taken root in the Ottawa area by the later 1970s.

Northern Telecom, Canada's rising multinational bright light in telecommunications, could be viewed as a symbolic legacy of the invention of the telephone in Ontario. It had major "branch plant" operations in the United States, and it had its head offices in Toronto by the mid-1970s. But the dozen largest industrial corporations headquartered in Ontario in the later 1970s (ranked by sales) suggested the continuing importance of Canadian-American manufacturing: General Motors of Canada Limited, Ford Motor Company of Canada Limited, Imperial

Oil Limited, Massey-Ferguson Limited, Chrysler Canada Limited, Shell Canada Limited, Gulf Canada Limited, Inco Limited, Canada Packers Limited, Texaco Canada Incorporated, Steel Company of Canada, Noranda Mines Limited, and Moore Corporation.

The major new economic development after the Second World War was a continuation of the shift into "the service sector" that had begun in the earlier twentieth century. Ontario moved from a labour force with a majority of blue-collar industrial workers, farmers, miners, and lumberjacks in the late 1940s to one with a majority of white-collar office workers and clerks in the late 1970s. By the mid-1950s the United States had become the first country in the world with a majority of its labour force engaged in the production of services rather than goods. Ontario reached the same point only a short while later. By the early 1980s almost two-thirds of the regional labour force was in the service sector: transportation, communication, and utilities; trade; finance, insurance, and real estate; community, business, and personal services; and public administration and defence.

Expansion of the service sector helped make new room for the trend toward direct female participation in the labour force, that had earlier been helped along by the two world wars. In the early 1950s, about one-quarter of Ontario's working-age women had jobs; by the late 1970s the figure had risen to about one-half. By the early 1980s women outnumbered men in general service occupations, clerical occupations, teaching occupations, and occupations in medicine and health.

New jobs gave women new freedom (enhanced by the technological innovation of birth-control pills, which also brought new freedom to both women and men). As elsewhere, new freedom brought new problems. In the late 1960s the divorce rate in Ontario suddenly more than doubled. By the late 1970s there were more than 225 divorces per 100,000 population annually, up from only 50 per 100,000 population in the early 1950s. In an ironic way, trends of this sort themselves became a force for more service sector expansion, such as counselling services to help deal with domestic breakdown and "stress" in the workplace.

Bethel (Lunau) Cemetery and Markham Hydro building: the old and the new in the Regional Municipality of York. The cemetery has tombstones that date from the late eighteenth century; the style of the building belongs unmistakably to the late twentieth century.

257

In a more traditional context, Eaton's and Simpson's remained in business. But Eaton's gradually lost its earlier dominance in the region's retail service sector. By the later 1970s it had discontinued its historic mail-order catalogue. Simpson's had become linked with the US-based Sears Corporation and with the Hudson's Bay Company (whose retail outlets were now known as The Bay) headquartered in Winnipeg. Sears Canada Incorporated was publishing the major mail-order catalogue in Ontario. The Bay had gained a new presence in Ontario retail markets, and specialty retail outlets were challenging all the more traditional department stores.

Suburban shopping centres as well as downtown shopping malls in such smaller southern Ontario cities as Peterborough and Chatham, helped bring the postwar revival of the new consumer society of the 1920s to virtually all parts of the old Upper Canada. Even the settled parts of northern Ontario were dominated by regional centres of the consumer society in North Bay, Sudbury, Sault Ste. Marie, and Thunder Bay.

By the early 1970s the four Toronto banks of the late nineteenth and earlier twentieth centuries had merged into two banks. This enhanced the traditional concentration among Canadian chartered banks (though by the early 1980s new federal legislation to encourage a degree of foreign banking competition was in place). The Bank of Nova Scotia, subsequently known as Scotiabank, had erected a major new Toronto office building in the 1950s. In the 1970s the Toronto-Dominion Bank, the Canadian Imperial Bank of Commerce, the Royal Bank of Canada, and the Bank of Montreal all erected steel and glass office towers that transformed the Toronto financial district.

The Montreal-headquartered Canadian National Railways erected the CN Telecommunications Tower, the tallest free-standing structure in the world, on the Toronto waterfront. In the early 1980s the Toronto Stock Exchange moved into new quarters at King and York streets. Toronto business life was affected as well by developments linked with the new immigration of the 1960s and 1970s, suggested in a late 1970s novel by the West Indian writer V.S. Naipaul (based in London, England):

All over the world money is in flight. People have scraped the world clean ... and now they want to run ... Koreans, Filipinos, people from Hong Kong and Taiwan, South Africans, Italians, Greeks, South Americans, Argentines, Colombians, Venezuelans, Bolivians, a lot of black people ... Chinese from every-where ... since Switzerland closed down, they are going to the United States and Canada ... Toronto, Vancouver, California ... Miami.

For the mass of the region's population, television was a major service sector innovation, which crossed boundaries that had stopped the press almost as readily as radio. The overwhelming majority of the Ontario population could receive signals broadcast by the major US networks from such places as Buffalo and Detroit. The publicly-owned Canadian Broadcasting Corporation (CBC) began English-language television broadcasting based in Toronto in the early 1950s. By the mid-1960s Toronto had its first French-language CBC radio station. By the late 1970s two privately-owned Canadian television networks were also broadcasting in Ontario, along with a multilingual television service and an educational television network funded by the provincial government. Ontario had twenty-six originating television stations broadcasting in English and two originating stations broadcasting in French.

Many Ontario-born Canadians with large ambitions, such as J.K. Galbraith from the rural southwest or the singer Paul Anka and the comic Dan Ackroyd (both from Ottawa), continued to pursue careers in the United States. But more"rare" kinds of services were also becoming more common in the region. In the 1960s Marshall McLuhan of Toronto (born in Alberta) became one of the first English-language writers to try to say what television meant, drawing on themes developed earlier in Harold Innis' writing on "the bias of communication". In the 1950s and 1960s Johnny Wayne and Frank Shuster brought a local variation on the continental tradition of the Jewish comic to Canadian television. In the later 1970s and early 1980s, the "slick and weird" comics of Second City Television (with earlier connections to Chicago) reached out for a continental audience from a Canadian base.

259

In the more traditional world of books, such writers as Margaret Atwood, Alice Munro, and Margaret Laurence (who moved from rural Manitoba to the rural village of Lakefield, Ontario) revived the much earlier regional tradition of "the gentlewoman in Upper Canada" in modern form. The New York critic Edmund Wilson helped give Morley Callaghan's career of the 1920s and 1930s a second lease on life.

In recorded music, Glenn Gould of Toronto became a noted interpreter of the classical piano music of Bach. By the early 1980s Oscar Peterson (who moved from Montreal, where his father had been a railway porter, to the Toronto satellite city of Mississauga) had become one of the world's most admired jazz piano players. Gordon Lightfoot from Orillia (the original "little town" in Stephen Leacock's *Sunshine Sketches*) brought the mood of the Great Lakes to North American country music.

In sports, the Toronto Maple Leafs won nine Stanley Cup championships from 1945 to 1967. A Canadian Football League flourished with teams in nine cities, including Ottawa, Toronto, and Hamilton. By the late 1970s Toronto had a North American major-league baseball team – the Blue Jays – competing in the "American League" (though the Detroit Tigers remained a sentimental favourite in southwestern Ontario).

Taken at large, if the regional society in the early 1980s still had an unfinished shape, Ontario was nonetheless a much different place than it had been at the end of the Second World War. The end of the long boom had brought new economic problems. But the long boom had also created new energies, new people, and new ambitions. "It is about time that Canada entered history," Charles de Gaulle had declared in the early 1960s. By the early 1980s, in Canada's most populous province, it seemed that it had.

14

A New Compromise

Ontario politics after the Second World War is about the adaptation of nineteenth-century public institutions to the new postwar society of the mid to late twentieth century. Two of the three major Ontario political parties that had evolved by the late 1930s assumed new names, following trends in Canadian national politics. The old Liberal Conservatives and then National Conservatives first ran as Progressive Conservatives in the provincial election of 1943. The CCF became the New Democratic Party (NDP) in 1961.

The Ontario Liberals were perhaps the least successful in accommodating new circumstances. Somewhat haunted by the turbulent legacy of Mitch Hepburn, they remained unimaginatively attached to the outlook of the old agrarian society, with their support concentrated in the pre-Confederation Grit stronghold of the southwest. They had increasingly little to say to the new urban industrial world that had become unambiguously dominant in regional public life by the early 1950s. Part of the explanation was that more innovative forces in Ontario Liberalism were preoccupied with Canadian federal politics.

The Liberals' one achievement in post Second World War Ontario, however, was to survive as a significant political force. This defied a much discussed view of the future, which saw Ontario politics following developments in the United Kingdom. There the progress of the industrial revolution had squeezed British Liberals into insignificance between a dominant democratic conservative party on the right and a dominant democratic socialist party on the left.

The most ardent proponent of this view was the CCF/NDP. Radically-minded Orangemen had been among the founders of the CCF in the 1930s. In some ways the post Second World War CCF/NDP in Ontario remained more loyal to the region's historic British political institutions than the Tories. If the party eventually became only mildly socialistic by European standards, the experience of the British Labour Party was highly influential among CCF/NDP activists. Ontario's left-wing party responded to changes in the region's cultural composition by broadening its vision to embrace the concerns of postwar "social democratic" parties in West Germany, France, and (particularly) Sweden.

The CCF/NDP's one achievement, especially after 1961, was to build a highly professional political party that did in many ways live up to its social democratic models. One of its problems was that, despite increasing similarities, the social structures of western Europe and North America remained different. During the period from the end of the Second World War to the early 1980s, the CCF/NDP actually formed provincial governments in three of the four provinces of western Canada. There (though British Columbia remained a different case again) it retained some institutional memory of "populism" and the old North American agrarian democracy, whose political vision was being inherited by much of the growing suburban, white-collar middle class. In Ontario, where it became more like a European labour party, it had to be content with replacing the Liberals as "Official Opposition" on three separate occasions – 1943, 1948, and 1975.

With both Liberals and CCF/NDP dividing the opposition, the Progressive Conservatives monopolized the power to govern. Without once winning a majority of the popular vote (it came closest in the mid-1950s), a new kind of Conservative Party won a majority of seats in the legislature again and again, and even on three occasions when it did not win a majority of seats, it retained the power to govern. It finally surpassed the old Great Reform record for political longevity in the region in the later 1970s.

Wasaga Beach in the summer of 1946: part of an earlier twentieth-century Ontario that had begun to change forever by the late 1940s.

"Colonel" George Drew, who began the postwar "PC" regime by forming a precarious minority government after the election of 1943, was a transitional figure, linking the Tory past with the Progressive Conservative future. The man who finally forged an up-to-date political compromise that would govern the province while the new society took shape was "Old Man Ontario", Leslie Frost, Provincial Treasurer under Drew and Premier from 1949 to 1961.

The Rise of the CCF

In 1943 it seemed quite possible that Ontario or even Canada as a whole was about to embark on a political journey pioneered during the previous two decades in the United Kingdom. The First World War had stirred up the radicalism expressed by the Farmer-Labour Government of 1919-1923. The Second World War stirred up a new radicalism, expressed in a dramatic surge of support for the Canadian socialism of the Co-operative Commonwealth Federation.

The CCF's first decade after its formation in 1932 had not been a conspicuous success. It had won one seat in the Ontario provincial election of 1934, and no seats in 1937. In the Canadian federal election of 1940, it won only one-twelfth of the national popular vote.

The Western alliance with the Soviet Union in the "fight against fascism" after 1941, however, helped insulate the CCF in Canada from the "red scare" rhetoric of the 1920s and 1930s. At the same time, Mackenzie King's Canadian federal government was imposing a wartime regime of national economic planning, similar in principle to what the CCF had long been proposing for peacetime. This did appear to have at last solved the problems of the 1930s depression. The centrally-guided wartime economy helped generate an increase of almost eighty per cent in Ontario manufacturing employment between 1939 and 1943.

The first concrete sign of political change came with a major CCF victory in a federal by-election in the Toronto area riding of York South early in 1942. By the end of that year, the Gallup Poll was reporting that, if an election were held at the moment thirty-two per cent of Ontario voters would support each of the Liberals and Conservatives. But as many as twenty-seven per cent would support the CCF. Subsequent polls showed steady increases in CCF support.

The "returned Rhodes scholar", Ted Jolliffe, had become the first provincial leader of the party in Ontario early in 1942, signalling a new CCF enthusiasm for provincial politics[1]. In some quarters, wartime sacrifices were helping to promote political radicalism. The old ex-Liberal CCF stalwart, Elmore Philpott, discovered that "the CCF represents to an ever increasing mass of ordinary people the hope of a better after-the-war world". By April 1943 The Ontario CCF was declaring itself "prepared to assume the responsibilities of office at the earliest occasion".

Though it could look back to Whitney and Hearst or even John A. Macdonald, in a very direct way postwar "progressive conservatism" was itself a creation of the sudden burst of CCF popularity in the early 1940s. The defeated Conservative in the York South by-election was Arthur Meighen, an old paragon of Canadian Toryism who had led the federal party in the 1920s, and had once again become Conservative leader. Meighen's by-election defeat at the hands of the CCF candidate, Joseph Noseworthy, precipitated the elevation of the surviving Canadian Progressive, John Bracken from Manitoba, as federal leader of a new Progressive Conservative Party.

In Ontario, George Drew elaborated the new theme by running in the 1943 provincial election on a "Twenty-Two Point Programme" of progressive conservative reform. Provincial Liberal advertising during the campaign featured a cartoon of Ted Jolliffe in a rowboat, with George Drew in the water beside him, asking for the loan of Jolliffe's boat: "I'll give it back after the election".

In Canadian federal politics, John Bracken would prove no match for Mackenzie King. But in Ontario, with the Liberals still suffering from the disarray of Mitch Hepburn's "phantom government", George Drew's new Progressive Conservatives won four more seats than the CCF in 1943 – enough to form a precarious minority government, committed to at least some reforms that the CCF felt bound to support. Nonetheless, marking the extent of electoral radicalism, along with thirty-four CCF seats, the 1943 Ontario election also saw seats go to Albert MacLeod and Joseph Salsberg of Toronto – members of a new "Labour Progressive Party", widely recognized as a Communist front.

To complicate matters, the defeated former Liberal Premier, Harry Nixon, with his supporters reduced to sixteen seats, engineered a return of the Liberal leadership to Mitch Hepburn late in 1944. Salsberg and MacLeod, following the Canadian Communist policy of the day, supported a progressive common front with the Liberals. And Hepburn, having now returned to his earliest view that "Toryism" was the ultimate problem in Ontario, tried to interest Jolliffe in a coalition government that could take over from Drew without a fresh election. Jolliffe heard him out, but refused. With Hepburn enjoying a final lease on political life, however, the position of Drew's minority government became increasingly precarious.

Yet once he had time to establish the credibility of his new progressive conservative regime, George Drew welcomed the prospect of a defeat in the Legislative Assembly, since he felt increasingly confident that he could win a majority in a fresh election. Hepburn had discredited himself by changing spots too many times. In 1943 the CCF had won only thirty-two per cent of the popular vote, with only fifty-eight per cent of the registered electorate voting. Its leadership was still very inexperienced. It had won strong support in the north and in the blue-collar urban areas of the south. But it had little appeal in the countryside or among the growing white-collar middle class.

Moreover, unlike its New Democratic successors of the 1960s and 1970s, the Ontario CCF of the 1940s preached a very fundamentalist brand of socialism. It believed in nationalization or public ownership of "the commanding heights of the economy", including the banks and the insurance companies. Not surprisingly, those who commanded the heights for the moment took it upon themselves to see that the electorate understood what such "state socialism" could mean for private property, personal freedom, and the "Canadian way – the spirit of friendly and open competition". When a CCF provincial government actually came to power under T.C. Douglas in Saskatchewan in June 1944 – claiming itself "a beachhead of socialism on a continent of capitalism" – private business funding for anti-socialist propaganda grew stronger.

266

By the spring of 1945, Drew's government had been defeated in the Ontario Assembly, and an election was called for early June (only one week before a decisive federal election of the same year). In the campaign Ted Jolliffe tried to launch his own propaganda by accusing "Colonel Drew", with some rather exaggerated justice, of keeping a secret political "Gestapo" to spy on CCF members. More than seventy per cent of the electorate voted, and when the results were counted Drew's Progressive Conservatives had won forty-four per cent of the popular vote and sixty-six seats. The Liberals had fourteen seats, and the CCF was reduced to eight seats, with twenty-two per cent of the popular vote. The Communists Salsberg and MacLeod retained their seats. But Mitch Hepburn and Ted Jolliffe lost theirs along with the CCF members Agnes Macphail and Mrs. Rae Luckock, who in 1943 had become the first women elected to the Legislative Assembly of Ontario.

Despite its reverses in 1945, the CCF had established itself as a significant new element in Ontario politics. In the provincial election of 1948 it staged a modest comeback. It won twenty-seven per cent of the popular vote and twenty-one seats. (Industrial manufacturing was reaching the peak of its relative importance in the regional labour force, and in the same year Henry Wallace ran as the last Presidential candidate of a Progressive Party in the United States. Down to the early 1980s, both the CCF and its New Democratic successor would never again quite equal the sudden socialistic surge of strength in 1943. "Ontario socialism" would live through a very lean period in the 1950s. But in the ten provincial elections from 1951 to 1981, the party would continue to win an average of about twenty-three per cent of the popular vote.

Imperial Twilight

Perhaps the Ontario CCF's largest achievement in the early 1940s, however, was to stimulate the creation of the Ontario Progressive Conservatives, as the CCF nationally stimulated a revival of the reforming spirit in Mackenzie King's federal Liberal Party. It is possible to dispute the importance of the shift to progressive conservatism after

267

1943, to point out that it had all happened before under Whitney and Hearst or even John A. Macdonald in the later 1850s. But the new PCs were clearly different from Howard Ferguson's Ontario Tories of the 1920s. And the formal identification with the old progressive cause had at least strategic significance.

On the one hand, it helped prevent more moderate strains in the earlier urban and (especially) rural progressive vote, that had finally given up on Hepburn's Liberals, from looking toward the CCF/NDP. On the other, it helped thwart any attempt by the post-Hepburn Liberals to take up some centre ground between conservative and socialist extremes. The progressive conservative strategy could not work in Canadian federal politics, where circumstances were different. Yet time would prove that it worked very well indeed in Ontario. As in the past, the price of success was to give up on something of an earlier Toryism. In some ways, the best historical precedent for the new governing regime was Oliver Mowat's Ontario Great Reform Government of the late nineteenth century, with its "blend of conservatism and reform, of caution and advancement".

George Drew was a somewhat unlikely figure to preside over the beginnings of the regime. He was the son of an old Loyalist political family from the Guelph area and the last Ontario Premier who identified strongly with the imperial civilization of the British Empire. He had made an early reputation writing books on Canadian military history. Throughout his life, his favourite article of clothing remained the red and blue artillery tie. He promoted British immigration to Ontario and had only a limited sympathy with French Canada. Like Howard Ferguson, he both served as his own Minister of Education and finally ended his political career as Canadian High Commissioner to the United Kingdom (from 1957 to 1963).

At the same time, perhaps only someone with George Drew's background could have mastered the transition from the Ontario Toryism of the 1920s and 1930s to the new reforming conservatism of the mid-twentieth century. During his period of enthusiasm for Hepburn's anticommunist "Union Government" proposal of the later 1930s, Drew had at least briefly come to doubt the continuing validity of the old "two-party system". In him, as in some others (Winston Churchill was perhaps the metropolitan model), the imperial spirit bred a broad-minded sense of historical change.

According to legend, Drew jotted down the "Twenty-Two Points" that formed the core of the new progressive conservative programme on the back of an envelope during the early days of the 1943 election campaign. Among the key points were:

- Municipal tax reform, with the province reducing total property tax burdens by paying fifty per cent of education costs;
- Major reform of the provincial education system to equalize educational opportunites;
- Publicly-supported medical, dental, and other health protection programmes;
- Establishment of an Ontario Housing Corporation;
- Immediate increases in mother's allowance, and increases in provincial old-age pensions;
- The "fairest and most advanced" labour laws in Canada;
- New marketing boards and public ownership of stockyards, in support of southern agriculture;
- Tax and other incentives for northern mining, and a major programme of timber management and reforestation.

The Twenty-Two points were an agenda for a generation of progressive conservatism, not a programme to be completely implemented during Drew's own five years in office. Many promises would take time to fulfill. Drew's original document would even be revived as an "Ontario Charter" in the provincial election of 1977, when the PCs once again felt themselves under strong pressure from the "social democratic" left.

Drew made a start on implementing the programme. He was also the last uncompromising defender of the Ontario regional state, however, and partly because of this his progress on the social policy dimensions of the Twenty-Two Points was halting. Nonetheless, Drew's government had a genuine reforming side, mixed in, as under Mowat, with strong doses of regional economic boosterism. He added three new ministers to the thirteen

269

cabinet positions that had developed by the end of Hepburn's Liberal government. The most important was Minister of Planning and Development, an office first filled by Dana Harris Porter from the Toronto riding of St. George. He was a fifteen year stalwart of the early PC regime, who would later serve as Minister of Education, Attorney-General, and Provincial Treasurer.

The other new positions were Minister of Travel and Publicity, and Minister of Reform Institutions, an area of at least social concern where some early progress was made. Under George Henry Doucette, Minister of Public Works and Highways (from the southeastern riding of Lanark), the Drew government also laid the foundations of southern Ontario's superhighway system. By 1949 the province's first four-lane restricted access highway – the Queen Elizabeth Way, from Toronto to the American border at Buffalo – had been completed[2]. Work had begun on an east-west Highway 401 from the Quebec border to the Michigan border at Windsor (southern Ontario's "Main Street"), and a "Holiday Highway" 400 from Toronto north to Barrie on Lake Simcoe (the most modern expression of the old Toronto Passage).

Two of Drew's particular reforms were linked with his ultimate departure from Ontario politics in 1948. By the later 1940s it had become clear that major new public investment in the Hydro-Electric Power Commission of Ontario would be required to accommodate a new era of economic growth, and to convert the region's 25-cycle electical system to the more efficient 60-cycle system that prevailed in both the United States and the Province of Quebec. Drew claimed he needed a fresh mandate from the people to sustain such an expenditure and called an election for early June 1948. It was speculated that, in fact, he anticipated the federal Progressive Conservative leadership would soon become available, and wanted to enter the federal leadership race on the heels of a provincial election victory.

The Ontario PCs dropped to fifty-four seats in the provincial election of 1948, with the CCF rising to twenty-one seats and the Liberals remaining at fourteen. This still left the PCs with a comfortable governing majority. But, not long before the election Drew's reforming instincts prompted him to introduce new elements of moderation into the draconian Ontario liquor laws left over from the ending of Prohibition in the late 1920s[3]. This was enough to bring about his personal defeat in the Toronto riding of High Park at the hands of the CCF teetotaler and staunch temperance advocate, William Temple. Despite this minor setback, early in October 1948 George Drew replaced John Bracken as leader of the federal Progressive Conservative Party at Ottawa, where he would prove that what had worked so well in Ontario could not defeat the "continentalist" Liberal regime that Louis St. Laurent had inherited from the grandson of William Lyon Mackenzie.

Old Man Ontario

Drew officially resigned as Premier of Ontario on 19 October 1948, appointing his popular 69 year-old Minister of Agriculture, T.L.Kennedy, as interim successor. In April 1949 the Ontario Progressive Conservatives held a convention to choose a new leader. To the surprise of many, the contest was finally won by Drew's Provincial Treasurer, Leslie Miscampbell Frost, from Lindsay in the central Ontario riding of Victoria. Frost assumed office in May 1949 and would remain Premier until November 1961, the second longest individual term of office after Oliver Mowat's twenty-four years.

A key ingredient in Frost's final victory at the 1949 convention had been the support of A.D. Mackenzie, a shy but brilliant political mechanic whom Drew had appointed PC party organizer in 1942. Under Mackenzie, the long-standing regional tradition of political management became a professional specialization. According to journalist Jonathan Manthorpe, he "had a Conservative ward heeler not merely in every riding, but in every poll of the province". It was said that scarcely a day of Frost's long regime went by without a meeting between the Premier and the PC party organizer. Mackenzie's death in 1960 was seen by many as an important factor in Frost's decision to resign as Premier in 1961.

By background and temperament, Frost was much more suited to the task of forging a new progressive conservative compromise than was Drew. Some saw him as "a

271

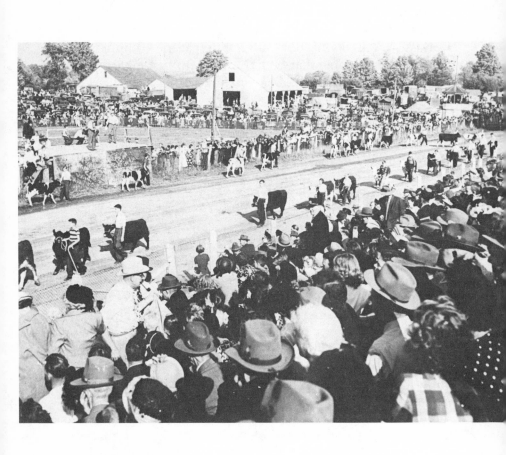

4H Club calves at Teeswater Fair, Bruce County, 1951: the sunset years of an old rural Ontario, that would itself be transformed into something quite different a generation later.

'small town' man with a limited intellectual horizon". But a magazine article of the mid-1950s noted that the Premier of Ontario

> has collected quite a library on Abraham Lincoln, though, characteristically, he admits to some senti-mental sympathy for the South.... He has sometimes been accused of being a Liberal at heart and certainly he is no flag-waving Tory of the old school; in fact, he disclaims any party philosophy.

Under "the Silver Fox" (Frost's hair had gone gray early), progressive conservatism in Ontario developed a remark-able capacity to bring diverse strands of the region's past together. Frost befriended Ontario's two Communist legis-lators, Salsberg and MacLeod, whom he saw simply as "radicals" with a rash zest for improving the province. (In fact, both men left the Communist Party of Canada when the Russians invaded Hungary in 1956). Salsberg finally lost his seat in the provincial election of 1955. MacLeod had lost his in 1951, but in the early 1960s he went to work as a civil servant in the Ontario Department of Education.

Frost also had a strong interest in the history of Ontario, especially the "forgotten history" of the region's French and Indian past. He played an important role in funding the excavation of the seventeenth-century Jesuit mission at Ste. Marie among the Hurons. He initiated a series of historical document collections in conjunction with a group known as the Champlain Society. And he encouraged the work of E.C. Drury (the "Farmer Premier" of 1919-1923) on the historical legacy of Huronia in the Simcoe County area. The last restrictions on the voting rights of Ontario Indians were removed in 1954[4]. After his retirement as Premier, Frost would write his own book on Ontario during the French and Indian period. His cabinet included two French Canadian ministers, George Doucette (an important supporter of Frost in the leader-ship race of 1949) and Louis Pierre Cécille from the Ottawa valley riding of Prescott.

At the centre of even progressive conservatism was the fundamental belief that govenment's primary economic role was "to clear the way for the private sector". Frost's programme, a newspaper editorial intoned shortly before the 1951 election, "can be summed up in one word – development ... development of Ontario's population, of its power resources, its highway system, its forest and mineral wealth, and its industrial strength". The Frost regime gave a particularly warm welcome to capital and business interests from the United States, prompting the President of the New York Stock Exchange to declare in 1953: "We envy the environment in which capital is encouraged to work in Canada and the respect accorded to the risk-taker".

At the same time, as the Twenty-Two Points implied, progressive conservative government was to be, in Frost's words, "a partnership between the two philosophies of economic advance and human betterment". Thus "Old Man Ontario" – Frost's favourite nickname and during the earlier twentieth century a political cartoon character in the old Toronto *Globe* – laid the foundations of the Ontario "service state", that would rise to its fullest height in the 1960s and early 1970s.

A Fair Employment Practices Act and Female Employees Fair Remuneration Act appeared in 1951. An increased mother's allowance and a new pension for the disabled appeared in 1952. There was a new Child Welfare Act in 1954. Extended provincial allowances to Indian bands and a new Rehabilitation Services Act came in 1955. In 1956 an Ontario Hospital Services Commission and a new Charitable Institutions Act appeared. There was a new General Welfare Assistance Act in 1958, and – an early sign of the region's increasing cultural diversity – an Anti-Discrimination Commission (renamed the Ontario Human Rights Commission in 1961).

The Frost regime also carried the highway building plans of the late 1940s forward vigorously and began a programme of new school construction that would blossom in the 1960s. It pursued reforms in municipal government and land-use planning and created the Municipality of Metropolitan Toronto in 1954 – the first working example of a "metropolitan federation" in North America. On advice from US President Dwight D. Eisenhower at an Ottawa dinner in 1953 ("don't let them ruin your water. We have ruined ours in the States"), Frost established an

Ontario Water Resources Commission under the chairmanship of John Robarts from London, Ontario.

Frost's version of active government was reflected in the provincial budget, which rose from about $300 million in 1949 to more than $1 billion in 1961. It was also reflected in a growing provincial civil service, which doubled from about 7,500 employees at the end of the Second World War to some 15,000 employees in the early 1950s and then doubled again by 1960.

Despite the growth in numbers, Frost's regime would be the last Ontario government where the tradition of political management remained close to the surface of day to day administration. For all his public geniality, the Premier played politics hard and was something of an authoritarian figure in cabinet. Frost served as his own Provincial Treasurer (like Mitch Hepburn) for the first six years of his regime, and it was said that he had his personal "spies" in every civil service department. Scandals in the Department of Highways and in connection with a new Northern Ontario Natural Gas Company fostered some early beginnings of change. But Frost continued to view problems of government management, as he liked to put it, from the standpoint of "the man in the barber's chair at Lindsay".

Federal-Provincial Co-operation and the New Party

At the end of the Second World War, both Ontario and Quebec took steps to recover the provincial tax powers surrendered to Ottawa as a wartime emergency measure in exchange for federal grants. In 1947 Mackenzie King's government had made arrangements to continue "renting" provincial tax powers from the other seven (soon to be eight) Canadian provinces for a five-year period. But George Drew in Ontario and Maurice Duplessis in Quebec refused the federal deal on behalf of the more than sixty per cent of the Canadian population who lived in the "central" provinces.

Drew, like Duplessis, also looked askance at new federal ambitions to set national standards and to assume new powers in such fields as old age pensions, unemployment assistance, health insurance, public works, and resource development. Quebec would continue its resistance to increased federal power in Confederation over the next three decades, a theme that would gradually become mixed in with a growing Quebec independence movement. But George Drew would be the last uncompromising defender of the tradition of the Ontario regional state begun by Oliver Mowat, with the support of Honoré Mercier in Quebec, some three quarters of a century before.

In 1949, the year after Drew left provincial politics, appeals of Canadian court decisions to the British Judicial Committee of the Privy Council, that had done so much to confirm Mowat's view of provincial rights, were discontinued by a statute of the Canadian federal parliament. Canada began the final steps in its long journey from colony to nation[5]. In 1950 Leslie Frost declared Ontario's intention to pursue a new "spirit of co-operation" in federal-provincial relations. Frost did not exactly give up on the old claims of the regional state, but he began a process of moderation that would carry through to the early 1980s (and beyond).

With some reservations, in 1952 Ontario joined a new round of five-year tax rental agreements with the federal government, though it rented only its rights to personal income not corporation taxes. In 1957 it accepted another round of agreements, incorporating the principle of "equalization grants" to less wealthy provinces as advocated by the Rowell-Sirois Commission in the early 1940s. Under Old Man Ontario, Canada's most populous province at last acknowledged Harold Innis' dictum of the 1930s: "an empire has its obligations as well as its opportunities". In an address to the Manitoba Union of Municipalities in 1953, Leslie Frost declared: "The flourishing conditions in Ontario are dependent upon similar conditions in other provinces".

It woud be wrong to imply that Ontario's motivations in its historic rapprochement with federal power which began in the 1950s were completely or even largely altruistic. Federal-provincial co-operation was crucial to the St. Lawrence Seaway, which brought Ontario new hydroelectric resources when it was finally completed in 1959. It was vital to the joint efforts of the Hydro-Electric Power Commission of Ontario and the Atomic Energy Commission of Canada, that led to Ontario's (and Canada's) first nuclear-powered electrical generating station at Rolphton on the

Leslie Miscampbell Frost: "Old Man Ontario" (also known as the "Silver Fox" and the "Great Tranquillizer"). Frost began his career as a small-town lawyer in Lindsay, Victoria County. In "the end," journalist Johnathan Manthorpe has written, "even Lindsay appeared to Old Man Ontario to have changed.... 'It's got so I don't know the people any more. And most of them don't know me.'"

Ottawa River in 1962. It played an important role in the Trans-Canada Highway that would do for northern Ontario what the QEW and Highways 400 and 401 were doing for the south. And it was at the centre of the Frost regime's early development of the Ontario social service state.

Moreover, with Toronto's growing strength in its historic commercial and financial rivalry with Montreal, Ontario had (for the time being, at least) outgrown the old strategy of province building. One of Frost's key economic development concerns was ensuring central Canadian access to western Canadian natural gas. The new federal-provincial co-operation proved its worth in 1952, when the federal Minister of Trade and Commerce, C.D. Howe, told Alberta Premier E.C. Manning, in Leslie Frost's presence, that Ottawa would not allow any gas exports to the American midwest "unless the needs of central and eastern Canada were provided for first". Frost and Howe developed a warm friendship based on a shared philosophy of postwar development in Canada. The grand design would ultimately grate against new province building aspirations in the West. But at the time of Howe's death and Frost's departure from Ontario politics in 1961, all this was in the future.

On his own testimony, Leslie Frost decided to resign as Ontario Premier in the early 1960s because he was getting older: "This is a young person's world. Young people should run it". He had won three elections – in 1951, 1955, and 1959. In 1951 and 1955 he had won well over three quarters of the seats in the Ontario legislature and almost (but not quite) a majority of the popular vote. The victory of 1959 was somewhat less impressive. Though Frost's PCS took just under three quarters of the seats, the Liberals, under J.J. Wintermeyer from the Kitchener area riding of Waterloo North, showed new strength with twenty-two seats (double their number in 1955) and thirty-seven per cent of the popular vote.

Frost's regime (and the general economic climate of the 1950s) had been particularly hard on the CCF. In his three elections they consistently won somewhat less than twenty per cent of the vote and managed only two seats in 1951, three in 1955, and five in 1959. In western Canada as

278

well, by the later 1950s the CCF had become what a book on the subject termed "A Protest Movement Becalmed". The great postwar boom had made the fiery socialism of the early 1940s, bred in the 1930s depression, seem fundamentally out of touch.

As the 1950s progressed, two different responses developed within the party, both in Ontario and in its western Canadian birthplace. Some saw a need to huddle around the glow of the old-time religion and take what Frank Underhill referred to as "peculiarly holy pleasure in punishing erring brethren". Others, following the lead of Hugh Gaitskell and the new Penguin volume *Twentieth Century Socialism* in the United Kingdom, saw a need to reach out for some broader status as, in the words of British Columbia CCF activist, Pauline Jewett, "a majority party of the moderate left".

By 1961 the supporters of a more moderate "New Party" had triumphed. During a very hot early August in Ottawa, the old CCF became the New Democratic Party, at the largest and longest political convention in Canadian history. The new party, it was reported, advocated "a planned economy, although not necessarily a socialist one". In Ontario the transition from the CCF to the New Democratic Party was not a major event. Donald MacDonald from the Toronto area, who had replaced Ted Jolliffe as Ontario CCF leader in the mid-1950s, remained as leader of the Ontario New Democrats. It was said that more active support from organized labour was an advantage of the new arrangements. But organized labour had been an important ingredient in the Ontario CCF since the 1940s. In 1952 Underhill, one of the authors of the "Regina Manifesto" that had given birth to the CCF in the early 1930s, complained that the Ontario CCF "is too much under the influence of the United Steelworkers and its close allies in the CCL"[6]. The CCL or Canadian Congress of Labour, which had become Canada's variation on John L. Lewis' CIO in the United States, broadened its own base when it joined with the earlier Trades and Labour Congress to form the Canadian Labour Congress in 1955. But above all else, Mitch Hepburn had made certain that the CCF/NDP would be Ontario's party of organized labour in the later 1930s.

279

The founding of the New Democratic Party on a new wave of youthful enthusiasm in 1961, however, did almost exactly coincide with Leslie Frost's announcement of his intention to resign as PC party leader and Premier of Ontario. In the United States the 43 year-old Democratic President John F. Kennedy had recently declared that "the torch has been passed to a new generation". And for the good of his party, Old Man Ontario had decided it was time to follow suit.

15

PC Dynasty

The 1960s and 1970s had a calmer surface in Ontario than in many other places. As elsewhere, the period began with a swing to the left politically and ended with a swing to the right. But these shifts were expressed by changes within the ruling Progressive Conservative dynasty, not by a change of the party commanding the governmental machine.

Improvements in the electoral fortunes of the opposition Liberals and New Democrats brought important pressures on the PCs. To no small extent, it was the willingness of successive PC regimes to accommodate these pressures that enabled the party to surpass the old Great Reform record for political longevity in 1977. Throughout the half dozen years from 1975 to 1981, the PCs actually governed while commanding only a minority of seats in the legislature.

Both practical events and the spirit of Leslie Frost, who had disclaimed "any party philosophy", continued to nibble away at the traditions of an earlier Toryism. By 1980 many (probably most) younger people in the province had never heard of "an Orangeman". The old British imperialist spirit – once a hallmark of Ontario Toryism – survived largely as a minor matter of local style and official imagery.

Similarly, the new compromise forged in the 1950s meant that in Ontario the swings to the left and then right which marked the 1960s and 1970s were characterized by, above all else, moderation. If John Robarts, who succeeded

Frost as Premier in 1961, was a "left-wing conservative", William Davis, who succeeded Robarts in 1971, proved to be a"right-wing progressive".

The Rise of the Service State

John Robarts became Premier of Ontario when, at the age of forty-four, he won a PC leadership convention held at Varsity Arena in Toronto during a late fall warm spell in 1961. His family had moved from Alberta to London, Ontario when he was thirteen. And he was the first Premier of Ontario born outside the province since Confederation.

Robarts had been a London lawyer and municipal politician before entering provincial politics in the early 1950s. After serving as first Chairman of the Ontario Water Resources Commission, he had become Frost's Minister of Education in 1959. He enjoyed hunting and fishing trips and struck one journalist as "an untormented political version of Ernest Hemingway".

Robarts retained progressive conservatism's particular respect for the economic capabilities of "the private sector". In 1963 the entrepreneurially-minded Stanley Randall became Minister of Economics (formerly Planning) and Development[1]. And Randall became known for a characteristic injunction to his civil servants: "Show me a resource, and I'll sell it."

Above all else, however, Robarts was, in his own words, "a management man" in "the era of the management man ... a complete product of the times." He himself would become known for his efforts to promote the human betterment side of the partnership with economic advance, by building a large-scale regional service state on a model that might be expected to attract a North American management man of the 1950s and 1960s.

Robarts' service state was a fulfilment of trends that had been developing for three-quarters of a century or more: spadework by Frost in the 1950s; Drew's Twenty-Two Points; appointment of new Ministers of Labour, Health, Public Welfare, and Municipal Affairs between the two world wars; Whitney and Hearst's early twentieth-century anticipations of progressive conservatism; and

282

John Robarts, Premier 1961-1971. Under Robarts, Progressive Conservatism in Ontario at last made substantial inroads on the historic Grit stronghold of the southwest. Robarts had decided to run for PC party leader at his friend Ernie Jackson's cottage in the Grand Bend area on Lake Huron, a traditional summer resort of the London business gentry. And the press would dub his cronies the "London Mafia".

even Mowat's early labour and social policy legislation of the late nineteenth century. In some of its aspects, the new service state could be traced back to the start of large-scale state support for mass education in the 1840s and 1850s.

In the form it had arrived at when Robarts left office in 1971, the Ontario service state had two main dimensions. One was an income security system for various minorities of the population who were temporarily, or in some cases permanently, not competing in the labour force or in private commerce and finance. Another was a more general system to enhance access for the broad "employed" majority to opportunities in such matters as education, housing, and health care.

Both dimensions were sustained by a complex network of federal, provincial, and municipal financial and administrative arrangements. Though federal money and a degree of homage to "national standards" were important, the province was at the focus of the bureaucratic mechanism, since that was where the fundamental power in such matters lay under the Canadian constitution inherited from the old British North America Act.

For the largest majority of the population, perhaps the two most important of the new public services were a guaranteed minimum pension or annual income for all persons sixty-five and older as well as a public health insurance system (finally named the Ontario Health Insurance Plan in 1972) which, for a small regular premium, paid virtually all hospital and doctor bills up to a minimum standard of service. The federal government played an important role in both programmes, in addition to providing for unemployment insurance from 1941 onward.

The federal and municipal governments also played important roles in those branches of the new Ontario service state that dealt with housing, social services, and education. Ontario's first modern "public housing" project at Regent Park in Toronto had been started by the Toronto city council in the late 1940s without provincial assistance. But an Ontario Housing Corporation was established in 1964, some twenty years after it was first promised in George Drew's Twenty-Two Points. With financial support from the federal Canada Assistance Plan, the pace of development in a wide variety of social programmes quickened after 1969 through the old provincial Department of Public Welfare. It ultimately became the new Ministry of Community and Social Services, with responsibility for more than thirty separate pieces of legislation, including a Charitable Institutions Act, a Child Welfare Act, a Day Nurseries Act, a District Welfare Administration Boards Act, a Family Benefits Act, a General Welfare Assistance Act, a Homes for Retarded Persons Act, a Homes for the Aged and Rest Homes Act, an Indian Welfare Services Act, a Training Schools Act, a Unified Family Court Act, and a Vocational Rehabilitation Services Act.

To no small extent, education was seen as the fundamental engine of progress in the new service state. In 1947 Harold Innis had contributed to a Manitoba Royal Commission on Adult Education. He himself had been educated in Ontario elementary and secondary schools as well as at McMaster University in Canada and the University of Chicago in the United States. He had become Dean of the School of Graduate Studies at the University of Toronto. Not long before his death in 1952, he would be elected President of the American Economic Association. He declared:

> We have assumed that government in democratic countries is based on the will of the governed, that people can make up their minds.... This implies that the state is concerned with strengthening intellectual capacity....
>
> ... It also implies that adults have been so trained in the education system that they can choose the facts and reach their own decisions. We should ... be concerned like the Greeks with making men, not with overwhelming them by facts.... Education is the basis of the state and its ultimate aim and essence is the training of character.

Under John Robarts' Minister of Education, William Davis, in the 1960s and early 1970s Ontario's old mass education system was dramatically expanded and reformed. At the elementary and secondary levels, the need to accommodate the postwar baby boom and new immigration and

285

a drive to equalize educational opportunities in urban and rural areas led to a major wave of new school construction. The old *Ontario Readers*, with their exhortations on the ideals of British imperial civilization, had long since vanished. The Hall-Dennis Commission of the mid-1960s popularized many of the themes urged earlier by Harold Innis and others[2], and it signalled the first major challenge to the region's old centralizing bias in education since the 1870s. By the early 1970s province-wide Grade 13 high school graduation examinations had been abandoned in response to what were seen at the time as more enlightened priorities of personal freedom and social variety.

At the post-secondary level, Ontario established a completely new system of some twenty "community colleges", specializing in technical and vocational training. The region's university system, traditionally dominated by Queen's, Western, and Toronto, was expanded. By the early 1970s there were two French language and more than a dozen English language universities in the province, including such smaller schools as Brock, Lakehead, Laurentian, Trent, Wilfrid Laurier, and Waterloo. Both the provincial and federal governments were involved in a system of student loans and grants designed to promote access to "higher education" for the mass of the population. The provincial government had established an Ontario Institute for Studies in Education and an Ontario Educational Communications Authority, which would ultimately operate what amounted to a publicly-funded regional television network.

In response to the priorities of the "management man", the provincial government made significant efforts to "rationalize" the financial and administrative base of the new elementary and secondary education. Many small local school boards, left over from an era when transportation and communications in the region were much slower, were consolidated. The process culminated with a completely new system of county school boards in 1968.

The same logic could be applied to Ontario's municipal system, a "creature of the province" and much involved in the provision of public services since its beginnings in the mid-nineteenth century. Under W. Darcy McKeough (the "Duke of Kent" from the Chatham area who became Robarts' Minister of Municipal Affairs in 1967), plans were developed for major new "regional government" reforms, that would extend the principles of the mid-1950s Metropolitan Toronto federation to other parts of the province. Provincial grants to municipalities would increase to the point where they accounted for about half of all municipal revenues. The provincial government assumed old municipal responsibilities for the administration of justice and property tax assessment, and plans were developed for major property tax reforms that would rationalize the municipal tax base.

The development of the new service state under Robarts helped promote a quadrupling of the provincial budget, from about $1 billion in the early 1960s to about $4 billion in the early 1970s (with health and education as the leading expenditure items). It was accompanied as well by growth in the provincial civil service from some 30,000 to almost 70,000 employees during the same period. By the early 1970s employees of municipal governments, such organizations as Ontario Hydro (officially renamed in 1974) and the Ontario Provincial Police, most teachers in the region, and most employees of hospitals and other health organizations were also paid largely by public funds, dependent in some degree on the provincial budget. A new regional "public sector" had become an important element in the wider postwar expansion of the service sector in the Ontario economy.

This created some worries, especially for an avowedly conservative government that still took pride and advantage in the market-oriented private sector as the fundamental engine of economic growth. In 1969 Robarts appointed a Committee on Government Productivity, composed of senior civil servants and private business executives and chaired by J.B. Cronyn, Director and Senior Vice-President of John Labatt Limited. The Committee's mandate was "to inquire into all matters pertaining to the management of ... and to make such recommendations as in its opinion will improve the efficiency and effectiveness of the Government of Ontario." Its work would ultimately lead to a major re-organization of the Ontario civil service.

The Confederation of Tomorrow

As in virtually every other Canadian province, close links between the federal government at Ottawa and the Ontario service state of the 1960s and early 1970s brought new conflicts to the Confederation. In the 1960s recurrent federal-provincial conferences became important – if to many rather mysterious – elements in Canadian public life.

From Ontario's standpoint, the era of genuine "co-operative federalism" that Leslie Frost helped launch in the 1950s came to an end in the mid-1960s. Increasingly, the expanding federal-provincial social service apparatus raised problems, since under the British North America Act the provinces had the bulk of constitutional power over the matters in question, while the federal government had the bulk of the revenues required to exercise these powers.

For official Ontario and some other provinces, the solution was for the federal government to give provincial governments "more tax room". Others attached to a rigorously "national" vision (or to the interests of the rapidly expanding postwar federal bureaucracy) saw the solution in some form of transfer of provincial powers to the federal government at Ottawa. The federal government's Medicare programme, which became the basis of provincial health insurance schemes, was perhaps the major bone of practical contention in the later 1960s. But by then it had become clear that the underlying issues were promoting a major debate on the nature of the modern Canadian Confederation, energized by the particular grievances of predominantly French-speaking Quebec.

John Robarts' memories of his Alberta childhood and, no doubt, the interests of a newly-matured Toronto business community helped prevent Ontario's return to the province-building posture of Oliver Mowat's regional state. But the new moderation toward the federal government implied not so much a softening of Ontario's determination to pursue its own provincial interests as a growing conviction that this interest (and in the Ontario government's view, the interests of all Canadian provinces) required the federal government to play a particular role in Confederation that it seemed increasingly unwilling to play.

Broadly, the perspective that Ontario brought to the Confederation debates of the late 1960s and 1970s envisioned a federal government that largely confined itself to defence, foreign policy, and general management of the national economy. Social policy was fundamentally a provincial responsibility; and as Ontario Treasurer Charles McNaughton declared in 1968: "Nothing short of comprehensive tax reform and a major redistribution of taxation fields will provide an intelligent solution to this problem." Ontario continued to support the principle of equalization grants to less wealthy provinces, albeit sometimes grudgingly, as a sign of its dissatisfaction with increasing federal power. But official Ontario's vision of Canada as something more than an alliance of regional states still implied vigorous provincial governments and much more "decentralization" of political power than had developed in the old model American federalism.

Beyond crude calculations of provincial self-interest, Robarts perhaps deserves more credit than he has typically received for his efforts to inject an element of national statesmanship into Ontario's role in the modern Canadian Confederation. Initially, this focused on the particular question of Quebec, Ontario's historic "sister province". Robarts organized a "Confederation of Tomorrow" Conference at Toronto in November 1967, as a forum at which Quebec (still under the moderate leadership of Daniel Johnson) could present its case for Canadian constitutional reform. This prompted other provinces to lay out their grievances in the Confederation as well: federal interference with provincial resources in Manitoba, Saskatchewan, and Alberta; "regional disparities" in Saskatchewan, Manitoba, and the Maritimes; new province-building aspirations in oil-rich Alberta and resource-rich British Columbia; widespread irritation with newly-expansive federal power and with the dominance of Toronto and Ontario generally in national life.

As Canada celebrated the centennial of the Confederation of 1867, Robarts' Confederation of Tomorrow Conference started a new era of constitutional debate that would not begin to reach a conclusion for another fifteen years. By 1968 Pierre Trudeau had arrived on the scene, first as Lester Pearson's federal Justice Minister at the first televised federal-provincial conference, then as Prime Minister of Canada. He brought a federal agenda for constitutional reform that, for one reason or another, almost everyone claimed to dislike, but that would nonetheless guide events.

In Ontario, the province with the largest French Canadian population outside Quebec, Robarts also announced the start of a major programme to gradually extend French language services in the operations of the provincial government and judicial system. The French language schools in the province that had been hobbling on since the resolution of the bilingual schools crisis in the later 1920s were given a fresh legislative mandate. Some eighty years after it was first advanced, Mowat's sense of "proper policy" for the French language in Ontario had begun to receive significant official support. Pursuing a historically-related theme in Ontario-Quebec relations, in the early 1960s Robarts had expanded provincial aid to Ontario separate schools, strengthening public support for the first ten years of the Catholic elementary and secondary school programme.

Beyond the question of Quebec, an unattractive side of the new constitutional debate, especially in Ontario, was that it sometimes seemed little more than a continuing squabble over power among newly-expanding and assertive government bureaucracies. After the Second World War, the Canadian federal government had begun to adopt the new professional bureaucratic management style pioneered earlier by large private corporations. The first province to follow suit was Saskatchewan, where the agrarian socialism of Canada's first CCF government was an inspiration to new bureaucratic experts and public-sector managers as well as old farmers and mechanics. The second province to adopt the new style was the Quebec of the quiet revolution and Premier Jean Lesage. And Quebec's delegations of talented analysts and aggressive advisors at the federal-provincial conferences of the early 1960s convinced Robarts that Ontario must join the trend. Some early concern with "planning" had appeared under Drew in the late 1940s, and the province had a tradition of earlier forms of expertise in public administration that could be traced back much farther. But the Ontario budget of 1966 and the new process by which it was put together marked a watershed in the management of a provincial bureaucracy that had grown some eight to nine times larger than it was in 1945.

In fact, the new budget process borrowed specific techniques from a traditional model for government innovation north of the Great Lakes: the "Mother of Parliaments" in the United Kingdom. In a more general way, however, Robarts the North American management man brought an end to the age of viewing provincial government operations in Ontario from the standpoint of gossip in a barber shop. To some later observers, his "Red Tory" reforms helped create an excessively professional public sector in the region, with overly aggressive instincts.

The Big Blue Machine and its Rivals

Following the precedent set by Leslie Frost, Robarts had concluded by the summer of 1970 that the Ontario Progressive Conservatives needed fresh leadership. He had won the provincial election of 1963 handily, taking forty-eight per cent of the vote and seventy-seven seats in a 108-seat legislature. But the election of 1967 was disappointing. The PCs dropped to forty-two per cent of the vote and sixty-nine seats in an expanded 117-seat legislature. The Liberals won thirty-two per cent of the vote and twenty-eight seats. And the new party strategy of the New Democrats at last seemed to be bearing fruit. They increased their share of the vote from sixteen per cent in 1963 to twenty-six per cent in 1967 and their number of seats from seven to twenty.

Shortly before the election of 1967, the Liberals had chosen a new leader, Robert Nixon, son of Harry Nixon, the old United Farmers activist and last Liberal Premier of Ontario. In the fall of 1970 the New Democrats chose a new leader, Stephen Lewis, son of David Lewis, the long-time principal national organizer of the old CCF, who would become leader of the federal New Democrats in 1971. New Democrats had formed a provincial government in Manitoba in 1969, and they would form governments in Saskatchewan in 1971 and in British Columbia in 1972.

In Ontario, Robarts resigned and was replaced by his Minister of Education, William Davis, at a convention held early in 1971 at Maple Leaf Gardens in Toronto. When Davis resigned as Premier almost fourteen years later, he would advise his party to avoid "simplistic slogans, easy solutions to complex issues, and the ideological prisons of the left or right." Like Oliver Mowat a century before, he was criticized for being "bland". His response was: "It is not the responsibility of government to entertain."

Shortly after assuming leadership, Davis called a provincial election for October 1971 and consolidated the fortunes of the governing party. The PCs took forty-five per cent of the vote and seventy-eight seats. The Liberals were reduced to twenty seats, and the New Democrats were held in check with nineteen seats.

Davis was helped a great deal by a revitalized PC political organization, dubbed "the Big Blue Machine" by the regional media. He was also helped by his opponents. The Liberal leader Robert Nixon was a much-respected last exemplar of the old virtues of progressive agrarian democracy north of the Great Lakes. But he had doubts about the changes that the 1960s and early 1970s were bringing to the region. "Sometimes", he once confesssed, "I just want to go back to the farm and roll up the driveway behind me." The New Democrats' Stephen Lewis was a confident social-democratic intellectual, a brilliant debater, and the darling of the Toronto radical intelligensia and the Ontario labour movement. But he lacked empathy with the mores of a wider Ontario society, where he sometimes seemed, in the words of Jonathan Manthorpe "an arrogant ruthless fanatic who would have the whole province cutting sugar cane given half a chance."

In one sense, Davis' success in the election of 1971 seemed to defy broader trends reflected by the New Democratic victories of the late 1960s and early 1970s in western Canada. As elsewhere, the international, national, and regional turmoil of the period brought at least gentle forms of social unrest to Ontario. For various reasons, there was dissatisfaction with the new service state that progressive conservatism and George Drew's Twenty-Two Points had been building since the 1950s.

William Davis and his wife Kathleen, on the last campaign trail in the election of 1981.

Some felt it had gone, or was going, too far. There were those who believed that the provincial Liberals were picking up support from this source. But others felt the new service state was too compromised and had not gone far enough. The New Democrats spoke for this view. Pressed by a "Waffle" splinter group on their far left, the New Democrats had also become the leading provincial spokesmen for concern over the service state's failure to confont increasing "foreign ownership" in the Canadian economy, based principally in the United States. This concern found some sympathetic echoes among the federal Liberals at Ottawa, though fewer among provincial Liberals in Ontario.

Others again, on both the left and the right, were in revolt against the "quality of life" promoted by the new service state and the wider social and economic trends in which it was rooted. The PC regime that William Davis inherited in 1971, with its various progressive and conservative tendencies, had some advantages in this context. Davis' first electoral victory as Premier owed something to his decision to cancel a planned Spadina Expressway in Toronto, in recognition of an early cause for a neighbourhood protection and community organizing movement that would bring a new Reform Council to power in Toronto municipal politics in 1972.

The decision on the Spadina Expressway itself owed something to the Robarts regime's planning and early development of a GO Transit regional commuter rail system as an alternative to mindless expansion of superhighways in central Ontario. By the mid-1970s GO Transit was serving the "Toronto-centred" area from Oshawa to Barrie to Hamilton. In effect, it was a partial revival of Adam Beck's radial electric railways proposal of the First World War era. And it was accompanied by major provincial government investment in a new Urban Transportation Development Corporation.

Similarly, the PCs had begun to take action on environmental concerns in the 1950s with the formation of the Ontario Water Resources Commission, which became the Ministry of Environment in 1972[3]. In response to complaints that the postwar economic boom had done little to improve "regional disparities" inside Canada's most populous province, a Northern Ontario Development Corporation had been established by the time Davis took office in 1971. An Eastern Ontario Development Corporation was established in 1974, and a new Ministry of Northern Affairs would be established in 1977. In response to the growing strength of "women's liberation", the contemporary revival of the long-standing progressive cause of women's rights, by 1973 William Davis had appointed Ontario's first woman cabinet minister, Margaret Birch. In response to complaints about housing shortages from Stephen Lewis and the New Democrats, he established a new Ministry of Housing in 1974.

At the same time, despite its success in the 1971 election, the early Davis regime had also inherited specific policies and programmes that were proving distinctly unpopular among many different groups in the region. Ontario Hydro, an increasingly unwieldy and insensitive bureaucracy in the eyes of some, had embarked on a major program of nuclear power development after the success of Rolphton in 1962. But new doubts were being raised about the future of nuclear power. Darcy McKeough's regional governments also began to take hold in the early 1970s. By 1975 ten new consolidated "regional municipalities" had been created, one in the Ottawa area, one in the Sudbury area, and eight in the area around the western end of Lake Ontario. They disturbed long-standing political and administrative relationships. Especially in rural areas, they became symbols of the new service state's tendency to place abstract efficiency before the old virtues of community life.

As elsewhere, student unrest in the late 1960s and early 1970s helped turn the new Ontario post-secondary education system that William Davis himself had created into something quite different from what its early supporters had envisioned. And at the centre of everything, the work of John Robarts' Committee on Government Productivity had led to a major reorganization of the Ontario civil service shortly after Davis became Premier. Government "Departments" became "Ministries", grouped into three new "policy fields": Justice, Resources Development, and Social Development. Policy-making was to be centralized in secretariats for each of the three fields, in a new Ministry of Treasury, Economics, and Intergovernmental Affairs, and in a streamlined Office of the Premier (under the former Executive Director of the Committee on Government Productivity – a management man trained at the Harvard School of Business).

The new arrangements seemed to have effects exactly opposite those intended. Instead of centralizing control of government policy with a small group of cabinet "superministers", they tended to shift power to unelected "superbureaucrats". The Big Blue Machine complained that the managerial Office of the Premier was isolating the Premier from day to day political realities.

The reorganized provincial civil service and the partly reorganized Ontario municipal system also had to cope with a new public-sector unionism that developed in the later 1960s. In the 1930s and 1940s the regional labour movement had at last made free collective bargaining of wage rates and working conditions an important element in the private industrial manufacturing sector. In the 1960s and 1970s it brought parallel techniques to the public component of the rapidly expanding service sector. Though the justice of the cause was widely ackowledged, it raised new and often difficult problems for government management.

Finally, the "energy-crisis" recession of 1973-74 and a surge of inflation unprecedented in the previous two decades signalled the beginning of the end of the long postwar economic boom. To some observers, the early signs of new economic troubles also raised new questions about the foundations of the regional service state that had been expanding since the 1950s. To others, they raised a need for more expansion.

In September 1975, William Davis called a provincial election, the results of which showed how much the thirty-two year-old Progressive Conservative hold on power had in fact been shaken by the social unrest of the late 1960s and early 1970s. Davis and the PCs remained in power, but as a minority government. They won only thirty-six per cent of the popular vote and fifty-one seats in a 125-seat legislature. The Liberals under Robert Nixon won thirty-four per cent of the vote and thirty-five seats. Under Stephen Lewis, who was trying to project a more moderate public image, the New Democrats won twenty-nine per cent of the popular vote and, better still, doubled their number of seats to thirty-eight to replace the Liberals as the Official Opposition.

The Slow Retreat

The New Democrats' rise to Official Opposition in 1975 was the culmination of more than a decade of inspired organizing and hard political work. But it would prove to be the end of an old era, not the beginning of a new one. True to the "neo-marxist" theorizing that attracted the party's most radical intellectual wing, the Ontario NDP's failure to grow beyond the revival of earlier CCF strength that it had achieved by the mid-1970s could be at least partly attributed to developments in the regional economy.

In Ontario, the end of the postwar boom that began in the mid-1970s had diverse aspects. As elsewhere in both North America and Europe, birth rates had fallen dramatically; population growth was suddenly much slower than in the 1950s and 1960s. The 1973-74 recession also cast a harsh light on new "structural" economic troubles beyond the more routine vagaries of the business cycle. New and increasingly "automated" technologies, aging plants, and new low-wage competition in the American south and such offshore locations as Taiwan and South Korea (and in a less direct way Japan) were bringing grief to the old manufacturing belt in the northeastern United States. Though aging plants were somewhat less of a concern, Canadian-American manufacturing in Ontario shared the grief.

Historically, average manufacturing wage rates in Canada had been less than in the United States. The smaller scale of Canadian industry necessarily made it somewhat less efficient. But in 1974, Canadian wage rates edged above those in the United States. The success of the Ontario labour movement in negotiating its wages had created new problems for Ontario labour, even if simple conceptions of economic justice made it difficult to confront these problems head-on.

The mines and forests of the north had entered a new period of difficulty as well. They faced both shifts in world demand and problems of resource depletion. At least modest reforestation programmes had been underway

297

since the earlier twentieth century. But Ontario now had to compete with forestry locations in more benign southern climates, where forests could be regenerated in shorter periods of time.

At the same time, the leftward shift and new political radicalism that had begun in the earlier 1960s had reached a peak in the earlier 1970s. One result was a federal Foreign Investment Review Agency, established by a Trudeau Liberal minority regime at Ottawa, governing in a parliament where the New Democrats held the balance of power. In Ontario itself, another result was a peak in democratic political pressure for further expansion in the service state and in the rights of women, minorities (especially visible minorities who had arrived with the new postwar immigration), and labour at large in the regional economy.

From the standpoint of the management of the Ontario provincial budget, the problem was paying for the expansion of the service state that had already taken place. In the 1969-70 fiscal year, Ontario had spent about $350 million on health programmes, the third largest expenditure item in the budget after education and highways. By 1974-75, expenditures on health had become the largest item in the budget at more than $2½ billion.

It was a sign of William Davis' skill as a practical politician that he successfully navigated such precarious waters through half a dozen years of PC minority government (and, it might be said, of his intuitions about an Ontario political tradition defined much earlier, not by Leslie Frost but by Oliver Mowat). After the disappointment of 1975, Davis tried to win back a majority in 1977 by running with the "Ontario Charter", an unabashed revival of Drew's Twenty-Two Points. The PCs picked up seven extra seats, but still finished five seats short of a clear majority. The New Democrats lost five seats, and the Liberals returned to their accustomed status as Official Opposition. After 1977 Davis settled down to four more years of minority rule. In the provincial election of 1981, he would at last win back a solid majority of seventy seats, with forty-four per cent of the popular vote – the ultimate test of his mastery of the skills of his profession.

Both the Liberals and New Democrats tried new leadership: the Montreal-born psychiatrist Stuart Smith

298

for the Liberals and Michael Cassidy from the Ottawa area for the New Democrats. But the Davis minority regime governed with increasing confidence. It played off the two sides of its divided opposition in the legislature (neither side of which was prepared to co-operate with the other). And it posed convincingly as the only political force with a coherent and realistic approach to the region's problems.

At the centre of the approach was a gradual and moderate retreat from the regional service state in place by the early 1970s along two broad paths – the "Politician's Art"[4] and economic development. Movement along both paths had at least begun before the 1975 election.

By instinct, Davis was more attuned to the traditional skills of the democratic party politician than to the bureaucratic skills of the management man so admired by Robarts. The controversy and confusion induced by the work of the Committee on Government Productivity in the early 1970s seemed to bear out this instinct. A key element in Davis' approach to the later 1970s was what amounted to a rehabilitation of the old regional tradition of political management in contemporary colours.

To some extent, the process had begun with the creation of the Big Blue Machine even before the election of 1971 – a reinvigoration of a PC political organization that had languished under Robarts. Of more consequence for public administration, however, Davis had begun by 1974 to replace the managerial Office of the Premier, inherited from the Committee on Governmental Productivity, with a more politically sensitive Premier's staff under the direction of E.E. Stewart. He was a progressive but quite politically-minded civil servant who had worked with Davis almost from the start of his earlier career as Minister of Education.

After the election of 1975, the new style in the Office of the Premier was gradually adopted in the civil service more generally. The Davis regime moved to restore political accountability of the service to the elected cabinet (still known as the Executive Council of Ontario), not to the legislature nor to the electorate and certainly not to the senior bureaucrats.

At the municipal level, the experiment with regional government was brought to an end. No new regional municipalities would be created. Even a bureaucratic

299

compromise known as county restructuring would gradually be abandoned, as would Darcy McKeough's companion plans for major property tax reform (though in this case a compromise would survive).

The new style did not imply any direct politicization of the working levels of the civil service. But with some two decades of PC rule behind it, the higher management of the service had been at least quite political even under Robarts. And there were significant numbers of non-civil service positions on boards, commissions, and other advisory bodies traditionally subject to political patronage.

To some extent, the new style did imply new respect for the more sordid side of the old political management. But it also implied more high-minded motivations in the appointments process. Such new Canadians as Sikhs in turbans, who like some Ontario Tories could still dimly remember an earlier British Empire, served on the provincial Rent Review Commission in Toronto, itself created in 1975 as another implication of the politician's art. In 1984 Ontario's leading Black historian, Daniel Hill, was appointed provincial Ombudsman, an office created in 1976 to deal with citizen complaints against the misdemeanours of the provincial bureaucracy.[5]

The Davis regime's approach to Ontario's new economic problems evolved more slowly. At first, it was largely inspired by Darcy McKeough, who had become Davis' Treasurer in 1971. McKeough resigned for a brief period as the result of a minor real estate scandal during his earlier tenure as Minister of Municipal Affairs. But he was back as Davis' Minister of the new Treasury, Economics, and Intergovernmental Affairs before the election of 1975.

Philosophically, McKeough was clearly to the right of Davis. He was also an extremely able and energetic cabinet minister, who presided over a combative civil service staff. His approach to the regional economic malaise that had appeared by the mid-1970s was bold and simple, backed by sincere conviction and the wilfulness of a son of the southwestern Ontario business gentry who, it was said, had been raised on "royal jelly". It had several interwoven strands: revive the longstanding PC faith in the private sector as the engine of economic growth and fundamental

300

Letting the private sector do it in downtown Toronto: Roy Thomson Hall and the new Sun Life headquarters on King Street West. Thomson made his first fortune in radio broadcasting in northern Ontario, and then went on to become a media magnate in the United Kingdom, ultimately known as Lord Thomson of Fleet. Sun Life decided to move its headquarters from Montreal to Toronto in the later 1970s.

source of long-term "productive" employment; bring the alarming expansion of the provincial budget in the early 1970s to a halt as quickly as possible; and "freeze" the size of the provincial civil service at its current levels.

McKeough's parallel vision of policy in federal-provincial relations was "disentanglement". In provincial-municipal relations, the province could not be as generous with municipal financial assistance as it had been in the past. The abandonment of regional government was proof of McKeough's own willingness to turn his back on a programme that he himself had been instrumental in developing during the later 1960s.

Yet especially after the election of 1977, the shift to the right inspired by McKeough's Treasury increasingly grated against the sensitivities of the new political management in an era of continuing minority government. After a series of struggles in cabinet, Darcy McKeough resigned in the late summer of 1978. Davis replaced him as Treasurer with Frank Miller from Muskoka, and responsibilities for federal-provincial and provincial-municipal relations were moved to separate ministries. Philosophically, Miller was to the right of the Premier as well. But unlike McKeough, he had something of a populistic touch. Miller had also survived a heart attack when, as Minister of Health, he had tried to close some hospitals in response to the earlier bold priorities and been met with stiff resistance.

After Darcy McKeough's resignation, it became clear that the retreat from the service state in Ontario would be a notably moderate and gradual one, careful to preserve hard-earned guaranteed pensions, health insurance, and similar programmes for the mass of Ontario people. Davis tried to avoid the tendency "for one group in society ... to confront another ... at odds with the broader objectives held by the rest of the population." Revived enthusiasm for the private sector as the engine of economic growth was not altogether one-sided. When William Davis himself announced his resignation as PC leader in 1984, the President of the Ontario Federation of Labour would concede that under him "we have made progress never given to labour from any other Tory Premier."

Nonetheless, the retreat from the service state was real enough. In the gradualist tradition, some piecemeal efforts were made to take a more positive approach to the new economic development priorities, culminating with the establishment of a Board of Industrial Leadership and Development – known in government advertising as "BILD". (More effective in improving Ontario's economic development climate, however, was a sharp decline in the value of the Canadian dollar in the late 1970s and early 1980s, which acted to reduce Ontario labour and resource costs relative to those in the United States.)[6]

In a more gradual and moderate form, Darcy McKeough's programme remained in place. With slower population growth and declining enrolments, public spending on education (especially higher education, now viewed by many progressive and other conservatives as a disappointment) lost its 1960s glamour and became a focus for financial restraint. Under Bette Stephenson, who became Minister of Education after McKeough's resignation in 1978, movement was begun toward more discipline in Ontario's elementary and secondary schools.

In fact, the Ontario provincial budget doubled even between the mid-1970s and early 1980s from about $10 billion to about $20 billion. But the lion's share of the increase was almost entirely attributable to inflation. Broadly, in 1982 it took about $1.90 to buy what $1 had bought in 1975. Nonetheless, as in the United States, inflation in Canada at large slowed dramatically in the 1980s. By 1983 growth in provincial spending was increasing at a distinctly slower rate than growth in the gross provincial product for the Ontario economy as a whole. In one sense, growth in the regional public sector had been brought to an unambiguous halt. In the early 1980s the Ontario civil service still had somewhat less than 70,000 "classified" employees, almost exactly the same as in the early 1970s[7]. It could at least no longer be said that, on the Government of Ontario's account, the private sector of the regional economy had "no room" in which to grow.

16

Modern Times

When William Davis announced his intention to resign as
PC leader and Premier of Ontario in the autumn of 1984,
he was asked if he saw "a single accomplishment that stood
out" during his term in office. He replied that it was "very
difficult to make such a choice." But, he suggested,
perhaps his "role in the constitutional debate could be considered".

In the first instance, Davis had inherited the role from
John Robarts and the Confederation of Tomorrow
Conference in 1967. He began to place his own mark on
events, however, as the debate moved to the centre of
Canadian public life in the late 1970s and early 1980s.

By this time, the debate had four main themes. The
first was the question of Quebec independence or at least
"sovereignty-association" – the ultimate incentive for
action. The second was federal-provincial conflict over a
constitutional amending formula that would at last permit
"patriation" of the old British North America Act from the
Parliament of the United Kingdom. Historically, this
flowed from the cry for provincial rights raised by Premier
Howard Ferguson of Ontario and others at the time of the
Statute of Westminster some half century before. The
third theme in the debate involved conflict over the
appropriate distribution of governmental powers and
financial resources, raised by the development of federal
and provincial social service states since the Second World
War (and by new enthusiasms for province-building in

western Canada). The fourth theme was Pierre Trudeau's proposed "Charter of Rights", designed both to guarantee French language rights in the Canadian Confederation and to give federalism in Canada the kind of democratic legitimacy that the American Bill of Rights gave federalism in the United States.

In Ontario, if Oliver Mowat was in some ways an apt historical precedent for William Davis' approach to provincial government, a more apt precedent for his approach to federal-provincial relations and the constitutional debate was the province's first post-Confederation Premier John Sandfield Macdonald. The analogy is not exact. The seventy-five year history of the regional state begun by Mowat had left marks that could not be erased. Davis saw the Government of Ontario as much more than "a glorified county council". Its "primary role ... relates to advancing the interests of this province."

Yet as for Sandfield Macdonald, in the Ontario that William Davis spoke for, "we have never been afraid to be Canadians first ... the ultimate priority is to ensure the existence of a stable and unified Canada." As the constitutional debate progressed, this implied fundamental co-operation between the Government of Ontario and the Government of Canada. From 1976 to 1981, Willam Davis and Pierre Trudeau went "hunting in pairs", not unlike John Sandfield Macdonald and John A. Macdonald from 1867 to 1871.

Ontario and National Unity

The final conflicts of the constitutional debate in the fall of 1981 pitted the government of Canada along with the provincial governments of Ontario and New Brunswick against the eight other provinces. In Quebec, Premier René Levesque and the Parti Québécois had lost a provincial referendum on sovereignty-association in May 1980 but then won a resounding victory in an April 1981 provincial election. Levesque allied with the seven other English-speaking provincial premiers around a proposal inspired by Alberta Premier Peter Lougheed that, in the words of the Toronto-based historian Ramsay Cook, "amounted to complete 'provincialization' of Canadian federalism".

305

The competing federal proposal, backed by Ontario and New Brunswick, included a veto over constitutional amendments for each of Ontario and Quebec as the still most populous and geographically largest provinces. As the debate developed, both Ontario and (somewhat accidently) Quebec agreed to forgo their claims to a veto over constitutional amendments. This opened the way for a compromise agreement, ultimately accepted by the federal government and all provincial governments except René Levesque's Quebec[1].

The agreement of November 1981 finally resolved the problem of a constitutional amending formula that had resisted successive attempts at resolution for more than half a century. The new amending formula required the approval of the Canadian federal parliament and at least two-thirds of the provincial legislatures (or seven of the ten current provinces), representing at least fifty per cent of the population of all the provinces. On this basis, the British North America Act was patriated from the Parliament of the United Kingdom as The Constitution Act 1867. This in turn was amended by The Constitution Act 1982, which added the amending formula, a Charter of Rights and Freedoms (including French and English language rights), and provisions regarding equalization and regional disparities, provincial control of natural resources, and "the existing aboriginal and treaty rights of the aboriginal peoples of Canada". During ceremonies held at Ottawa on 17 April 1982, Queen Elizabeth II formally severed the last constitutional links between the United Kingdom and Canada[2].

It seems possible to discern two guiding principles behind the unwavering support of William Davis and the Government of Ontario for Pierre Trudeau and the Government of Canada throughout the Canadian constitutional debate of the later 1970s and early 1980s. The first was that Canada without Quebec was inconceivable, and vice-versa. In March 1980, less than three months before the Quebec referendum, Thomas Wells – Ontario's Minister of Intergovernmental Affairs, with primary responsibility for managing the province's role in the constitutional debate – declared in Toronto: "We reject categorically the Parti Québécois option of sovereignty-association." On the other hand, Wells made clear that Ontario was very serious about constitutional reform. A "non" vote in the referendum would be taken not as a "confirmation of the status quo", but as a "signal that the planning for comprehensive constitutional change can at last begin." And Wells proposed a federal-provincial conference that would be held four weeks after the referendum to begin the process.

The second principle behind Ontario's co-operation with Ottawa was that, no matter what the appropriate relations between federal and provincial governments in other fields may be, the federal government must have a primary responsibility for management of "the national economy". This ultimately found constitutional expression in the conception of the Confederation as an "economic union", which entailed "mobility rights" ensuring that any citizen of Canada could "pursue the gaining of a livelihood in any province". And these mobility rights became part of the Charter of Rights and Freedoms in The Constitution Act 1982[3].

In other provinces, and especially in western Canada, Ontario's particular concern for the national economy was often seen as no more than the old Ontario regional state's traditional solicitude for the interests of the Toronto financial community, updated for an era in which Toronto had at last replaced Montreal as the economic capital of Canada. Now that Ontario had itself outgrown the old strategy of province building, it wanted to make it unconstitutional for anyone else.

This view of Ontario's motivations was particularly strong in Alberta where Peter Lougheed stood up for the principles of Oliver Mowat's old Ontario regional state in a new setting. Ever since C.D. Howe had told Ernest Manning, in Leslie Frost's presence, that the federal government would not permit exports of Alberta gas to the midwest United States until the needs of central and eastern Canada had been met first, the disposition of Alberta's modern oil and gas wealth had been a contentious point of dispute between Alberta and Ontario. Alberta and other parts of western Canada tended to see Ontario's staunch commitment to national unity as pious rhetoric that masked a longstanding Ontario habit of viewing the West as an economic colony of central Canada.

Both the Trudeau government's National Energy Policy of the later 1970s and Trudeau's victory in the federal election of 1980 (when his policy on Canadian oil and gas prices helped him win fifty-two of ninety-five seats in Ontario) were read by many as support for this "western-alienated" sense of Ontario's underlying agenda. And this sense found echoes in virtually all other provinces as well.

Even in the late 1970s, there perhaps was a side to Ontario opinion that saw some revival of the spirit of C.D. Howe and a central Canadian national vision of the 1950s and early 1960s as the best possible solution to the problems of the modern Confederation. But ultimately, it seems hard to fit William Davis, with his penchant for accommodating all forms of reality, into quite this mold. By the 1970s it had become clear that, whatever else might be true, Toronto was not the economic capital of Canada in the late twentieth century in the way that Montreal had been in the nineteenth and earlier twentieth centuries.

Toronto had not simply inherited the old Empire of the St. Lawrence from Montreal in some new North American form. The Empire of the St. Lawrence, like the British Empire and the "Empire Ontario" that Harold Innis had written about in the 1930s, had retreated into history. Moreover, to view the Confederation of 1867 itself as a political and constitutional arrangement "in which central Canada, principally Ontario, has been 'favoured' at the expense of the other regions" contradicted the ultimate direction of post Second World War development in Canada. Following continental trends, "power" was, in fact, shifting west, as it was shifting south and west in the United States. In 1921 the combined population of British Columbia and Alberta had amounted to thirty-eight per cent of the population of Ontario. The figure had risen to forty-six per cent by 1951 and fifty-eight per cent by 1981. By the early 1980s Ontario had only the third highest average family income in all ten Canadian provinces, behind Alberta and British Columbia and just ahead of Saskatchewan, Manitoba, and Quebec.

From the standpoint of someone living in Ontario in the early 1980s, the one financial centre that genuinely did cast a prospective shadow over the autonomy of all Canadian provinces was Montreal's oldest rival in the Canadian hinterland, New York City. By now, New York had clearly replaced London, England as the world's leading financial centre[4]. Toronto's long history of playing off New York and Montreal to rise within its own province had ended. Even some traders on the Toronto Stock Exchange were expressing concern that Canada's leading stock broker "has only 4% of the capital of Merrill Lynch & Co., the largest US broker." In this context, only some form of strong national economic management could protect provincial rights in all parts of the Confederation.

Finally, the new Constitution Act 1982 made distinct bows to all regions of the country. Along with French language rights and economic mobility rights, it included constitutional protection for the principle of equalization payments (at the insistence of the Maritimes). An amendment also made clear that all provinces (including the three prairie provinces "created" by the federal government) had constitutional jurisdiction over their own "nonrenewable natural resources" – in response to the one historic grievance of western Canada on which everyone could agree[5]. Both the Charter of Rights and the amending formula also included special protections for provincial powers. Ontario, like Quebec, had given up its claim to a veto over constitutional amendment during the course of the constitutional debate. For the Premier of Ontario to accept all this and still call for "national unity" gave his rhetoric at least a note of sincerity.

Ontario's Forgotten History

As a practical matter, the political significance of official Quebec's refusal to endorse the constitutional compromise of November 1981 was blunted in the Canadian federal election of 1984. Following the resignation of Pierre Trudeau as leader of the federal Liberals, the Quebec electorate joined the Maritimes, Ontario, and western Canada in giving Brian Mulroney's federal Progressive Conservatives a dramatic majority at Ottawa. Mulroney was an "English-speaking" native of Quebec (of Irish extraction), who also spoke fluent and colloquial Quebec French. He was a warm admirer of Trudeau's constitutional achievements as opposed to his partisan politics. And in effect, the federal

309

The City of North Bay, on the shore of Lake Nipissing, Canada Day 1980. Like most of northern Ontario, the railway town of North Bay had moved from raw frontier to the consumer society of the late twentieth century in only three generations.

election of 1984 ended the first phase of the constitutional debate with a show of national solidarity.

Yet the continuing official dissent of the Province of Quebec remained a loose end that would have to be faced again. In this context, Pierre Trudeau's greatest disappointment with William Davis (a disappointment largely shared by Brian Mulroney) was that Davis would not declare Ontario "officially bilingual" under the Charter of Rights, as Richard Hatfield and Louis Robichaud had done in New Brunswick. Official bilingualism in Ontario, a former leading Trudeau advisor declared shortly after William Davis' announcement of his resignation, "would put another nail in the coffin of the Parti Québécois."

As matters stand, Section 16 of the Charter of Rights in The Constitution Act 1982 "entrenches" English and French as "the official languages of Canada" with "equality of status and equal rights and privileges" in all institutions of the federal government. It does the same for all institutions of the provincial government of New Brunswick (where some thirty-four per cent of the population reported French as their "mother tongue" in 1981) and makes provision for other provinces to follow New Brunswick's lead. Sections 17 to 20 spell out more specific implications of official bilingualism in legislatures, legal statutes, and courts.

Beyond particular provisions regarding official bilingualism, Section 23 of the Charter entrenches the right of "Citizens of Canada", regardless of which province they live in, to have their children receive primary and secondary school education in either English or French, where numbers warrant[6]. This section formed one of the Province of Quebec's specific objections to the Charter, since it rendered unconstitutional Quebec provincial legislation of the 1970s designed to secure the status of French as the dominant language of Quebec (and more broadly, infringed on provincial powers in education under The Constitution Act 1867).

In Ontario, only about 5½ per cent of the population reported French as their mother tongue in the census of 1981 (though more than ten per cent reported "both English and French" as their "official language"). But in absolute numbers, Ontario had more than twice as many people reporting French as their mother tongue as New Brunswick and the largest French Canadian population outside Quebec. Thus, in one of his last acts before he resigned as Prime Minister of Canada in the spring of 1984, Pierre Trudeau once again publicly urged William Davis to declare Ontario officially bilingual under Section 16 of the Canadian Charter of Rights and Freedoms.

In fact, Davis' response to the issue had simply been to continue the policy of gradual extension of French language services and French education in Ontario, begun under John Robarts in the late 1960s, in final recognition of the "proper policy" suggested by Mowat almost a century before. The policy was pursued with genuine vigour; by the early 1980s bilingual services in Ontario were at least quite close to what they would in fact become under Section 16 of the Charter of Rights. As one of his final acts before resigning as Premier of Ontario, Davis also announced the extension of full public support for Catholic separate schools through to the end of the secondary level, at last acceding to a demand that had at least been historically linked with French language rights (though also of interest to Ontario's modern Irish, Italian, Polish, and Portuguese communities).

In the words of one Trudeau advisor, Davis' policy amounted to implementing "the substance" of official bilingualism in Ontario, without formally acknowledging its "symbolism.... Yet it is precisely symbolism that is required." Only the future, however, can tell whether the failure to accept Trudeau's own position on this issue constitutes a genuine blemish on William Davis' record as a "Canadian first". It may in fact not be in the Canadian national interest for Ontario, or any other province, to embrace the Trudeau Liberal's partisan zest for putting nails "in the coffin of the Parti Québécois".

Trudeau defeated the Parti Québécois in the sovereignty-association referendum of 1980. But he did not defeat the modern Province of Quebec's aspirations to fortify its regional "national state" as a solid base for French culture in North America. Similarly, with The Constitution Act 1982 all Canadian provinces except Quebec acknowledged the formal symbolism of official bilingualism in the Canadian federal state. As a practical matter, it

312

seems clear, this means that all future Prime Ministers of Canada must be able to at least converse intelligibly in both English and French, a new reality reflected in the first televised French language debate among all three party leaders held during the 1984 federal election campaign.

With French/English dualism thus guaranteed at the federal level, an Ontario that stops short of the symbolism of official bilingualism – while recognizing the practical principle that French language minority rights in Ontario must be identical to English language minority rights in Quebec (which also stops short of official bilingualism) – may be a stronger force for Canadian unity than an Ontario that lives up to the highest abstract ideals of Pierre Trudeau or even Brian Mulroney. The path of future progress on the language issue in Canada may have more to do with "provincializing" the spirit of Section 23 of the Charter of Rights, that Quebec itself has objected to, than with provincializing the spirit of Section 16.

In the Canadian census of 1981, 77½ per cent of Ontario residents reported their mother tongue as English, 5½ per cent as French, and some 17 per cent as a language other than English or French. Above all else, history is at the root of the case for French language rights in Ontario, as in other parts of Canada. And from the standpoint of Ontario's own "forgotten history" as a region, Ontario society before the start of English-speaking mass settlement was not predominantly French-speaking, but "French and Indian", with the Indian peoples very much in the majority.

Trudeau's own thinking had itself stressed the "polyethnic" legacy of Canada's earliest French and Indian history (which also included the English experience on Hudson Bay) since the start of his career as a public figure in the 1960s. Ultimately, his long-term vision of Canada was the vision of Champlain, suggested in the Ontario "Farmer Premier" E.C. Drury's 1959 study of Huronia: the "production, here in North America, of a new race, stronger for the mingling ... of many and varied strains."

At Trudeau's final federal-provincial conference held not long before his resignation in 1984 (and mandated by The Constitution Act 1982), the federal government proposed an amendment to the new Constitution that would go beyond entrenching the existing aboriginal and treaty rights of the aboriginal peoples of Canada and entrench the principle of "aboriginal self-government." But the proposal could not win the required approval of at least seven provinces, representing at least fifty per cent of the population of all the provinces.

It did win the approval of three provinces, representing just over forty-two per cent of the population: New Brunswick, Manitoba, and William Davis' Ontario. For the time being, however, the nation building of the 1960s and 1970s had reached its limits[7].

Ontario, Canada, and the North American Economy

If the failure to achieve provincial official bilingualism was the Trudeau Government of Canada's major disappointment with the Davis Government of Ontario, the Davis regime's major disappointment with the Trudeau regime at Ottawa was its failure to make substantial progress on the issue of national economic management. By the 1980s this was a complex issue in Ontario. Some observers (especially outside the region) tended to stress two simplistic points: first, the significance of the province's industrial manufacturing sector, particularly that part of it dependent on the protectionist legacies of the old National Policy; and second, the comparatively large amount of "foreign-owned" (chiefly American) industry in the region. From this viewpoint, the crux of national economic management in Ontario involved trade policies tilted toward preserving the region's protected manufacturing sector and the kind of "nationalist" economic legislation illustrated by the Foreign Investment Review Agency (FIRA) created by the Trudeau regime in 1973.

Davis' Ontario, however, was never entirely comfortable with FIRA[8]. Similarly, the region's economic strength in the twentieth century had not been even predominantly rooted in its industrial manufacturing sector (and the still relatively small Canadian market), but in a diversified economic base that stressed resource and service industries as well as manufacturing and that depended to no small extent on exports to the United States. In any candid Ontario historical perspective, there was a vaguely unreal

314

quality to the crusade against foreign investment from the start. Reciprocity with the United States had accompanied the province's first great economic boom in the mid-nineteenth century. Macdonald's National Policy had only been devised after it became clear that the United States would not renew reciprocity. The reciprocity election of 1911 in Ontario had expressed a popular protest against the prospect of political annexation by the American republic, at least as much as a protest against a particular economic policy. After the First World War, in the strategic Ontario sectors of forestry, mining, agricultural machinery, and ultimately even automobiles, embracing the North American market had proved the path to prosperity.

The Trudeau regime itself took perhaps at most a half-hearted approach to FIRA. Nonetheless, its fundamental approach to Canadian-American relations was still to "create counterweights" against the influence of the United States. Thus, Trudeau tried to replace the old Canadian commercial links with the United Kingdom and the British Empire with a new "contractual link" to the European Economic Community. And he tried to invest the post-colonial heritage of the Commonwealth of Nations with economic significance by promoting "North/South" issues and reaching out to the economic hope and promise of the so-called Third World. There was significant sympathy with this approach in Ontario, where (as in British Columbia and other parts of Canada) the newest migrations were in fact giving the region new links with a wider European heritage and with the vast human diversity beyond Europe and America[9]. Yet in the real world of economics, Trudeau's "Third Option" represented at best early gropings toward new policies for the long-term future. For a province that was sending more than eighty per cent of its exports to the United States in the later 1970s, a strategy of Canadian national economic management that did not at least have Canada-us economic relations as a central mid-term focus did not make much practical sense.

As both the race to succeed Davis as provincial PC leader late in 1984 and the emergence of a new provincial Liberal government in 1985 suggested, Ontario's warmth toward the North American economy did not imply a commitment to unrestricted Canadian-American "free trade" in the spirit of the "commercial union" proposals of the late nineteenth century. A complete economic integration of Canada and the United States would be impossible without a significant surrender of Canadian political sovereignty. And Canada's most populous province retained its traditional antipathy toward annexation by the American republic. Much of the modern regional economy in Ontario looked to markets south of the Great Lakes for future growth. But Canada, with a population only somewhat larger than that of California (spread over a territory larger than that of all the United States), could not expect to enjoy the kind of access to the US market that California enjoyed, without itself becoming a State of the Union and abandoning its own past.

Yet only at the radical New Democratic fringes of Ontario political culture did the quest for a new national economic management imply any kind of rigorous economic nationalism. In the Ontario mainstream, the balanced forces of economic self-interest seemed to suggest some durable framework for trade relationships between Canada and the United States, that brought mutual benefits to both sides.

The required new kind of "national policy", in other words, also involved some new kind of "reciprocity". This was open to the traditional objection that the United States was not prepared to give Canada the kind of reciprocity agreement that would serve Canadian national interests. In the later twentieth century, however, Canada was at least in a stronger position in this respect than it had been a century before.

The United States was the single largest destination for exports from Canada. But Canada was also the single largest destination for exports from the United States. In 1982 the United States sent some $34 billion worth of exports to Canada, compared with just over $30 billion, all told, to twenty different Latin American republics, about $21 billion to Japan, some $10½ billion to the United Kingdom, $10 billion to West Germany, and $7 billion to France.

316

Some New Directions

The Trudeau regime at Ottawa did begin to move toward a recognition of the need for national economic management in a North American context during its final moments. It began discussions with Washington on the prospects of "sectoral" Canada-us free trade agreements in steel, agricultural machinery, telecommunications and computers, and urban transportation equipment, on the model of the existing auto free trade agreement. Not long after Brian Mulroney's federal Progressive Conservatives came to power, the us Congress passed the Trade and Tariff Act of 1984, which among other things empowered the President to enter into negotiations on sectoral free trade with the Government of Canada.

At the same time, the old nineteenth-century debate over tariffs versus free trade was not quite the issue at stake. By the early 1980s some two-thirds of us exports to Canada and about eighty per cent of Canadian exports to the United States were crossing the border duty free. The issue was what kind of Canadian national economic management could best structure the more intensive economic relations between Canada and the United States that had developed since the Second World War in order to guarantee Canadian political sovereignty and maximize benefits to what the new Constitution called "the Citizens of Canada". In Ontario, there was still no real consensus that simple extensions of the Canada-us Auto Pact of the 1960s were what was required. The issue was complex and would take time to resolve. As in the past, prudence and caution were cardinal virtues.

The broad principle Ontario had brought to the constitutional debate of the late 1970s and early 1980s, however, was that some form of national economic management remained a requirement of making the Canadian Confederation work. Culturally, Canada (even in Quebec) was simply another version of the varied themes that dominated experience in the United States. But politically Canada was independent because this made practical as well as patriotic sense. Toronto, Hamilton, London, Thunder Bay, and Ontario at large were better off than they would be without the border between Canada and the United States. But so were Halifax, Montreal, Winnipeg,

317

Calgary, and Vancouver. Without the will to national unity that gave meaning to the border, everyone's regional rights were threatened.

It could be said that there remained one last logical flaw in the argument. Neither Trudeau's Government of Canada nor Davis' Government of Ontario had quite faced up to the potential injustice of any national unity forged exclusively in a federal parliament where the old "central Canada" of Ontario and Quebec together still contained more than sixty per cent of the country's population. The constitutional debate had shown that it was not easy to make national economic policy at federal-provincial conferences, and the debate itself could not go on forever. But neither the Trudeau nor Davis regimes demonstrated much sympathy toward proposals for an elected federal Senate of the sort advocated by Oliver Mowat in the original Confederation debates of the 1860s to strengthen "regional" representation from the Maritimes, western Canada, and ultimately perhaps the far north in the federal parliament. Like the federal-provincial division of powers and financial resources and a more satisfactory long-term accommodation for Quebec, this was an issue for the future.

Whatever the future might hold, with the resignations of both Trudeau (in the spring) and Davis (in the autumn), 1984 marked the end of one more era in the history of the Canadian region west of the Ottawa River and north of the Great Lakes. And by 1984 it was a fact that Canada at large had survived some two decades of often bitter internal dissension intact and without any resort to major violent conflict. Despite recurrent predictions of its imminent demise from its beginnings, the Canadian Confederation had lasted for well over a century – perhaps a testimony to the wisdom in *The Times* of London's observation in 1867: the "freer and less binding relations sometimes last the longest." In 1980 Ontario's leading French Canadian historian, Robert Choquette, declared: "l'Ontarien franco-phone n'est pas un Québécois en exil, ni un citoyen de deuxieme classe. L'Ontario et le Canada sont sa patrie. Il est ici pour rester." In Ontario, as elsewhere, the historical vision of a separate Canadian political unity in northern North America could be traced back nearly four centuries.

In 1984 Ontario, like Canada at large, was a place where many things were still possible. And in Ontario, as in other parts of the country, the modern history of Canada had only just begun. By the time William Davis announced his intention to resign as provincial Premier in the autumn of 1984, he had surpassed Leslie Frost's earlier record for the second-longest individual term in office, next to Oliver Mowat's twenty-four years. There were those both inside and outside the Premier's party who thought it would be best for all concerned if William Davis would continue to pursue the record set by Mowat himself. But the Premier's own judgement was that, as the middle of the 1980s drew within sight, it was time for "a new approach, new personalities and perhaps some new directions."

The 1985 Election

By the summer of 1985, it was clear that Davis' resignation had indeed brought new directions to Ontario politics and perhaps ultimately to the regional society at large. But the exact shape of change was not quite what the former Premier himself might have wished.

After the provincial election of 1981, both the opposition Liberals and New Democrats had chosen new leaders. The New Democrat's choice, Bob Rae, was a former Toronto-area member of the federal parliament and a somewhat aristocratic-looking "returned Rhodes scholar", vaguely reminiscent of Ted Jolliffe, the first provincial leader of the Ontario CCF. The Liberals had chosen David Peterson, a young small businessman from the old Grit stronghold of the southwest in London, Ontario.

Throughout the last few years of the Davis regime, however, neither the Liberals nor the New Democrats seemed able to make headway against the governing Progressive Conservatives. A strong performance by the North American auto sector had helped pull Ontario out of the 1981-82 recession. Youth employment remained a serious problem, and immediate prospects for a new economic boom still appeared dim. But under Davis' leadership, Ontario had weathered the political and economic storms of the later 1970s and early 1980s intact. The Premier, one of his principal advisors suggested, was a

319

Bob Rae and his wife Arlene Perly on the campaign trail in the election of 1985, with the New Democratic candidate for the Kitchener riding, Tim Little.

leader with whom the people of Ontario felt comfortable.

The situation changed when Frank Miller from Muskoka succeeded Davis as PC party leader and Premier of Ontario at a convention held in Toronto in January 1985. Though it was clear that Miller's victory did signal some new directions for the PC regime, to most observers the governing party's hold on power at first seemed as strong as ever. A Gallup Poll taken in March 1985 showed the PCs under Miller with the support of some fifty-one per cent of the Ontario electorate, compared with only twenty-nine per cent for David Peterson's Liberals, and twenty per cent for the New Democrats under Bob Rae. The Ontario PC dynasty, already in its 42nd consecutive year in office, seemed almost certain to remain in office for some time yet.

With reasons to be confident about his chances of success, Frank Miller called an election for 2 May 1985, anticipating that once again the Ontario electorate would ratify the Progressive Conservative party's selection of a new provincial Premier. By the later part of April, however, it was suddenly clear that the governing party would not have an easy victory.

Only the future can provide the kind of perspective on the 2 May Ontario election that makes a balanced assessment possible. And in fact, Frank Miller's PCs did no worse in the spring of 1985 than Davis' PCs had done in the summer of 1975. Nonetheless, the 1985 election ultimately led to the end of the Progressive Conservative dynasty that had first come to power in the summer of 1943.

A variety of explanations have been offered. Frank Miller, for instance, was somewhat to the right of Davis, possibly something of a "right-wing populist" in the manner of British Prime Minister Margaret Thatcher and American President Ronald Reagan. As events after the election would show, ideology was far from decisive for Miller. But he could at least be pictured as having abandoned the Ontario PC's traditional claim on the vital political centre, at last leaving an opening for the provincial Liberals.

Especially in the Toronto area, Miller's populism was also read by some as symbolic of an insular "little Ontario", that wanted to turn its back on the cosmopolitan and outward-looking dynamism which had taken root in the region during the past quarter century. This too was a misleading and, in its own way, narrow-minded perception. But in some quarters, it became influential. Two of the three Toronto newspapers officially endorsed Peterson as the next Premier.

As a sign that he did indeed intend to bring new directions to the PCs, Miller had moved to replace key figures in the Big Blue Machine with his own appointees. One result was that the 1985 PC campaign was run by less experienced organizers who sometimes made such elementary mistakes as failing to ensure that adequate crowds turned out for televised campaign meetings. This helped erode the vaunted PC image of cool competence and managerial efficiency, skilfully built up during the later years of the Davis regime.

Miller could also blame Davis himself for some of his problems. Davis' decision to extend "full funding" for Ontario's Catholic separate schools through to the end of the secondary level was officially endorsed by all three provincial parties. But as in the past, the issue proved contentious among the Ontario electorate. As the 1985 campaign developed, PC organizers reported that they sensed some of their voters would stay away from the polls in protest.

In the flush of his victory at the recent PC convention Miller had warned the opposition parties that after the next election they could be holding their caucus meetings in a telephone booth. To some, perhaps, this suggested the arrogance of an old regime that was not quite as closely in touch with the mood of the Ontario electorate as it imagined.

The 1984 federal election, for instance, had shown that the swing to the right of the later 1970s and early 1980s was not about to obliterate the New Democrats in Ontario. Rae had not managed to turn the Ontario NDP into a serious alternative government. But he had given the province's left-wing party the credibility of an articulate yet moderate leader, with family roots in the Canadian diplomatic establishment and a brother who was active in the federal Liberal Party[10].

The defeat of the federal Liberals in 1984 had also liberated the Ontario Liberals from the albatross of the late Trudeau regime's unpopularity at Ottawa. It freed up regional Liberal resources that had long been obsessed by federal politics and brought them to the aid of the provincial party. And it reminded some that, since the later nineteenth century, the Ontario electorate had a recurrent tradition of preferring governments of different political colouration at Ottawa and Queen's Park.

Perhaps more important than anything else, as the 1985 provincial campaign developed, Peterson proved a far more effective performer than virtually anyone except he and his wife had earlier thought possible. Peterson had never looked strong in the desultory carping and back-biting of the Ontario Legislative Assembly, where the opposition-minded New Democrats typically seemed more impressive. But in the 1985 election campaign, he found his feet, and at last he gave the provincial Liberals the appearance of having come to grips with the dynamic diversity of modern Ontario. He ran an aggressive campaign, picturing the Liberals as a progressive alternative to a faltering 42-year-old Tory regime, that was losing touch with the new regional society which had emerged from the great economic boom of the post Second World War era.

When the ballots were counted on the evening of 2 May, David Peterson's Liberals had won thirty-eight per cent of the province-wide popular vote, compared with thirty-seven per cent for Frank Miller's PCs, and twenty-five per cent for the New Democrats under Bob Rae. The exact configuration of seats in the Assembly see-sawed back and forth all evening in the first genuine "cliff-hanger" Ontario election since 1943. In the end, the PCs hung onto a slim plurality of fifty-two seats, compared with forty-eight seats for the Liberals, and twenty-five for the New Democrats.

Geographically, the distribution of seats reflected Ontario's traditional diversity. In northern Ontario (the part of the province that was in some respects most similar to western Canada), the Liberals took only one seat while the remainder were divided evenly between the PCs and the NDP. Here alone, the New Democratic theory of a "three-party system in transition" remained a serious view of the future.

In Metropolitan Toronto, the three parties divided up the available seats almost evenly, with the Liberals showing a dramatic improvement over their performance in the elections of the 1970s and earlier 1980s. In the old "loyal east" of southern Ontario, the PCS retained the traditional Tory primacy (though the Liberals made some significant gains). In the southwest, the Liberals returned to their former dominance. Geographically, in fact, the base of support for David Peterson's resurgent Liberal party had striking similarities with the base of support for Mitch Hepburn in the 1930s and for Oliver Mowat's Great Reform Government in the later nineteenth century.

A New Political Alliance and a New Government

Perhaps the most common immediate reaction to the 1985 Ontario election was to compare it with the election of 1975. Frank Miller's PCS had actually won one more seat and one per cent more of the popular vote than Davis' PCS had won a decade before. Davis had gone on to preside over six years of minority government and then to win a majority of seats in the election of 1981. Hoping to do the same, Miller, still with the largest number of seats of any single party, formed a government and prepared to meet the new Legislative Assembly in June.

Yet ultimately, Ontario's parliamentary democracy, like parliamentary democracies everywhere, gives the reins of government not to the party leader who commands a plurality of seats in the Legislative Assembly, but to the party leader who can command a majority – or in 1985 at least sixty-three seats. "Majority rule" in this sense was in fact the principle that the Reformers of the earlier nineteenth century had fought for and finally won with the triumph of Baldwin and Lafontaine in 1848.

In this context, the great difference between 1975 and 1985 was the relative strength of the Liberals and New Democrats. In 1975 the two "opposition" parties, who together held a clear majority of seats in the legislature, could have formed a coalition to defeat the PCS. But the Liberals then held thirty-five seats to the New Democrats' thirty-eight seats (and the PCS fifty-one). The New Democrats still anticipated that they could ultimately replace the Liberals in a new two-party system and had no intention of co-operating with them. The Liberals themselves were suspicious of the NDP. Throughout the period from 1975 to 1981, Premier Davis had been able to play off his divided opposition, governing sometimes with the support of one party and sometimes with that of the other.

In 1985, however, the Liberals had almost twice as many seats as the New Democrats (and only four fewer than the PCs). For the first time in more than a generation, they could plausibly be seen as a future alternative government. As a practical matter, this meant that Frank Miller's PC minority government would likely have to depend on the New Democrats alone to remain in office.

Yet Frank Miller had said harsh things about the NDP in the heat of the election campaign. And the public perception of Miller as something of a right-wing figure would make it awkward for the New Democrats to prop up his government for any length of time. Moreover, the Liberals had run on a moderately "progressive" campaign platform, that was unambiguously closer to the New Democratic vision than the PC platform. Though Peterson was clearly a businessman in politics, not a labour leader or a social democratic intellectual, his father had in fact been among the signers of the Regina Manifesto which gave birth to the CCF in the early 1930s.

The New Democrats held meetings with both the PCs and Liberals in the weeks that followed the election. And it gradually became clear that, when the Legislative Assembly met in June, the New Democrats would ally with the Liberals to defeat the PCs and bring in a new Liberal Government of Ontario. The basis of the alliance was a written "Accord" which became public late in May. By this document the NDP agreed to support a Liberal government for two years in return for two key commitments. The first was to implement, "within a framework of fiscal responsibility", certain "common campaign proposals", dealing with such issues as rent review, environmental regulation, and public accessibility to government. The second was a commitment on the part of the new Liberal government not to call an election for two years.

Frank Miller, still for the moment Premier of Ontario, did his best to act as if the Liberal/NDP alliance did not exist. When the legislature met in June, his PC government put forward a Throne Speech that set out a progressive

David Peterson and his cabinet in the early summer of 1985.

legislative programme remarkably similar to that envisioned in the Liberal/NDP Accord. This showed some that Miller was prepared to be far less of a right-wing populist than had been claimed by his opponents (and showed others that the tottering PC dynasty would do anything to hold onto the reins of power). Nonetheless, when the first opportunity presented itself, in the early evening of 18 June 1985, the Liberals and New Democrats at last joined forces to defeat the PC government by a vote of seventy-two to fifty-two.

The next afternoon, Lieutenant-Governor John Black Aird asked David Peterson to form a government as the twentieth Premier of Ontario[11]. A week later Peterson's new Liberal cabinet was sworn into office. It included, among others, two women (Elinor Caplan and Lily Munro), two French Canadians (René Fontaine and Bernard Grandmaitre), a Roman Catholic as Minister of Education (Sean Conway), and Ontario's first Black cabinet minister (Alvin Curling from the Toronto-area riding of Scarborough North). It did not include any New Democrats. The NDP would support the Liberals on the basis of the written Accord. But it would not actually be part of the new government. And Peterson made it clear that his minority government would also be open to co-operation with the PCs on specific pieces of legislation.

The arrangement was constitutionally quite correct, but it represented something of an innovation in Ontario political history, with risks for all involved and with no exact analogies in the past. The events of May and June 1985, however, did suggest at least three rather inexact historical precedents.

In some ways, for instance, the end of the PC dynasty resembled the end of Ontario's other long-lived political dynasty – Mowat's Great Reformers. The Great Reform regime had begun to falter with the rise of the Patrons of Industry and the earliest manifestations of Ontario's modern three-party system in the election of 1894. But it was another decade before Whitney's Conservatives replaced the Reformers, with a new regime that brought more of a change in style than in substance.

Similarly, it might be said that the modern PC dynasty had begun to falter with the election of 1975 when the New Democrats rose to the status of Official Opposition. A decade later, the PCS were replaced by a Liberal regime that also seemed to some to promise more of a change in style than in substance. David Peterson, the Queen's Park columnist of the *Globe and Mail* suggested, was in fact the real heir of William Davis.

In other ways, the Liberal/NDP Alliance that brought David Peterson to power resembled E.C. Drury's Farmer/Labour coalition government of 1919-1923. In both cases, the electoral outcome had taken most observers by surprise, and the modern Liberals were in some respects heirs of the old United Farmers, as the modern New Democrats were heirs of the old Independent Labour Party. Moreover, Peterson's new Treasurer was Robert Nixon, whose father had been not only the last previous Liberal Premier of Ontario but also a member of the Farmer/Labour cabinet of the early 1920s and a leading figure in the Ontario Progressive movement of the later 1920s and early 1930s.

In other ways again, the outcome of the 1985 election resembled the outcome of the 1943 election, when the Ontario Progressive Conservatives had begun their forty-two years in power, with a minority government that lasted for two years, informally supported by Ted Jolliffe's CCF.

Each of these inexact precedents held out the prospect of a somewhat different fate for the new Liberal government and its supporters and opponents. Whatever the future would bring, however, in its own way democracy in Canada's most populous province had shown it had the imagination and courage to try fresh approaches to the difficult problems and challenges of a new era. On the one side there was risk; on the other there was opportunity.

By the mid-1980s Ontario at large seemed in many ways a region in the midst of change. Though there were many reminders of the past, the regional society did not have the homogeneity of a century before. Yet Ontario in the mid-1880s itself had been dramatically different from the region in the mid-1780s. And there were crucial differences between the region in the mid-1780s and the region in the mid-1680s. A century from now, it will no doubt be possible to see Ontario today in a clearer light. In history, Harold Innis declared to an audience in the province's capital city in 1947 (quoting the German philosopher, Hegel): "Minerva's owl begins its flight only in the gathering dusk...."

Notes

Chapter One

1 Even today there are quite large parts of northern Ontario still very thinly populated and only lightly touched by the modern society.

2 There were "upwards of Forty" portages on the Ottawa-French River route, though the rapids were not so fierce. Like Lake Erie, lakes Huron and Superior are also higher than Lake Ontario. Lake Superior is somewhat higher than Lake Huron, and rapids were a problem as well on the St. Mary's River linking these two lakes.

3 As proof that the primitive terror invoked by the Shield was more than an abstract emotion, the Group of Seven acquired its own martyr; in 1917 Tom Thomson died in a mysterious way while on a solitary canoe trip and painting expedition in Algonquin Park.

Chapter Two

1 In the farthest north, it seems that there were also a very few Inuit or Eskimo peoples, as there are today.

2 It is often noted in this context that early seventeenth century Europe itself still indulged in such practices as public execution by drawing and quartering. The anthropologist John Witthoft has suggested that living with the prospect of death by ceremonial torture was the price Iroquoian men paid for having women do all the work of the agricultural economy (and women did take an active part in the torture of captured warriors).

3 In the 1950s and 1960s the remains of Ste. Marie were excavated and many of the original buildings restored with financial assistance from the Government of Ontario. It can now be visited as a tourist attraction.

4 Queen Anne of England sent a silver tea service to the Six Nations in the early 1700s as a reward for their loyalty to the English Crown. At the end of the American War of Independence in the early 1780s, when some of the Six Nations moved north into what would later become the British Province of Upper Canada, the service was divided in half. It remains in the possession of the Six Nations today.

5 La Salle also built the first European boat used on the Great Lakes (the "Griffin"), though the canot de maître would remain dominant for another century.

6 Kent County is now a relatively small area in the deep southwest. But it began as an area that covered much of the more northerly part of southern Ontario and virtually all of the more southerly parts of northern Ontario. It was the "French and Indian county" of Upper Canada, represented on the Executive Council by a member of the fur-trading Bâby family.

7 There were also "Panis" or Indian slaves, usually taken as captives in the warfare that periodically accompanied the trade.

Chapter Three

1 There were a few Catholics in the Thirteen Colonies, chiefly in Maryland and Pennsylvania. But estimates made for the mid-1770s suggest that Catholics accounted for no more than one per cent of the total population. There were also a few French Protestants on the lower St. Lawrence.

2 France would regain Louisiana briefly during the early 1800s, and Napoleon would then sell it to the new United States.

Chapter Four

1 Jean Baptiste Rousseau, for instance (also known as "Mr. St. John"), was "the last citizen of the old French Toronto and the first of the new English York." He cultivated cherry trees along the Humber River, that "are said to have supplied cuttings for numerous pioneer orchards."

2 Forty shillings was the requirement in rural areas. In "towns" it was five pounds. "Annual value" has never made the kind of sense in North America that it makes in Europe, where real estate has real and not just theoretical connections with the feudal society of the Middle Ages. In practice, virtually all adult males who owned farms or houses of some size in urban centres could vote.

3 Simcoe named and re-named various parts of the region. The Six Nations chief Joseph Brant quipped: "Governor Simcoe has done a great deal for this province. He has changed the name of every place in it."

4 The fees were sometimes a source of complaint, but even with them, the cost of land remained well below the cost of comparable acreages in the new United States.

5 Tecumseh Park on the Thames River in Chatham is named for the Shawnee chief who died in Canada's defence in 1813.

6 In effect, this revived a proposal of the late 1770s (never acted on) for an Indian "fourteenth colony" that would be admitted to the Continental Congress at Philadelphia.

7 In the 1970s Fort William, as it existed in the early nineteenth century, was restored with financial assistance from the Government of Ontario. It can now be visited as a tourist attraction.

Chapter Five

1 Anna Jameson wrote *Winter Studies and Summer Rambles in Canada* in 1838. There are two other well-known "gentlewomen of Upper Canada" who wrote books in the first half of the nineteenth century: Catharine Parr Traill (*The Backwoods of Canada*, 1836); and Susannah Moodie (*Roughing it in the Bush*, 1852). In somewhat the same mode, Simcoe's wife, Elizabeth, kept a diary in the early 1790s, which has subsequently been published.

Chapter Six

1 As a demonstration of the "bi-cultural" unity achieved by the French and English moderate Reformers in the 1840s, Lafontaine sat for the Fourth Riding of York in Canada West in 1843 and Baldwin for Rimouski in Canada East.

2 The intent of the original Negro separate school legislation, like that for Anglicans and Catholics, was to permit those Blacks who wished to do so to send their children to separate schools. In virtually all parts of the province outside Toronto, however, the legislation came to mean segregated schools for Blacks. Though the schools had disappeared by the twentieth century, the legislation remained part of Ontario statute law until the 1960s.

3 In 1861 two Southern Confederate envoys to the United Kingdom were seized from the British steamer *Trent* by a Union ship of war. Prospects of war between the Union and the United Kingdom were avoided when the two envoys were set free. In 1864 a group of Southerners who had sought refuge in Canada East

raided the adjacent town of St. Albans in Vermont. Prospects of war were avoided when the government of the United Province seized the raiders on their return to Canada. Both events, however, created genuine war scares in British North America.

Chapter Seven

1 With the exception that, in Ontario, the old Legislative Council was abolished.

2 There was some brief experimentation with multiple member constituencies in Ontario during the nineteenth century, none of which have survived to the present.

3 A typical farmer's house of the day was worth about $1,000. In the mid-1880s a solid brick eight-room house with bath and gas could be bought in Toronto for about $1,500.

4 In higher education, the University of Western Ontario was established at London in 1878, but without financial or other assistance from the provincial government.

Chapter Eight

1 This was also the argument Lord Elgin had used in 1854 to convince Southern senators that Reciprocity was their best protection against the admission of the British North American colonies as new free states in the Union.

2 From smallest to largest: St. Catharines, Guelph, Belleville, St. Thomas, Brantford, Kingston, London, Ottawa, Hamilton, Toronto.

Chapter Nine

1 The federal Senate that finally appeared in the British North America Act of 1867 was an heir of the pre-Confederation Legislative Council, with a modified form of regional representation but with members appointed for life (now until the age of 75) by the federal government of the day.

2 Interestingly enough, Ontario's position in the boundary dispute amounted to a contention that the claims of the old French regime in northern Ontario took precedence over the claims of the Hudson's Bay Company.

3 Another side of the era's taste for alcohol is suggested by the cure for the common cold proposed by Sir William Osler, the most famous product of late nineteenth-century Toronto medicine: "Put your hat on the bedpost. Go to bed with a bottle of whiskey. Drink the whiskey until you see two hats."

Chapter Ten

1 The other major Atlantic bank, the Merchant's Bank of Halifax, had moved its headquarters to Montreal in 1901 and became the Royal Bank of Canada.

2 The TNOR changed its name to Ontario Northland Railway in 1945 to avoid confusion (it is said) with the Texas and New Orleans Railroad, whose bills were sometimes mistakenly sent to the TNOR of the north.

3 The official Canadian census definitions of urban and rural changed in the 1950s and 1960s. In the earlier definition, urban meant any municipally-incorporated city, town, or village. In the later one it came to mean any place of at least 1,000 people with a density of at least 400 people per square kilometer. Published estimates of trends in the 1920s, 1930s, and 1940s using the new definition suggest no stall in rural decline during the 1930s. But these are only estimates, and the old city, town, and village data at least conform with popular folklore.

Chapter Eleven

1 According to John Ross Robertson, editor of the *Toronto Telegram*: "You could throw a brick through the window of any country lawyer in Ontario and hit a better man than Whitney."

2 Early labour history in the province is marked by factional antagonisms. The first Independent Labour Party had formed in 1899 but was "virtually defunct" by the start of the First World War. A second Independent Labour Party was formed in 1917.
3 Drury also supported the retail distribution plans of the Farmers' co-operative manager, T.P. Loblaw. Morrison and the dominant leadership did not, on ideological grounds. Loblaw left the United Farmers co-operative movement (which survives today) and started what would become a major private chain of regional supermarkets.

Chapter Twelve
1 Nixon ran as UFO in 1919 and 1923, Progressive in 1926 and 1929, Liberal-Progressive in 1934, and Liberal in 1937. As a furthur sign of the extent to which old political attachments were mixed up in the earlier twentieth century, the Nixon family of Brant County were proud United Empire Loyalists who had traditionally supported the Conservatives.
2 Every province but Quebec had adopted Prohibition by 1916, and the federal government imposed nation-wide Prohibition under the War Measures Act late in 1917. Federal Prohibition, however, ended after the War in 1919.
3 In his memoirs of his youth, John Kenneth Galbraith, who grew up in the same part of southwestern Ontario as Hepburn, has his father perform this legendary stunt. Hepburn himself performed a variation on the theme as Premier in the late 1930s – standing on a mechanical manure spreader. A voice from the crowd cried out: "Throw her into high gear, Mitch. She's never had a bigger load on."
4 The life of the provincial parliament elected in 1937 was extended to 1943 as a wartime measure. The Canadian constitutional expert, Eugene Forsey, has pointed out that "provincial legislatures can constitutionally extend their own lives indefinitely, subject only to the use of rarely used sections of the BNA Act" (now the Constitution Act 1867).
5 Hepburn pointed out to Aberhart: "My position here is more difficult in view of the fact that Toronto is the centre for entrenched finance for the Dominion, and the Press, generally speaking, are very hostile."
6 The governments of Australia and New Zealand simply declared war with the United Kingdom on 3 September, without consulting their parliaments. After some internal dissension and a change of governments, South Africa declared war on 6 September.

Chapter Thirteen
1 In the 1981 census it was possible, for the first time, to report"multiple" ethnic origins. The complete statistics (based on sample data) are: Single British origins – 52.6 per cent; Single origins other than British or French – 30.6 per cent; Multiple origins – 9.2 per cent; Single French origins – 7.6 per cent.
2 The record is not entirely consistent. Ontario joined the Diefenbaker victories of 1957 and 1958 and sent a majority of Conservatives to Ottawa in 1979. In 1972 it sent more Conservatives than Liberals, but its Liberal and New Democrat (old CCF) contingents combined outnumbered the Conservatives. It sent clear Liberal majorities to Ottawa in 1962, 1963, 1965, 1968, 1974, and 1980. With the exception of nine months in 1979-80, the Liberals were in power in Ottawa from 1963 to 1984.

Chapter Fourteen
1 Jolliffe's parents were United Church missionaries, and he had in fact been born in Lucknow, China. While studying on his Rhodes Scholarship in England, he became a member of the British Labour Party.
2 Work on the QEW had begun in the mid-1930s. It was named not after the

present Queen Elizabeth II but after her mother, the wife of George VI.

3 Ferguson's end to Prohibition had permitted the purchase of liquor from government stores for consumption in the home only. Hepburn had brought back public "beer parlours" in 1934. Drew legalized the sale of hard liquor in public bars, with a particular eye on the region's growing tourist industry.

4 The same year as the U.S. Supreme Court's "Brown vs the Board of Education" decision, which helped launch the Civil Rights movement of the 1960s. Ontario's moribund Negro separate schools legislation would only be officially removed from the provincial statutes several years later at the instigation of Leonard Braithwaite, the Liberal Black member for the Toronto riding of Etobicoke.

5 The power to amend the Canadian constitution would remain with the British Parliament until federal-provincial agreement on an amending formula was at last secured in 1981.

6 The career of Underhill, who had been born in Ontario as "a North York Presbyterian Grit", illustrates an important side of the region's reforming energies from the 1930s to the 1960s. In the early 1940s he almost lost his job at the University of Toronto for radical remarks in public. In the 1950s he became sceptical about the future of the CCF. In 1960 he dedicated a collection of his writings, entitled *In Search of Canadian Liberalism*,"For Mike Pearson".

Chapter Fifteen

1 The name was changed shortly after Robarts took office in the wake of the late 1950s/early 1960s recession. The surviving planning organization, designed to promote municipal land-use planning, was transferred to the Department of Municipal Affairs.

2 Hilda Neatby, *So Little for the Mind* (Toronto, 1953) was an influential book.

3 Though in 1967 John Robarts told a journalist "that until then it had been a fairly common practice of governments to look the other way when large corporations (with large tax bills) broke such regulations as there were to protect the water supply". It had been, he implied, "the price of progress".

4 An article with this title by the British journalist residing in America, Henry Fairlie, published in the December 1977 issue of *Harper's* magazine, was required reading at an Ontario PC think-tank retreat held in 1978.

5 As a variation on the new pluralistic themes, in the late summer of 1985 Prime Minister Brian Mulroney appointed Lincoln Alexander (from the Hamilton area) Ontario's first Black Lieutenant-Governor to replace the retiring John Black Aird.

6 In an early 1980 address to a Toronto audience, the liberal US economist, Lester Thurrow, had drawn attention to a successful Austrian strategy for economic prosperity: keep industrial labour costs somewhat below those in adjacent parts of West Germany as an inducement to German investment. The health of the Ontario auto-sector recovery after the "Great Recession" of 1981-82 owed much to a similar logic.

7 Taking classified and unclassified staff together (where "unclassified" means employees without permanent civil servant status), the number of provincial government employees declined from just over 87,000 in 1975 to just over 81,000 in 1983.

Chapter Sixteen

1 The compromise had its beginnings in an informal meeting among Jean Chretien, federal Justice Minister; Roy Romanow, Attorney General of Saskatchewan; and Roy McMurtry, Attorney General of Ontario.

2 In her own right, Elizabeth II remained "Queen of Canada", reflecting a characteristic gradualism in Canadian political development.

3 Like other rights in the Charter, these were qualified by a general provincial

power to override rights by legislation that declared it was doing so through a "notwithstanding" clause. Mobility rights were also qualified by specific provincial powers regarding residency requirements for social service programmes and special programmes in areas of high unemployment.

4 New York had begun to rival London as a leading financial centre in a major way by the end of the First World War.

5 Until the early 1980s, all provinces but Ontario had at one time or another qualified for the equalization payments that began in 1957, using formulas based sometimes on a national average and sometimes on a 'highest two provinces' average. One impact of the end of the long boom in Ontario (combined with the heady late-1970s blossoming of the oil economy in Alberta) was that Canada's most populous province qualified as well in the early 1980s, though it declined the payments. Ed Broadbent, leader of the federal New Democrats (which had twenty-seven of their thirty-five seats in the 1980 federal election west of the Ontario-Manitoba border), was instrumental in securing the amendment on natural resources.

6 Again, there are some qualifications: to be eligible for this right, a citizen of Canada's mother tongue must be either English or French, or his or her children must have already been partly educated in English or French in another province.

7 At a conference early in 1985, Brian Mulroney's government did manage to secure the required provincial consensus for a "watered-down" resolution on self-government. But this could not win sufficient support from Indian and Inuit representatives.

8 A 1976 Ontario Treasury study noted that during the period 1969-73 some thirty-two per cent of all Ontario "non-financial corporations", as measured by employment (and forty-six per cent as measured by taxable income), were controlled in the United States. It also noted that, contrary to popular impressions, the percentage of US-controlled industry in the province had been declining in the recent past, a trend that became clearer by the early 1980s. Only about fifteen per cent of all applications to FIRA between 1974 and 1976 were turned down.

9 Late in 1984 the Government of Ontario made plans to open a trade office in Singapore, adding to similar offices in Atlanta, Boston, Chicago, Dallas, Los Angeles, New York, Philadelphia, San Francisco, Brussels, Frankfurt, Hong Kong, London, Paris, and Tokyo.

10 Rae's brother in fact had run Jean Chretien's campaign in the federal Liberal leadership race that followed Trudeau's resignation.

11 Technically, Aird (an appointee of the late Trudeau regime at Ottawa) also had the option of calling a fresh election. By constitutional convention, however, he could only do this if he had a significant reason to doubt Peterson's ability to command a majority in the legislature, and such doubt was foreclosed by the written Liberal/NDP Accord.

Illustration, photograph and map credits

Front cover: Untitled [1897 The Legislative Building Queen's Park seen from University Avenue] by "N.W." [artist unknown]. Government of Ontario Art Collection, gift of Mr and Mrs D B Sutherland to the Ontario Heritage Foundation, 1983; on loan to the Government of Ontario. Photographed by J E Moore Photography.

In all cases illustrations, photographs and maps are from the Ontario Archives, with the following exceptions:

Page 25, Map: by Shelley Laskin.

Page 31, Ste Marie: Sainte-Marie Among the Hurons, Midland, Ontario. Ontario Ministry of Tourism and Recreation.

Page 77, Old Fort William: Old Fort William, Thunder Bay, Ontario. Ontario Ministry of Tourism and Recreation.

Page 236, Map: Ontario Bureau of Statistics and Research, 1947.

Page 243, Tourism Advertisement: Ontario Department of Travel and Publicity, 1959.

Page 257, Bethel Cemetery and Markham Hydro Building: by Christopher White.

Page 293, William Davis: Ontario Progressive Conservative Service Bureau.

Page 301, Letting the private sector do it in downtown Toronto: by Christopher White.

Page 320, Bob Rae: Ontario New Democratic Party.

Page 326, David Peterson and his cabinet: Press Office, Office of the Premier.

Statistical Appendices

Appendix A:
Lieutenant-Governors
of Upper Canada, 1791-1840

Name	Date Appointed
John Graves Simcoe	1791
Peter Russell*	1796
Peter Hunter	1799
Alexander Grant*	1805
Frances Gore	1806
Isaac Brock*	1811
Roger Hale Sheaffe*	1812
Francis de Rottenburg*	1813
Gordon Drummond*	1813
George Murray*	1815
Frederick P. Robinson*	1815
Francis Gore	1815
Samuel Smith*	1817
Peregrine Maitland	1818
John Colborne	1828
Francis Bond Head	1836
George Arthur	1838
Charles Poulett Thomson	
(Lord Sydenham)	1839
George Arthur	1840

During the Union of the Canadas the office of Lieutenant-Governor ceased to exist.

*Acted as Lieutenant-Governor without official appointment: known as President of the Executive Council, Administrator, or (in the cases of Drummond, Murray, and Robinson) Provisional Lieutenant-Governor.

Appendix B:

Lieutenant-Governors
of Ontario, 1867-1985

Name	Date Appointed
Henry William Stisted	1867
William Pearce Howland	1868
John Willoughby Crawford	1873
Donald Alexander Macdonald	1875
John Beverly Robinson*	1880
Alexander Campbell	1887
George Airey Kirkpatrick	1892
Oliver Mowat	1897
William Mortimer Clark	1903
John Morison Gibson	1908
John Strathearn Hendrie	1914
Lionel Herbert Clarke	1919
Henry Cockshutt	1921
William Donald Ross	1926
Herbert Alexander Bruce	1932
Albert Matthews	1937
Ray Lawson	1946
Louis Orville Breithaupt	1952
John Keiller Mackay	1957
William Earle Rowe	1963
W. Ross Macdonald	1968
Pauline E. McGibbon	1974
John Black Aird	1980
Lincoln Alexander	1985

*Second son of the John Beverly Robinson who played so important a role in the politics of the old Province of Upper Canada.

338

Appendix C:
Premiers* of Ontario,
1867-1985

Name	Party Affiliation	Date Appointed
John Sandfield Macdonald	Coalition	1867
Edward Blake	Liberal	1871
Oliver Mowat	Liberal	1872
Arthur S. Hardy	Liberal	1896
George W. Ross	Liberal	1899
James P. Whitney	Conservative	1905
William H. Hearst	Conservative	1914
E.C. Drury	United Farmers/Labour	1919
G. Howard Ferguson	Conservative	1923
George S. Henry	Conservative	1930
Mitchell F. Hepburn	Liberal	1934
Gordon D. Conant	Liberal	1942
Harry C. Nixon	Liberal	1943
George A. Drew	Progressive Conservative	1943
Thomas L. Kennedy	Progressive Conservative	1948
Leslie M. Frost	Progressive Conservative	1949
John P. Robarts	Progressive Conservative	1961
William Davis	Progressive Conservative	1971
Frank Miller	Progressive Conservative	1985
David Peterson	Liberal	1985

*Some "Premiers" of Ontario (most recently John Robarts) have preferred to be known as "Prime Ministers". Since Whitney, the official cabinet position of the first minister has been President of the Executive Council – a practice foreshadowed much earlier by Blake.

Appendix D:
Population of Upper Canada,
Canada West,
and Ontario, 1831-1981

Year	Population (thousands)	Percentage of National Pop.	Rural* Percentage of Ontario Pop.
1831	237	-	-
1842	487	-	-
1851	952	-	86
1860	1,396	-	82
1871	1,621	44	78
1881	1,927	45	70
1891	2,114	44	61
1901	2,183	41	57
1911	2,527	35	47
1921	2,934	33	42
1931	3,432	33	39
1941	3,788	33	38
1951	4,598	33	27
1961	6,236	34	23
1971	7,703	36	18
1981	8,625	35	18

(Source: Statistics Canada)

*Until 1951, the rural population was defined as people living outside cities, towns and incorporated villages. Since 1951, it has been defined as people living outside minimum clusters of population size and density, as specified by federal statisticians: currently, areas with a population concentration of 1,000 or more, and a population density of 400 or more per square kilometre.

Appendix E:
Changing Birthplaces
of the Ontario Population,
1851-1981

Place	1851 Percentage	1901 Percentage	1931 Percentage	1981 Percentage
Ontario	58	82	72	65
Other Canada	1	3	5	10
United Kingdom	35	11	15	6
United States	5	2	2	1
Other Places	1	2	6	18

(Sources: *Ontario Statistics 1978*. Statistics Canada.)

Appendix F:
Changing Occupational Structure
of the Ontario Labour Force,
1881-1981

Sector	1881 Percentage	1921 Percentage	1951 Percentage	1981 Percentage
Agriculture & Resources	49	28	13	5
Manufacturing & Construction	32	33	36	30
Service Sector	19	39	51	65

(Sources: Ray *et al.*, *Canadian Urban Trends*. Statistics Canada)

Appendix G:
Growth of Ontario Cities

Five Largest Urban Places in Upper Canada, 1830

Place	Population
Kingston	3,587
York (Toronto after 1834)	2,800
London	2,415
Hamilton	2,013
Brockville	1,130

(Source: Brian S. Osborne, "Kingston in the Nineteenth Century: A Study in Urban Decline", in Wood *Perspectives on Landscape and Settlement in Nineteenth Century Ontario*, p. 161.)

341

Ten Largest Cities in Ontario, 1881

Place	Population	Place	Population
Toronto	86,415	Guelph	9,890
Hamilton	35,961	St. Catharines	9,630
Ottawa	27,412	Brantford	9,616
London	19,746	Belleville	9,516
Kingston	14,091	St. Thomas	8,367

(Source: Statistics Canada)

Ten Largest Cities in Ontario, 1931

City	Population	City	Population
Toronto	631,207	Kitchener	30,793
Hamilton	155,547	Brantford	30,107
Ottawa	126,872	Fort William	26,277
London	71,148	St. Catharines	24,753
Windsor	63,108	Kingston	23,439

(Source: Statistics Canada)

Ten Largest Census Metropolitan Areas in Ontario, 1981
(Statistics Canada Boundaries)

City	Population	City	Population
Toronto	2,998,947	London	283,668
Ottawa	547,399	Windsor	246,110
Hamilton	542,095	Oshawa	154,217
St. Catharines-Niagara	304,353	Sudbury	149,923
Kitchener	287,801	Thunder Bay	121,379

(Source: Statistics Canada)

Ten Largest Cities in Ontario,
1981 (Municipal Boundaries)

City	Population	City	Population
Toronto	599,217	Etobicoke	298,713
North York	559,521	Ottawa	295,163
Scarborough	443,353	London	254,280
Mississauga	315,056	Windsor	192,083
Hamilton	306,434	Kitchener	139,734

(Source: Statistics Canada)

Selected Bibliography

General Works

Allen, Robert Thomas. *The Great Lakes.* Toronto: The Illustrated Natural History of Canada, 1970.

Bishop, Olga B., Barbara I. Irwin, and Clara G. Miller. *Bibliography of Ontario History 1867-1967.* 2 vols. Toronto: University of Toronto Press, 1980.

Bowle, John. *The Imperial Achievement.* London: Martin Secker & Warburg, 1974.

Brebner, John Bartlet. *North Atlantic Triangle.* New York: Columbia University Press, 1945.

Careless, J.M.S. *Canada: A Story of Challenge.* Toronto: Macmillan of Canada, 1963.

Chapman, L.J., and D.F.Putnam. *The Physiography of Southern Ontario.* Toronto: University of Toronto Press, 1966.

Choquette, Robert. *L'Ontario français, historique.* Montreal: Éditions Études Vivantes, 1980.

Easterbrook, W.T., and Hugh G.J.Aitken. *Canadian Economic History.* Toronto: Macmillan of Canada, 1956.

Firth, Edith G., ed. *Profiles of a Province.* Toronto: Ontario Historical Society, 1967.

Gentilcore, R.L., ed. *Ontario.* Toronto: University of Toronto Press, 1972.

Glazebrook, G.P. de T. *Life in Ontario.* Toronto: University of Toronto Press, 1968.

Hall, Roger, and Gordon Dodds. *A Picture History of Ontario.* Edmonton: Hurtig, 1978.

Hutton, C.L.A., and W.A.Black. *Ontario Arctic Watershed.* Ottawa: Information Canada, 1975.

Lower, Arthur R.M. *Colony to Nation.* Don Mills: Longmans Canada, 1964.

Moon, Barbara. *The Canadian Shield.* Toronto: The Illustrated Natural History of Canada, 1970.

Morison, Samuel Eliot. *The Oxford History of the American People.* New York: Oxford University Press, 1965.

Ontario. *Ontario Statistics 1978.* Toronto: Ministry of Treasury and Economics, 1978.

Spelt, Jacob. *Urban Development in South-Central Ontario.* Toronto: McClelland and Stewart, 1972.

Wilderness Romance, 1610-1791

Burt, A.L. *The Old Province of Quebec.* Toronto: McClelland and Stewart, 1968.

Drury, E.C. *All for a Beaver Hat.* Toronto: The Ryerson Press, 1959.

Eccles, W.J. *The Canadian Frontier 1534-1760.* New York: Holt, Rinehart and Winston, 1969.

Frost, Leslie M. *Forgotten Pathways of the Trent.* Don Mills: Burns and MacEachern, 1973.

Innis, Harold A. *The Fur Trade in Canada*. Toronto: University of Toronto Press, 1956.

Jenness, Diamond. *The Indians of Canada*. Ottawa: National Museum of Man and University of Toronto Press, 1977.

Jury, Wilfred, and Elsie McLeod Jury. *Sainte Marie Among the Hurons*. Toronto: Oxford University Press, 1954.

Lajeunesse, Ernest J. *The Windsor Border Region*. Toronto: University of Toronto Press, 1960.

Mealing, S.R. ed. *The Jesuit Relations and Allied Documents*. Toronto: McClelland and Stewart, 1963.

Morison, Samuel Eliot, ed. *The Parkman Reader*. Boston: Little, Brown, 1955.

Preston, Richard A., and Leopold Lamontagne. *Royal Fort Frontenac*. Toronto: University of Toronto Press, 1958.

Rich, E.E. *The Hudson's Bay Company, 1670-1870*. Vols. 1-2. Toronto: McClelland and Stewart, 1960.

Robinson, Percy J. *Toronto During the French Regime 1615-1793*. Toronto: University of Toronto Press, 1965.

Trigger, Bruce G. *The Huron*. New York: Holt, Rinehart and Winston, 1969.

Wright, J.V. *Ontario Prehistory*. Ottawa: National Museum of Man, 1972.

Pre-Confederation, 1791-1867

Armstrong, F.H., H.A.Stevenson, and J.D.Wilson, eds. *Aspects of Nineteenth Century Ontario*. Toronto: University of Toronto Press, 1974.

Arthur, Elizabeth. *Thunder Bay District 1821-1892*. Toronto: University of Toronto Press, 1973.

Careless, J.M.S. *Brown of the Globe*. 2 vols. Toronto: Macmillan of Canada, 1959 and 1963.

———. *The Union of the Canadas*. Toronto: McClelland and Stewart, 1967.

———. ed. *The Pre-Confederation Premiers*. Toronto: University of Toronto Press, 1980.

Cowan, Helen. *British Emigration Before Confederation*. Ottawa: Canadian Historical Association, 1968.

Craig, Gerald M. *Upper Canada: The Formative Years, 1784-1841*. Toronto: McClelland and Stewart, 1963.

———. ed. *Lord Durham's Report*. Toronto: McClelland and Stewart, 1963.

Crawford, Kenneth Grant. *Canadian Municipal Government*. Toronto: University of Toronto Press, 1954.

Creighton, Donald. *John A. Macdonald*. Vol. 1. Toronto: Macmillan of Canada, 1952.

———. *The Empire of the St. Lawrence*. Toronto: Macmillan of Canada, 1956.

Douglas, R.Allan. *John Prince 1796-1870*. Toronto: University of Toronto Press, 1980.

Dunham, Aileen. *Political Unrest in Upper Canada*. Toronto: McClelland and Stewart, 1963.

Dunlop, William. *Tiger Dunlop's Upper Canada*. Toronto: McClelland and Stewart, 1963.

Earl, David, ed. *Family Compact: Aristocracy or Oligarchy*. Toronto: Copp Clark, 1967.

Gagan, David. *Hopeful Travellers*. Toronto: University of Toronto Press, 1981.

Glazebrook, G.P. de T. *A History of Transportation in Canada*. Vol. 1. Toronto: McClelland and Stewart, 1964.

Gourlay, Robert. *Statistical Account of Upper Canada*. Abridged by S.R.Mealing. Toronto: McClelland and Stewart, 1974.

Hill, Daniel G. *The Freedom Seekers*. Agincourt, Ontario: Book Society of Canada, 1981.

Hodgins, Bruce W. *John Sandfield Macdonald*. Toronto: University of Toronto Press, 1971.

Innis, Mary Quale, ed. *Mrs. Simcoe's Diary*. Toronto: Macmillan of Canada, 1965.

Johnson, J.K., ed. *Historical Essays on Upper Canada*. Toronto: McClelland and Stewart, 1975.

Jones, Robert L. *History of Agriculture in Ontario, 1613-1880*. Toronto: University of Toronto Press, 1946.

Kilbourn, William. *The Firebrand*. Toronto: Clarke, Irwin, 1956.

Landon, Fred. *Western Ontario and the American Frontier*. Toronto: McClelland and Stewart, 1967.

Masters, D.C. *The Reciprocity Treaty of 1854*. Toronto: McClelland and Stewart, 1963.

Moir, John S. *Church and State in Canada West*. Toronto: University of Toronto Press, 1959.

Morton, W.L. *The Critical Years*. Toronto: McClelland and Stewart, 1964.

Reaman, G.Elmore. *The Trail of the Black Walnut*. Toronto: McClelland and Stewart, 1957.

Splane, Richard B. *Social Welfare in Ontario, 1791-1893*. Toronto: University of Toronto Press, 1965.

Strachan, James. *A Visit to the Province of Upper Canada*. New York: Johnson Reprint Corporation, 1968.

Thomas, Clara. *Ryerson of Upper Canada*. Toronto: The Ryerson Press, 1969.

Tiffany, Orrin Edward. *The Relations of the United States to the Canadian Rebellion of 1837-1838*. Toronto: Coles Reprints, 1972.

Upton, L.F.S., ed. *United Empire Loyalists: Men and Myths*. Toronto: Copp Clark, 1967.

Walker, Franklin A. *Catholic Education and Politics in Upper Canada*. Toronto: Dent, 1955.

Winks, Robin W. *Canada and the United States: The Civil War Years*. Montreal: Harvest House, 1971.

Wood, J.David, ed. *Perspectives on Landscape and Settlement in Nineteenth Century Ontario*. Toronto: Macmillan of Canada, 1978.

Confederation to the Present, 1867-1985

Armstrong, Christopher. *The Politics of Federalism*. Toronto: University of Toronto Press, 1981.

Arnopoulos, Sheila McLeod. *Voices from French Ontario*. Kingston and Montreal: McGill-Queen's, 1982.

Biggar, C.R.W. *Sir Oliver Mowat*. 2 vols. Toronto: Hunter Rose, 1905.

Bliss, Michael. *A Living Profit*. Toronto: McClelland and Stewart, 1974.

Brown, Robert Craig, and Ramsay Cook. *Canada: A Nation Transformed, 1896-1921*. Toronto: McClelland and Stewart, 1974.

Buck, Tim. *Yours in the Struggle*. Toronto: NC Press, 1977.

Caplan, Gerald L. *The Dilemma of Canadian Socialism*. Toronto: McClelland and Stewart, 1973.

Clement, Wallace. *Continental Corporate Power*. Toronto: McClelland and Stewart, 1977.

Creighton, Donald. *John A. Macdonald*. Vol. 2. Macmillan of Canada, 1955.

————. *Harold Adams Innis*. Toronto: University of Toronto Press, 1957.

Drury, E.C. *Farmer Premier*. Toronto: McClelland and Stewart, 1966.

Glazebrook, G.P. de T. *A History of Transportation in Canada*. Vol. 2. Toronto: McClelland and Stewart, 1964.

Granatstein, J.L., and Peter Stevens, eds. *Forum*. Toronto: University of Toronto Press, 1972.

Innis, Harold A. *Essays in Canadian Economic History*. Edited by Mary Q. Innis. Toronto: University of Toronto Press, 1956.

Johnson, Harry G. *The Canadian Quandry*. Toronto: McClelland and Stewart, 1977.

Lang, Vernon. *The Service State Emerges in Ontario*. Toronto: Ontario Economic Council, 1974.

Leacock, Stephen. *The Social Criticism of Stephen Leacock*. Edited by Alan Bowker. Toronto: University of Toronto Press, 1973.

Lower, Arthur R.M. *My First Seventy-Five Years*. Toronto: Macmillan of Canada, 1967.

MacDonald, Donald C., ed. *Government and Politics of Ontario*. Toronto: Macmillan of Canada, 1975.

Mallory, J.R. *The Structure of Canadian Government*. Toronto: Macmillan of Canada, 1971.

Manthorpe, Jonathan. *The Power and the Tories*. Toronto: Macmillan of Canada, 1974.

Martin, Joe. *The Role and Place of Ontario in the Canadian Confederation*. Toronto: Ontario Economic Council, 1974.

Marshall, Herbert, Frank Southard Jr., and Kenneth W. Taylor. *Canadian-American Industry*. Toronto: McClelland and Stewart, 1976.

McKenty, Neil. *Mitch Hepburn*. Toronto: McClelland and Stewart, 1967.

Mulvey, Thomas. "The Provincial Executive Organization." in *Canada and its Provinces*. Vol. 17. Edited by Adam Shortt and Arthur G. Doughty. Toronto: Publishers Association of Canada, 1914, pp. 189-240.

Nelles, H.V. *The Politics of Development*. Toronto: Macmillan of Canada, 1974.

Neufeld, E.P. *A Global Corporation: A History of the International Development of Massey-Ferguson Limited*. Toronto: University of Toronto Press, 1969.

Oliver, Peter. *Public & Private Persons*. Toronto: Clarke, Irwin, 1975.

——— *G. Howard Ferguson, Ontario Tory*. Toronto: University of Toronto Press, 1977.

Prang, Margaret. *N.W.Rowell: Ontario Nationalist*. Toronto: University of Toronto Press, 1975.

Ray, D. Michael, Graham Murchie, Terrence W. Irwin, Margaret L. Pendleton, and David H. Douglas, eds. *Canadian Urban Trends*. Vol. 1. Ottawa: Ministry of State for Urban Affairs, 1976.

Schindeler, F.F. *Responsible Government in Ontario*. Toronto: University of Toronto Press, 1969.

Schull, Joseph. *Ontario Since 1867*. Toronto: McClelland and Stewart, 1978.

Siegfried, André. *La Canada, les deux races*. Paris: Librarie Armand Colin, 1906.

Sissons, C.B. *Church and State in Canadian Education*. Toronto: The Ryerson Press, 1959.

Smith, Goldwin. *Canada and the Canadian Question*. Toronto: University of Toronto Press, 1971.

Stamp, Robert M. *The Schools of Ontario, 1876-1976*. Toronto: University of Toronto Press, 1982.

Swainson, Donald, ed. *Oliver Mowat's Ontario*. Toronto: Macmillan of Canada, 1972.

Underhill, Frank H. *In Search of Canadian Liberalism*. Toronto: Macmillan of Canada, 1960.

Waite, P.B. *Canada: Arduous Destiny, 1874-1896*. Toronto: McClelland and Stewart, 1971.

Wallace, Elisabeth. *Goldwin Smith: Victorian Liberal.* Toronto: University of Toronto Press, 1957.

Wallace, W.S. "Political History 1867-1912," in *Canada and its Provinces.* Vol. 17. Edited by Adam Shortt and Arthur G. Doughty. Toronto: Publishers Association of Canada, 1914, pp. 103-185.

Wilson, Barbara M. *Ontario and the First World War.* Toronto: University of Toronto Press, 1977.

Wilson, Edmund. *O Canada.* New York: The Noonday Press, 1965.

Winks, Robin W. *The Relevance of Canadian History.* Toronto: Macmillan of Canada, 1979.

Young, Scott, and Astrid Young. *Silent Frank Cochrane.* Toronto: Macmillan of Canada, 1973.

Zaslow, Morris. *The Opening of the Canadian North 1870-1914.* Toronto: McClelland and Stewart, 1971.

Index

350